JOSEPH II

T.C.W. BLANNING

Longman

An imprint of **Pearson Education**

Harlow, England · London · New York · Reading, Massachusetts · San Francisco
Toronto · Don Mills, Ontario · Sydney · Tokyo · Singapore · Hong Kong · Seoul
Taipei · Cape Town · Madrid · Mexico City · Amsterdam · Munich · Paris · Milan

Pearson Education Limited
Edinburgh Gate
Harlow, Essex CM20 2JE, England
and Associated Companies throughout the world

Visit us on the World Wide Web at:
http://www.pearsoneduc.com

First published 1994

ISBN 0 582 052734 CSD
ISBN 0 582 052726 PPR

British Library Cataloguing-in-Publication Data

A catalogue record for this book is
available from the British Library

Library of Congress Cataloging-in-Publication Data

Blanning, T. C. W.
Joseph II / T.C.W. Blanning
p. cm. – (Profiles in power)
Includes bibliographical references and index.
ISBN 0-582-05273-4. – ISBN 0-582-05272-6 (pbk)
1. Joseph II, Holy Roman Emperor, 1741-1790. 2. Austria-Politics and
government–1740–1789. 3. Austria–Kings and rulers–Biography. I. Title. II. Series:
Profiles in power (London, England)
DB74.3.B58 1994
943.6'03–dc20   93-29516
                                                                                                    CIP

10 9 8 7 6 5 4 3
04 03 02 01 00

Set by 13 in 11/12 pt Bookman
Produced by Pearson Education Asia Pte Ltd
Printed in Singapore (B&JO)

CONTENTS

PREFACE

In 1970 I published a short book on Joseph II entitled *Joseph II and enlightened despotism* in the 'Seminar Studies in History' edited by the late and much lamented Patrick Richardson. It was my first publication and was based on lectures I had given in Cambridge when a research fellow. It concentrated on the relationship between Joseph's reform programme and the Enlightenment. Since its publication a great deal of distinction has been published on the Habsburg Monarchy in general and Joseph in particular. Although I myself worked mainly on German, French and British history during the 1970s and 1980s, I maintained my interest in the Monarchy and continued to work occasionally in the Viennese archives. So when I discovered that my first-born had been allowed to go out of print, it seemed appropriate to replace it.

This new book is not intended to be an 'up-date'. It is an entirely new creature, written without reference to its predecessor and with a different object in mind. Nor is it in any sense a biography – it would be both foolhardy and unnecessary to attempt such a thing, given the existence of the first volume of Derek Beales' magnificent and definitive work and the likelihood that it will be completed by a second in the near future. Taking the title of this present series 'Profiles in Power' as its conceptual focus, this book seeks to analyse the constraints under which Joseph operated, his attempts to overcome them and the reasons for his failure. A constant theme is his ill-fated attempt to construct a modern state and the baleful effects this misguided exercise had on the Habsburg Monarchy, the Holy Roman Empire and Europe in general.

The debts I have incurred in writing this book are many. It will be readily apparent how much I rely on those historians who have produced so much of distinction during the past twenty years or so, especially Robert Evans, Peter Dickson, Grete Klingenstein, Peter Hersche and Derek Beales. I have tried the patience of archivists and librarians in many institutions, notably the Haus-, Hof- und Staatsarchiv, the Nationalbibliothek and the Stadtbibliothek in Vienna, the Staatsbibliothek in Munich, the Staatsbibliothek in Berlin, the British Library in London and, above all, the University Library in Cambridge, which manages to combine wealth of resources and ease of use to a degree which is quite unique in my experience. The research for this book has been financed by the Master and Fellows of Sidney Sussex College, the University of Cambridge, the British Academy and the Leverhulme Foundation; I am deeply grateful to all of them and welcome the opportunity to say so. The ideas I advance in this book have been hammered out in discussion – or more usually in argument – with several generations of undergraduates taking the course on German history I run with my colleague Jonathan Steinberg, who has always been a constant source of encouragement, assistance and constructive criticism. The same can be said of Derek Beales and Hamish Scott, who gallantly read a first draft and have saved me from many errors, distortions and over-statements. But they could not save me entirely from myself and are in no way responsible for those which remain. This is the first occasion on which I have had the opportunity to thank my wife Nicky in print for her loving support, sound advice and occasional reprimand. I look forward to an early opportunity to repeat the tribute.

Tim Blanning
Cambridge
May 1993

ABBREVIATIONS

Arneth and Flammermont	Alfred Ritter von Arneth and Jules Flammermont (eds), *Correspondance secrète du comte de Mercy-Argenteau avec l'empereur Joseph II et le prince de Kaunitz*, 2 vols (Paris, 1889-91)
Arneth, *Joseph II. und Katharina*	Alfred Ritter von Arneth (ed.), *Joseph II und Katharina von Russland. Ihr Briefwechsel* (Vienna, 1869)
Arneth, *Joseph II. und Leopold*	Alfred Ritter von Arneth (ed.), *Joseph II und Leopold von Toscana. Ihr Briefwechsel von 1781 bis 1790*, 2 vols (Vienna, 1872)
Arneth, *Marie Antoinette, Joseph II. und Leopold II.*	Alfred Ritter von Arneth (ed.), *Marie Antoinette, Joseph II. und Leopold II. Ihr Briefwechsel* (Vienna, 1866)
Arneth, *Maria Theresia und Joseph II.*	Alfred Ritter von Arneth (ed.), *Maria Theresia und Joseph II. Ihre Correspondenz sammt Briefen Joseph's an seinen Bruder Leopold*, 3 vols (Vienna, 1867-8)
Beer	Adolf Beer, *Joseph II., Leopold II. und Kaunitz. Ihr Briefwechsel* (Vienna, 1873)

ix

Handbillets	Vienna, Haus-, Hof- und Staatsarchiv, Handbilletenprotokolle
Schlitter	H. Schlitter (ed.), *Geheime Correspondenz Josefs II. mit Trauttmansdorff. 1787–1789* (Vienna, 1902)
Beales	Derek Beales, *Joseph II*, vol. I: *In the shadow of Maria Theresa 1741–1780* (Cambridge, 1987)
BL	British Library, London
Dickson	P.G.M. Dickson, *Finance and government under Maria Theresa 1740–1780*, 2 vols (Oxford, 1987)
Österreich im Europa der Aufklärung	Richard Georg Plaschka and Grete Klingenstein (eds), *Österreich im Europa der Aufklärung. Kontinuität und Zäsur in Europa zur Zeit Maria Theresias und Josephs II. Internationales Symposion in Wien 20.-23. Oktober 1980*, 2 vols, (Vienna, 1985)
PRO	Public Record Office, London

The publishers would like to thank Cambridge University Press for permission to reproduce a map taken from D. Beales, *Joseph II*, vol 1.

FOR NICKY

Chapter 1

JOSEPH II AND THE HABSBURG INHERITANCE

. . .

ASSETS

'Everything in politics is very simple – but even the simplest thing is very difficult'. This paraphrase of Clausewitz's dictum on war would have carried conviction on the lips of Joseph II. On 1 January 1781, only a month after the death of his mother (on 29 November 1780), he wrote to the Grand Duke and Duchess of Russia that his elevation to sole rule had brought crushing burdens which kept him at his desk from early in the morning until late at night. He lamented that in such *une vaste et grande machine* as the Habsburg Monarchy, good could be achieved only slowly and with great difficulty, while the slightest mistake did harm very quickly. With rueful humour, he added that when a German bureaucrat, trying to speak French, mispronounced his place of work as a *bourreau* [hangman] when meaning *bureau* [office], he spoke truer than he knew.[1] After less than ten years of torment at the hands of the hangman, Joseph died (on 20 February 1790), exhausted, prematurely aged, embittered and deeply disappointed by his apparently total failure. As his own despairing epitaph put it: 'Here lies a prince whose intentions were pure, but who had the misfortune to see all his plans collapse'.[2]

When assessing the validity of this crushing self-indictment, it is difficult but important to avoid the 'teleological trap'. By that is meant the knowledge that the Habsburg Monarchy lurched from one crisis to another after Joseph's death (1797, 1801, 1805, 1809, 1848, 1859, 1866 and so on) and was finally

1

expunged from the map of Europe altogether by the peace settlement which followed the First World War. Once the final destination – the *telos* – is known, all previous events can be seen as rites of passage on a journey as preordained as is every human's route from birth to death. Oscar Jászi's influential work *The dissolution of the Habsburg Monarchy* begins with the very foundation of the dynasty's fortunes in the late thirteenth century, while those of A.J.P. Taylor and C.A. Macartney on the same theme take Joseph II as their point of departure.[3] Whatever the theoretical preconceptions of the author, this is history with a sense of inevitability built-in. It necessarily stresses problems and failures at the expense of assets and achievements. Not only does it distort the eventual collapse by exaggerating its inevitability, it also leads to a misunderstanding of the nature of the past, especially by the application of anachronistic concepts taken from a later period.

Although it is clearly impossible to forget what came afterwards, it is not necessary to write the history of Joseph II as if it were one episode in the pre-history of the *Fall of the house of Habsburg*.[4] An attempt, at least, can be made to follow Ranke's dictum that 'every age stands in direct relationship to God', or in other words that every age has its own identity and validity and should be studied on its own terms and for its own sake. With specific reference to the Habsburg Monarchy during the life of Joseph II (1741–1790), this requires a recognition of opportunities that were missed as well as traps that were blundered into.

First and foremost, it requires the recognition that the European states-system in the mid-eighteenth century was exceptionally fluid. In 1700 the largest country in Europe in terms of area (with the exception of Russia) had been Poland-Lithuania, the greatest empire had been ruled by Spain, while the richest, most populous and most powerful state had been France. By the time Joseph II died, a truncated Poland-Lithuania was sliding towards total elimination from the map, the Spanish empire in Europe had been partitioned and its hegemony overseas had been wrested by the British, while France was immobilised by revolution. Other casualties included the Swedish empire in the Baltic, conquered by Peter the Great of Russia in the Great Northern War (1700–21) and the possessions of the Ottoman Turks around the Black Sea, conquered by Catherine the Great of Russia in the two wars of 1768–74 and 1787–92. In the course of the eighteenth century, four empires (the Spanish, the Swedish, the Polish and the French) collapsed, a fifth (the Holy Roman Empire) began to totter terminally and a sixth (the Ottoman) was pushed back to the European periphery.

As the frontiers of eastern and southern Europe waxed and waned, opportunity knocked with the same insistence that danger threatened. Countries with the will and ability to adapt could move from obscurity to hegemony in just a few generations. In 1657 Louis XIV sent a letter to Tsar Michael of all the Russias, unaware that he had been dead for twelve years;[5] in 1735 a Russian army marched to the Rhine; in 1759 a Russian army raided Berlin; and in 1779 Russia became a guarantor of the peace of Teschen and thus a guarantor of the *status quo* in Central Europe. Poland, by contrast, lost about a third of her territory and population in the first partition of 1772, about a half of what remained in the second partition of 1793 and all the rest in the third partition of 1795. She was to remain conspicuously absent from the European map for 124 years.

The Habsburgs were well-placed to take advantage of this territorial upheaval. Prudent and lucky marriages dating back to three all-important unions with the heiresses of Burgundy (1477), Castile and Aragon (1496) and Hungary and Bohemia (1515) had created an empire which stretched across the breadth and much of the length of Europe, not to mention the New World. Despite the division into separate Spanish and Austrian branches in 1521–2 and the extinction of the former in 1700, resulting in the cession of Spain and the overseas possessions to a Bourbon, there was plenty left by the time Joseph II was born in 1741 to form a collection of territories impressive in both its quantity and its quality. In the Austrian Netherlands (covering much of present-day Belgium and Luxemburg) and the duchy of Milan there were towns, high population-density and wealth; in parts of Bohemia, Moravia, Silesia and Lower Austria there were rural industries; in Styria, the Bohemian massif and the mountains of Upper Hungary, there were deposits of iron ore; on the great plains of Hungary, bisected by the navigable Danube, there was at least the potential to make the entire Monarchy self-sufficient in agricultural produce; on the southern and eastern periphery of the Monarchy there was

3

a great deal of empty space awaiting settlement and development.

In the great-power currency of the day, what mattered most was population. Although difficult to credit, there was a widespread belief that the population of the world had been declining steadily since classical times, so there was no perception of the problems which could arise from demographic pressure. By this yardstick, the Habsburg Monarchy was well-placed. With its total population of about 25,000,000, it was rapidly overhauling France (28,000,000 in 1789) and not so very far behind the Russian empire. The figures yielded by the conscription of 1791 revealed the following provincial distribution:

Bohemia	2,896,497
Moravia	1,600,367
Lower and Upper Austria	1,625,238
Styria	810,026
Carinthia	293,190
Carniola, Görz and Gradisca	530,841
Galicia and Bukovina	3,440,075
Tyrol (1789)	680,204
Vorderösterreich (1789)	337,858
Hungary (1787)	7,116,789
Transylvania (1787)	1,403,401
Total	20,734,486
Plus estimates for	
Istria	30,000
Trieste and the coast	30,000
Lombardy	1,340,000
Austrian Netherlands	2,000,000
Military frontier	350,000
Total	3,750,000
Grand Total	24,484,000[6]

Moreover, the core of the Monarchy, centred on the Danube valley, was ringed by a cordon of natural obstacles – the Bohemian forest, the Moravian Heights, the Carpathian mountains, the Transylvanian Alps, the Dinaric Alps and the Alps proper – which invaders always found very difficult to penetrate. As no less a person than Frederick the Great ruefully conceded in 1744 after his failed invasion:

> It must be allowed that it is more difficult to make war in Bohemia than in any other country. This kingdom is surrounded by a chain of mountains, which render invasion and retreat alike dangerous.[7]

Of all the Habsburg Monarchy's numerous and varied enemies, only Napoleon ever succeeded in taking Vienna.

Relatively secure behind this natural rampart, the Habsburgs were well placed to influence, if not dominate, events in the Balkans, eastern, central and southern Europe. In addition, the scraps of territory in south-western Germany (known collectively as *Vorderösterreich* or 'anterior Austria') and the substantial possessions in the Low Countries brought western Europe too within their orbit. Only the Baltic lands clearly lay beyond their grasp, although even here a Habsburg presence was maintained by virtue of the fact that northern Germany as far east as the Leba (not far from Danzig) formed part of the Holy Roman Empire. Indeed, the imperial nexus gave the Habsburg emperor influence, both formal and informal, right across German-speaking Central Europe.

This relationship between the Habsburg Monarchy and the Holy Roman Empire was as important as it is confusing. As the map on page 220 shows, the two overlapped but were by no means identical. Founded by Charlemagne's coronation as emperor by Leo III in Rome on Christmas Day 800, the Empire had developed over the centuries into a decentralised amalgam of princes great and small, both secular and ecclesiastical, together with fifty-odd self-governing municipalities, and all presided over by an elective emperor. By the mid-eighteenth century, there were nine electors: three ecclesiastical (the archbishops of Mainz, Cologne and Trier), and six secular (the king of Bohemia and the electors of the Palatinate, Saxony, Bavaria, Brandenburg and Hanover).

From 1452 onwards these electors had always chosen a Habsburg as emperor, so there was a natural tendency to assume that the Holy Roman Empire and the Habsburg Monarchy merged into each other. Their essential separability, however, was demonstrated in 1740 when the emperor Charles VI died without a male heir. The possessions he had ruled by virtue of being head of the house of Habsburg – the Habsburg

Monarchy – passed to his daughter Maria Theresa, who ruled them using the most senior of the many titles she had inherited – 'King of Hungary'. However, under the Salic law which governed the Holy Roman Empire, as a woman she could not have been elected empress, even if the electors had been inclined to do so. Attempts to secure the title for her husband – Francis Stephen – failed, the electors preferring one of their own number, Charles Albert of Bavaria, whom they elected as emperor Charles VII in 1742. It was not until 1745, following Charles' brief and unhappy reign, that Francis Stephen could be elected as emperor Francis I and the connection between Holy Roman Empire and Habsburg Monarchy restored.

It is important to realise, however, that the connection was still only personal – it was based on the essentially contingent fact that the Holy Roman Emperor, Francis I, and the ruler of the Habsburg Monarchy, Maria Theresa, were married to each other. Their son Joseph was elected 'King of the Romans' in 1764, which in effect gave him the automatic right to succeed his father as emperor on the latter's death. When that happened the following year, Joseph became the emperor Joseph II, but the government of the Habsburg Monarchy remained firmly in the hands of his mother. He did become 'coregent' of the Monarchy, but this was due solely to the generosity (or cunning) of Maria Theresa. As we shall see in a later chapter,[8] the relationship between the Holy Roman Emperor and the Queen of Hungary – between son and mother – was not always amicable. It was not until Maria Theresa's death in 1780 that Holy Roman Emperor and head of the house of Habsburg (or, more correctly, the house of Lorraine or perhaps Lorraine-Habsburg) were one and the same person once again.

In other words, between 1740 and 1780 there was a separation between Holy Roman Empire and Habsburg Monarchy, although it was only between 1740 and 1745 that the separation was total. It will be argued later that this separation, caused simply by the inability of the last of the Habsburgs – Charles VI – to sire a legitimate male heir, had a profound and mainly detrimental effect, not only on the Habsburg Monarchy but also on Germany and even Europe as a whole.[9] Here what needs to be stressed is the influence which the emperor was able to exercise and the benefits this brought to the Habsburg Monarchy.

As with so much else relating to the politics of eighteenth-century Europe, it mainly concerns religion. When the religious upheavals of the sixteenth and seventeenth centuries finally abated and both Catholics and Protestants were obliged to accept that they could not achieve total victory, about two-thirds of the population of the Holy Roman Empire had become Protestant.[10] This denominational balance was not reflected, however, in the political structure of the Empire. On the contrary, there the ratio was almost exactly reversed. This was due mainly to the survival of most of the ecclesiastical principalities – eighty-odd archbishoprics, bishoprics, monasteries, even nunneries, which all enjoyed princely status, or in other words were full self-governing members of the Empire, were not subject to any other prince and were represented in the imperial parliament (*Reichstag*).[11]

These prelates naturally gravitated towards the Habsburg emperor on that most reliable of political principles: 'my enemy's enemy is my friend'. The enemy in question was the group of larger secular princes, most of whom were Protestant and all of whom sought to increase their independence from imperial control and to add the remaining ecclesiastical territories to their existing hoard. A straight fight between – say – the duke of Württemberg and the prince-abbot of Kempten could have ended only with the absorption of the latter's lilliputian territory by the former. It was only the imperial constitution, maintained by the emperor, which kept the prince-abbot and the rest of the small fry afloat.

Even the largest of the ecclesiastical principalities could not compete with Württemberg, let alone Prussia, Saxony or Hanover, but collectively they were of considerable importance. Firstly, they provided the Habsburg emperor with a large and generally reliable bloc of votes at the imperial parliament. At the very least, that allowed the Habsburgs to prevent the Empire from doing anything contrary to their interests. Secondly, the strategic location of many of them – notably the three Rhenish archbishoprics, which dominated the Rhine and Moselle valleys – made it much easier for Austrian armies to operate in Germany. Thirdly, their own lack of power-political ambitions allowed them to make financial contributions to the Habsburg war-effort.

It was not only the ecclesiastical principalities which helped to extend Habsburg influence throughout the Holy Roman

Empire. There were three other groups equally threatened by the ambitions of the greater secular princes: the free imperial cities, the smaller secular princes and the imperial knights. Many of these were Protestant, but their political vulnerability kept them huddled together in the protective embrace of the emperor. Once again, their individual frailty should not lead to an underestimate of their collective weight. If political influence means making individuals and corporate groups behave as one desires, then the imperial nexus did extend the influence of the Habsburgs far and wide. In free imperial cities, especially those with strong imperial traditions such as Aachen, Regensburg, Frankfurt and Nuremberg, the writ of the emperor still ran.

As we shall see, in the age of the power-state, which began its relentless progress in just this period, such little territories came to seem anachronistic, because they could not assemble great armies and conquer other states. It is easy to mock – as Treitschke did – the Prince of Hohenlohe who erected statues of the world's greatest conquerors (Ninus, Cyrus, Alexander and Caesar) outside his castle at Weikersheim or the geriatric soldiers of the prince-bishop of Hildesheim whose caps bore the timid motto 'Grant us peace in our time, Oh Lord!'.[12] But there is more than one way of ruling Germany and ultimately 'the Prussian way' did not prove to be an unqualified success. 'The Austrian way' traditionally involved the use of groups such as the imperial knights (*Reichsritter*), nobles who were not full princes because they were not represented in the imperial parliament but were not subject to any other prince either, being directly and solely subject to the emperor. In round figures, they constituted 350 families, ruling 1500 estates comprising 13,000 square kilometres and 350,000 people.[13] They supported the Habsburg emperors by serving in their armies and administrations and by ensuring that the numerous ecclesiastical states they dominated toed the Austrian line. Such important servants of the Habsburg Monarchy as Count Stadion and Prince Metternich were imperial knights by origin.

It was not only mutual self-interest which held the Holy Roman Empire together. Like every other successful polity, it was also maintained by law and culture. During its thousand-year existence, it had developed institutions, practices and values which satisified both the material and cultural aspirations of many of its inhabitants. If oppression, exploitation, poverty and ignorance were common, their incidence compared favourably with almost every part of Europe. Even after the political success of France or the economic success of Great Britain advertised the apparent superiority of the nation-state, there were still many in the Holy Roman Empire who preferred their own unique combination of centrifugal dispersion of political authority counterbalanced by the centripetal forces of imperial law and German culture.

In summary, the Holy Roman Empire of the eighteenth century can be divided into six constituent parts: i) the emperor; ii) the ecclesiastical states; iii) the free imperial cities; iv) the imperial knights; v) the smaller secular princes; vi) the greater secular princes. Groups one to five were united by opposition to group six. In the event, it was this last group which triumphed, when the French Revolution and Napoleon foolishly and fatally destroyed the Holy Roman Empire and allowed group six to expropriate groups two to five. As a result, Bavaria, for example, acquired no fewer than eighty-three separate territories (not including myriad imperial knights' estates), which increased its area and population by at least 50 per cent, with the elector being made a king into the bargain.[14] Admittedly, this was not the first time that the aggrandisement of the strong at the expense of the weak had been mooted. At the beginning of the century Louis XIV had enticed Max Emanuel of Bavaria into an alliance by the promise of annexing neighbouring prince bishoprics and free imperial cities. A generation later, in the very year that Joseph II was born, the new main threat to the Habsburg Monarchy – Frederick the Great – floated the idea of building a more secure territorial basis for the new Bavarian emperor Charles VII by the same process.[15]

For the time being, the balance of forces within the Holy Roman Empire was too even to allow such a fundamental change. It was not until the revolutionary armies brought force and folly of truly modern dimensions that Humpty Dumpty could be dislodged. In the meantime, the Habsburgs had at their disposal a web of patronage and mutual interest which stretched the length and breadth of German-speaking Europe. It was fragile, delicate, and required very deft and delicate handling, but it was what held the European states-system together. Joseph's failure to appreciate its value, and the fissures he tore in it by his determination to create an Austrian power-state, brought tragedy not only to him and the Habsburg Monarchy but also to the entire continent, with consequences which are still being suffered today.

. . .

PROBLEMS

The assets of Joseph II as he took control of the Habsburg Monarchy were therefore formidable, but there were problems to match. One of the penalties of its location at the centre of Europe was a corresponding ethnic diversity. This can be conveyed in many striking ways. One effective example was provided by a pamphlet of 1790 containing the funeral oration delivered by Father Joseph Scheller in St Stephen's cathedral, Vienna, which listed by way of preface Joseph's various titles:

> Joseph II, Roman Emperor, Apostolic King of Hungary, Bohemia, Dalmatia, Croatia, Slavonia, Galicia, Lodomeria, Archduke of Austria, Duke of Burgundy, of Styria, of Carinthia and of Carniola; Grand Prince of Transylvania, Margrave of Moravia, Duke of Brabant, of Limburg, of Luxemburg, of Geldern, of Württemberg, of Upper and Lower Silesia, of Milan, of Mantua, of Parma, of Piacenza, of Guastalla, of Auschwitz and Zator; Prince of Swabia, Prince-Count of Habsburg, Flanders, the Tyrol, of Hennegau, of Kyburg, of Görz and Gradisca, Margrave of the Holy Roman Empire, of Burgau, of Upper and Lower Lusatia, Count of Namur, Lord of the Windisch March and of Mecheln; Duke of Lorraine and Bar; Grand Duke of Tuscany.[16]

Even this list was not exhaustive, as the author recognised by ending with 'etc. etc.'. Another way of making the same point is to record that the Habsburg Monarchy of Joseph II's day included all or part of the present-day countries: Belgium, Luxemburg, the Netherlands, Germany, Austria, the Czech Republic, Slovakia, Poland, the Ukraine, Rumania, Hungary, Serbia, Croatia, Slovenia and Italy. As Harold Temperley observed, the Habsburg Monarchy was not so much a country as a continent, all by itself.

Within this great conglomerate lived a wonderful variety of peoples. Leaving aside the French- and Flemish-speaking inhabitants of the Austrian Netherlands, five main groups of languages can be identified: the German speakers, concentrated in Austria and the Alpine provinces, but also strongly represented in Bohemia, the towns of Hungary, and Transylvania; the Italian speakers, forming a relatively homogeneous bloc in southern Tyrol (but which also included – as it still does – a minority of 'Ladins' speaking a form of Latin similar to the Romansch language of Switzerland), Milan, Parma, Piacenza and Tuscany; the Magyar speakers of Hungary and Transylvania; the Romanian speakers of Transylvania; and, finally, the speakers of Slavonic languages. This last-named group needs to be subdivided further into three: those with a long-standing sense of cultural identity and a written language, such as the Czechs of Bohemia and Moravia or the Poles of Galicia; those with an embryonic sense of separate identity but without yet a clear national consciousness, such as the Croats and Serbs of Hungary; and those 'submerged nationalities', concealed by illiteracy, whose existence awaited discovery by the ethnologists of the nineteenth century, such as the Ruthenians (or Ukrainians) of Galicia or the Slovaks of northern Hungary.[17] In addition, there were large Jewish minorities in Galicia (200,000–250,000), Hungary (80,000), Bohemia (40,000), and Moravia (30,000).[18]

Even this bewildering categorisation fails to do justice to the complexity of the situation, by failing to record adequately just how *mixed* each area was. Especially in Bohemia, Moravia and throughout the vast kingdom of Hungary and Transylvania, a plethora of different ethnic groups lived together with varying degrees of mutual animosity. In the Banat of Temesvár, for example, the census of 1770–5 counted 189,640 Romanians, 78,778 Serbs, 43,201 Germans, 8,683 Bulgarians, 5,572 gypsies, 3,000 Italians and French, and 353 Jews.[19]

These were people divided by language, history, dress, customs, religion: in a word, by culture. Religious differences were particularly important, as they defined so much more than object and method of worship. Although the official ethos of the Habsburg Monarchy was firmly Roman Catholic, there were few varieties of European religious experience which could not be found somewhere. With the possible exception of the Austrian Netherlands and the Tyrol, which were overwhelmingly

Catholic, no province of the Monarchy was monolithic in its denominational make-up. In the kingdom of Hungary and Transylvania there were 1,900,000 Greek orthodox, 1,300,000–1,500,000 Calvinists, 600,000 Lutherans, 500,000 Uniates or Greek Catholics (who used the orthodox rite but acknowledged the primacy of the Pope), 80,000 Jews and 4,000,000 Catholics.[20] In Bohemia, a notorious centre of heresy since the days of John Hus, there was a rich sub-culture of unorthodox religion worthy of twentieth-century Southern California, while in many German-speaking regions 'clandestine Protestants' (*Geheimprotestanten*) sullenly conformed to Catholic ritual while awaiting the day of deliverance from the hands of anti-Christ.

Even in a Europe hitherto untouched by the standardising forces of modernisation, the Habsburg Monarchy stood out for its flamboyant 'otherness'. Visitors to Vienna were intrigued by the sights, sounds and smells of a dozen alien cultures. As the author of the best contemporary description of the city recorded:

> A striking visual drama is presented here by the variety of national costumes from different countries. Vienna is not dressed in the uniform, conventional clothes to be found in most other European cities. There are always many Hungarians, Poles, Serbs, Croats, Wallachians, Moldavians, Greeks and Turks to be found here, all of whom retain their national costume and stand out from the crowd as graphic counterpoints. The dominant and most commonly spoken language is German, but almost as much French and Italian can be heard, a good deal of Illyrian [Slavonian] and modern Greek, as well as Polish, Czech, Magyar, Croatian and Slovakian.[21]

Cultural confusion may have made Vienna an exciting place for foreign tourists, but it did not make the Habsburg Monarchy easy to govern. On the contrary, by impeding communication, it imposed a handicap on the Habsburgs which they were never able to surmount. Quite rightly, theorists of modernisation have identified ease of communication as the crucial determinant in the rate of change. Modernisation both requires and accelerates linguistic standardisation, as the relentless progress of the English (or rather American) language in the later twentieth century so clearly demonstrates. As Ernest Gellner has written, in industrial society for the first time in human history, explicit and reasonably precise communication becomes generally, pervasively used and important...A society has emerged based on a high-powered technology and the expectancy of sustained growth, which requires both a mobile division of labour, and sustained, frequent and precise communication between strangers involving a sharing of explicit meaning, transmitted in a standard idiom and in writing when required.[22]

The truth of this maxim was demonstrated whenever a Magyar tried to talk to a Slovak, a Romanian to a Serb, a Croat to a Slovene, or – more importantly – whenever a Viennese bureaucrat tried to talk to almost anybody out in the provinces. There was not even agreement as to what different places should be called: the city the Germans call Pressburg, for example, was (and is) called Bratislava by the Slovaks, Pozsony by the Magyars and Pozun by the Croats.[23] As we shall see, when Joseph II tried to grasp the nettle of linguistic diversity he was well and truly stung.[24] This deficiency would have been less serious if the Habsburg Monarchy had been surrounded by similarly multi-ethnic empires. But by the time Joseph II assumed power, it was clear that the major threat came from Prussia. There were non-German speakers in Prussia too (Poles in Silesia and Wends in Brandenburg) but by comparison with the Habsburg Monarchy it was monoglot: and correspondingly better-placed to modernise. The great economic gulf which opened up between the two rivals for the domination of Central Europe derived not least from this linguistic contrast.

It also derived from a similar disparity in ease of physical communication: the incidence of physical and symbolic communication are of course closely connected. In an age of instantaneous communication, it is difficult to conceive of the problems posed to the state – especially an interventionist state – by distance. At the height of his problems in the autumn of 1789, Joseph II complained bitterly that he was helpless in the face of the Belgian revolt for the simple reason that any report took eight days to reach him and any response on his part took eight more days to return, by which time both documents would have been rendered irrelevant by changing circumstances.[25] Plans which seemed so lucid and so logical in Vienna became blurred and frayed by the time they reached their intended targets in the localities. As Peter Dickson has drily observed: 'The Hobbesian characteristics of law, authenticity, clarity, communicability, proved elusive'.[26]

It was a cruel trick of geography that the Habsburg Monarchy was almost totally land-locked. Its only port of any significance was Trieste, which could be reached from Vienna only after a long, arduous and often dangerous journey over the Alps. An attempt to turn the equally remote port of Ostend in the Austrian Netherlands into a major port was crushed by British jealousy in 1727. Joseph himself felt this deficiency acutely; as he wrote in 1783:

> Nothing in the world could be more advantageous for the Monarchy than if a gigantic earthquake were to plunge all the Turkish provinces into the ocean and thus create a coastline from Dalmatia to the Dniestr. In that case I would gladly renounce all further acquisitions and Hungary would be like Belgium and Holland.[27]

There was little he could do beyond lamenting his fate. Although it can only be a rough guess, it has been estimated that two-thirds of the Habsburg Monarchy consisted of either forest or mountain.[28] Until mechanical equipment became available to create roads and tunnels, they would remain impenetrable or impassable. Moreover, geography had also cheated the Habsburgs by denying them the only pre-modern substitute for railways and motorways – navigable waterways. Certainly their monarchy was bisected by the greatest river in Europe, the Danube, but that was a river which was difficult to navigate due to rapids, rocks and large areas of swamp.[29] Worse still, it inconveniently flowed in the wrong direction, away from the rich markets of western Europe and towards the under-developed Balkans and the Black Sea. Most of the other rivers of the Monarchy betrayed their Alpine origins: frozen in winter, in spate in spring, dried up in summer and falling too steeply in any season to be of much use for transport. How different was the situation in Prussia, for which nature had provided access to one of the best navigable river-systems in Europe. Down these torpid waterways, as they wound their way gently across the great north European plain, could be floated the large surpluses of grain which western and southern Europe needed whenever the extra demand generated by population growth exceeded local supplies. It was a traffic which created in its wake a social and economic system which allowed the Hohen-zollerns to challenge, check and finally to overcome the Habsburgs.

These structural reasons for Habsburg backwardness had been exacerbated by historical development. In the late six-teenth century the Monarchy had enjoyed 'a brief Golden Age, peaceful, prosperous, and expansive on the whole, when the Danube lands...belonged perhaps more nearly to Western Europe than at any time before or since'.[30] But after 1600 four interacting crises brought this encouraging phase to an abrupt halt and threw it into reverse. Firstly, a long war against the Turks (1593–1606), civil war and of course the Thirty Years War (1618–48) inflicted profound material and cultural dam-age. Secondly, the brutal suppression of Protestantism and other forms of heresy brought an end to the pluralism of the sixteenth century, imposed a new orthodoxy and led to the expulsion of the most enterprising groups in society. More than 150,000 Protestants left Bohemia alone after their defeat at the battle of the White Mountain in 1620 (to put this in perspec-tive, it should be remembered that about 200,000 Protestants left France in the much more celebrated expulsion following the revocation of the edict of Nantes by Louis XIV in 1685). Thirdly, everywhere towns collapsed, ceasing to exercise a commercial or industrial function and increasingly confined to communities of semi-peasants, engaging only in a little hand-icraft or retailing and unable to raise credit for anything more ambitious: 'the new order of the seventeenth century held little place for the towns or for the serious use of urban resources'.[31] Fourthly, in the countryside a 'second serfdom' emerged, as noble landowners expropriated peasants, tied them to the soil and increased their obligations to provide forced labour for the great estates which increasingly dominated the rural economy.

There were two main beneficiaries of this process. Pride of place was taken by the magnates, the great aristocrats with the political power and material resources to pick up the pieces of a crumbling society. When the dust settled on the turmoil of the seventeenth century, it was they who stood out head and shoul-ders above the debris. Both relatively and absolutely they had advanced their position in economy, society and the state at the expense of the bourgeoisie, the peasantry and the lesser nobil-ity. In Bohemia, for example, the noble Estate numbered only eighty-five families by 1650, owning 62 per cent of all peasants;

a century later the thirteen families sporting the title of 'prince' owned a quarter of all dominical revenue.[32] Eighty estates of over 25,000 acres were confiscated by the Czechoslovak government after 1918, including 500,000 acres each from the Schwarzenbergs and the Schönborns, 400,000 from the Liechtensteins and 170,000 from the Kinskys.[33] In Hungary the concentration of land, wealth and power in the hands of a few magnates was even more pronounced, for here 'the greater part of the wealth of the country' was owned by just fifty landowners.[34] Any visitor to Vienna can still see how this wealth was spent and this power was expressed in the great representational palaces which dominate the old city and were almost all built at this time. In the fifty years which followed the raising of the Turkish siege in 1683 nearly 300 were erected.[35]

The other victor was the Roman Catholic church. By 1600 the population of the Habsburg Monarchy was predominantly Protestant, with the unimportant exceptions of 'anterior Austria' in south-western Germany and the Tyrol. What followed during the next century gave the lie to the liberal illusion that the only effect of persecution is to strengthen the faith of the oppressed. The Catholic revival was achieved not only by rack, rope and deportation, however. Together with the coercive stick went the carrot of conversion, especially in the form of more, better-trained and better-behaved priests, new proselytising religious orders, popular missions and, last but emphatically not least, the personal example set by the Habsburg rulers. Ferdinand II, the hammer of the heretics, created so powerful a sacral image by demonstrative devotion that he also founded a new ideology for his dynasty – the *pietas Austriaca*.[36] We can still gain at least an inkling of the confidence and militancy which characterised counter-reformation Catholicism in the Habsburg Monarchy by visiting the great baroque churches and monasteries which proved to be its most durable and agreeable mementoes. The theology which informed their fabulous decorative schemes was unashamedly, aggressively Roman Catholic, stressing just what separated them most from the heretics: the real presence, the immaculate conception, the cult of the Virgin and the Sacred Heart, the veneration of miracle-working saints, relics and pilgrimage places, and so on and so forth. Visual, tactile, theatrical and emotional, this is the culture of images: anything associated with the Word is conspicuously absent. This was a form of piety which suited dynasty and magnates perfectly: 'baroque Catholicism was far more tied than its medieval predecessor to both dynastic government and the entrenched system of self-sufficient *Herrschaften*; indeed the Church might at times seem little more than the estate-owners at prayer'.[37]

In summary, it can be said that out of the various crises of the seventeenth century came a Habsburg Monarchy which had a distinctive identity. Centred on the dynasty, it was based socially on the great magnates, economically on land and culturally on baroque Roman Catholicism. As the casualties had included Protestantism, the bourgeoisie, the towns and urban culture, it was a Monarchy which was essentially static, conservative and defensive. Its future was seen to lie in regaining the past, not in progressing to some hitherto unexperienced goal. The Monarchy always seemed to be a generation or so behind the rest of Europe. The great witch-craze, for example, did not arrive until it had ceased everywhere else: indeed, 'witches' were still being burned in Hungary in the 1750s.[38] Only the Irish appear to have persecuted their witches for longer.[39]

Geography and history thus conspired to create for Joseph II an inheritance for which such adjectives as 'different' or even 'unique' seem woefully inadequate. From his own point of view, the most serious failing of the Habsburg Monarchy was that it was clearly not a state. In the attractive formulation of R.J.W. Evans: 'the result [of developments in the seventeenth century] was a complex and subtly-balanced organism, not a "state" but a mildly centripetal agglutination of bewilderingly heterogeneous elements'.[40] This was the most unwelcome legacy Joseph could have received, for, as we shall see, he worshipped the state.

If a state is 'that agency in society which has a monopoly of legitimate force' (Max Weber), then the Habsburg Monarchy of 1741 did not qualify, for its nominal ruler did not possess that monopoly. Rather he was a partner in a triad of authority, the other two members being the Church and the nobility. In every Catholic country the Church formed a state-within-a-state, by virtue of its essentially international nature and its recognition of the primacy of the Pope, by virtue of its wealth and by virtue of its traditional right to control important areas of public policy, notably censorship, education and social welfare. What

17

was special about the Habsburg Monarchy was the power exercised by bishops who were not subjects of the ruler but were princes of the Holy Roman Empire in their own right. The prince-archbishop of Salzburg and the prince-bishops of Augsburg, Freising, Regensburg, Passau, Trent and Brixen all exercised metropolitan and diocesan jurisdiction respectively over significant parts of the Monarchy (not to mention the Bavarian bishop of Chiemsee and the Venetian bishops of Feltre, Padua and Verona who had rights in the Tyrol[41]). This intrusion of the jurisdiction of the imperial Church provided perhaps the best possible evidence that the Habsburg Monarchy was not a state. Even wholly indigenous prelates such as the archbishop of Vienna or the archbishop of Prague enjoyed a status and a self-regard which placed them in a special category.

The political power of the nobility was even more obvious. Everywhere they dominated the 'Estates' (*Stände*),[42] the corporate organisations which represented the various component parts of the Monarchy. It is impossible to find an appropriate English word to denote its territorial units. The word 'province' springs most readily to mind but is far too weak to convey the sense of autonomy noisily asserted by its Estates, for it suggests a degree of subordination to a greater whole which did not exist. The most eloquent statement of a separate identity was made by a Tyrolean noble, Count Lodron, in 1790, at the height of local resistance to centralisation:

> What does it matter to the Tyroleans what is happening in Bohemia, Moravia and in other states [*Staaten*]? The Tyroleans have their own laws, their own constitution, their own country [*Land*]. It is merely accidental that their prince rules other states as well. It is certainly flattering for them that they should have as their protector such a great monarch, a ruler of so many provinces [*Provinzen*], but they do not wish to pay so dearly for this honour, especially they do not wish to pay with the loss of their fundamental laws, which are guaranteed by God and the Estates.[43]

That a contemporary should use three words in one paragraph – *Staat*, *Land* and *Provinz* – is an indication of the scale of the problem. In the same year the Estates of neighbouring Carniola used another word – *Nation*, but not in the sense of a nation of free and equal citizens currently being popularised by the

French Revolution, rather in defence of regional particularism and social inequality.[44]

If such sentiments could be voiced so stridently in 1790, how much more natural had they seemed fifty years earlier, before the programme of centralisation had begun. Then 'Estates government was parallel to royal government, and partly overlapped with it'.[45] In every province (the word cannot be avoided after all) of the Monarchy, the Estates performed most of the important tasks of government, raising money and raising soldiers, organising land surveys, supervising the judicial system, attending to the building and maintenance of roads, even levying their own tolls and tariffs. It would be quite wrong to suppose that this situation had arisen out of conflict between centre and periphery. On the contrary, successive Habsburg emperors since the sixteenth century had reconstructed the Monarchy on the twin pillars of Catholic orthodoxy and magnate support.[46] Mutual support and comfort since the dark days when the allied enemy forces of Protestantism and gentry radicalism seemed certain to triumph had allowed the triad of dynasty, Church and magnates first to survive and then to flourish. By the middle of the eighteenth century, however, such an arrangement was beginning to seem anachronistic in an age of sovereign power-states. This was why Maria Theresa criticised the power of the Estates so sharply in her *Political Testament*. In particular she complained that even her senior advisers regarded themselves as representatives of the Estates against the monarch rather than the other way round: 'they flattered themselves that they were to be regarded not as mere "ministers", as at other courts, but as co-regents or at least *pares curiae*'.[47]

Although she did not use the word, what Maria Theresa lacked was a bureaucracy. Max Weber identified the following main characteristics of a modern bureaucracy: fixed and official areas of jurisdiction governed by generally applicable laws and regulations; a hierarchy of command, accessible by appointment on the grounds of skill, not election or patronage, with promotion determined by merit; the conduct of business in writing (so that permanent records can be preserved in files) by full-time professionals, who have received expert training and are paid a regular salary (rather than being dependent on fees or bribes).[48] By this token, the Habsburg Monarchy did not possess a bureaucracy. It might reasonably be objected that

Max Weber was presenting an 'ideal type' and that no mid-eighteenth century European state measured up. However, ideal types do serve a purpose in helping to identify *relative* positions between a number of competitors. For the historical and geopolitical reasons identified earlier, the Habsburgs were a long way behind some of their rivals, most notably and fatally Prussia.

This may well invite the charge that the 'teleological trap', against which a warning was hoisted at the beginning of this chapter, is about to claim another victim. It seems a risk worth taking, for even if models of modernisation inflict distortion by introducing categories drawn from a later period and introduce an unwelcome air of inevitability, they do also put the peculiarities of the Habsburg Monarchy into sharper focus. For that reason, it is helpful to summarise the main features of traditional and modern societies (see Table 1).

Table 1   The main features of traditional and modern societies

	Traditional	Modern
economy	agrarian, self-subsistence	industrial technology
technology	low	high
pattern of settlement	rural	urban
productivity	low	high
mobility	low	high
incomes	low, major inequalities	high, tendency towards equalisation
social structure	homogeneous, stable, local groups	heterogeneous, high mobility
stratification	'deferential community', Estates	egalitarian divisions, based on professional achievement
family structure	dominance of large primary groups	nuclear family
social mobility	stable	mobile
professions	simple, stable	differentiated, fluctuating
functions	diffuse	specialised
life-expectancy	low	high
degree of organisation	low, informal	high
government	local, personal	centralised, anonymous
political participation	low	high
recruitment to posts	closed, by invitation	open, competitive
social control	direct, personal	indirect, bureaucratic
conflicts	open, disruptive	institutionalised, suppressed

law	religious, personal	abstract, formal, contractual
religion	dogmatic, state-supportive	secularisation, separation of church and state
literacy	low	high
communications	personal	media-based
attitudes	inward-orientated	outward-orientated
values	particularistic	universalist
norms	consistent	inconsistent
roles	general	specialised[49]

Every application of this check-list consigns the Habsburg Monarchy to the middle column; it was the traditional polity, economy, society and culture *par excellence*. This would not have mattered so much if a number of other European states had not begun edging into the right-hand column. It was a growing discrepancy which had been masked during the late seventeenth and early eighteenth centuries by the dramatic successes gained against the Ottoman Turks and the French. After the siege of Vienna in 1683 had been raised – significantly by means of an international effort – the Habsburgs embarked on a great *reconquista* in the Balkans. Although they had nominally ruled the entire kingdom of Hungary since the last Jagiellon king fell fighting the Turks at the battle of Mohács in 1526, they had been able to make good their claim only to the north-western fringe. The rest became part of the Ottoman empire. The peace of Karlowitz of 1699 placed all of Hungary, including Transylvania, under Habsburg rule *de facto* as well as *de jure*. A second war of 1716–18, ended by the peace of Passarowitz, added the Banat of Temesvár, northern Serbia and western Wallachia. Meanwhile, fruitful cooperation with the Dutch and the British in the war of the Spanish Succession brought victory over the French and a substantial share of the Spanish inheritance: a large part of the Italian peninsula and what now became known as the Austrian Netherlands.[50]

Success in the west and success in the east franked the system which had developed in the course of the seventeenth century with those most potent forms of legitimation: military victory and territorial expansion. Just as the *reconquista* in Spain had given their cousins a dangerous sense of divine mission, this latest defeat of the forces of Islam made the Austrian

Habsburgs over-confident. While it would be churlish to suggest that these great gains were wholly illusory, for the Habsburgs did retain most of them for two centuries, Nemesis was soon an unwelcome visitor. She came partly in the form of the failure of Charles VI (1711–40) to produce a legitimate male heir. The last twenty years of his reign were dominated by a search for domestic and international recognition of the 'Pragmatic Sanction', a document which declared the indivisibility of the Habsburg possessions and which gave priority to the claims of Charles's daughters over those of his elder brother and predecessor Joseph I (1705–11). It was an indication of how far the Monarchy was from statehood and the objectivisation of political authority that accident of birth should have assumed such importance.

Nemesis also appeared on the diplomatic and military scene. In 1733 the Monarchy became involved in a major war with France, the oddly named 'war of the Polish succession'. While France was supported by Savoy and Spain, Austria had to fight alone. Two years of defeat on the Rhine and in Italy showed just how much Habsburg victories in the past had owed to the money and manpower of Great Britain and the United Provinces and to the fortuitous genius of Prince Eugene of Savoy, now a crippled and senile septuagenarian. The peace settlement of 1735 (not formally ratified until 1738 as the treaty of Vienna) obliged Maria Theresa's husband Francis Stephen to give his duchy of Lorraine to France in exchange for the right of succession in Tuscany and ceded Charles VI's kingdoms of Naples and Sicily to a Spanish Bourbon. The acquisition of the duchy of Parma was scant compensation. In the crushing verdict of Derek McKay: 'In her unreformed state and without outside financial support, the position of Austria as a great power had proved a myth'.[51]

Worse was to come. In 1737 Charles VI felt obliged to intervene in the war between the Russians and the Turks, both to maintain his alliance with the former and to control their expansion into the Balkans. Not for the last time, the Turks proved to be more formidable opponents than had been expected and instead of providing easy victories, inflicted humiliating defeats. At the treaty of Belgrade in 1739 Charles VI was obliged to give up two of the great gains made at Passarowitz in 1718 – western Wallachia and northern Serbia, including Belgrade.

Defeat at the hands of the French and the Turks in the 1730s was serious but not critical, for it did not signify a structural failure. Neither of these traditional enemies had devised anything fundamentally new in the way of warfare or the mobilisation of resources. They owed their success to the more efficient use of traditional methods and to the decay of the Habsburg equivalents. The future of the Monarchy was not at stake in 1735 or 1739 – what had been lost could well be regained. But quite a different kind of problem erupted after the unexpected death of Charles VI in October 1740. Frederick the Great's invasion of the Habsburg province of Silesia in December of the same year was a truly world-historical moment, after which nothing could ever be the same again. For the first time a wholly German power, a prince of the Holy Roman Empire, had emerged to challenge the Habsburgs for the domination of German-speaking Europe. By seizing and retaining Silesia, Frederick created the problem of dualism, a problem which would remain on the agenda until the peace of Prague of 1866, when the Habsburgs were excluded from Germany following their defeat at Königgrätz. It was not so much what Frederick did, but the way he did it. As we shall see in the next chapter, there were many contributions to Prussia's victory over the Habsburg Monarchy in the three Silesian wars of 1740–63, but essentially it was the victory of the idea of the state (*Staatsidee*) over the idea of empire (*Reichsidee*), the victory of modernity over traditionalism.

Joseph was born on 13 March 1741, just a month before the Austrian defeat at Mollwitz indicated that the reconquest of Silesia would be difficult if not impossible. If Thomas Hobbes could claim that he and fear were born together in 1588, the year of the Great Armada, Joseph too could have claimed that an unhappy augur attended his own birth. As we have seen, his inheritance was as various as it was problematic. Twenty-four years were to pass before he could get one hand on the rudder and thirty-nine years were to pass before he could gain undisputed control of the cockpit. Much changed in the meantime, but the fundamental features of the Habsburg Monarchy remained deeply rooted in history and geography. To revert to Clausewitz's dictum paraphrased at the beginning of this chapter, it proved to be Joseph's misfortune that nature had given him the intellect to make everything very simple but not the temperament to recognise that everything was very difficult.

. . .

NOTES

1. Handbillets, vol. 5 (18), no. 7, fo. 15.
2. Quoted in Lorenz Mikoletzky, *Kaiser Joseph II. Herrscher zwischen den Zeiten* (Göttingen, 1979), p. 96.
3. Oscar Jászi, *The dissolution of the Habsburg Monarchy* (Chicago, 1929), p. 33; A.J.P. Taylor, *The Habsburg Monarchy 1809–1918. A history of the Austrian Empire and Austria-Hungary* (London, 1948) – the title notwithstanding, this begins with the reign of Joseph II; the same applies to C. A. Macartney, *The Habsburg Empire 1790–1918* (London, 1968).
4. The title of a popular work by Edward Crankshaw.
5. M.S. Anderson, *Europe in the eighteenth century* (London, 1961), p. 173.
6. *Krieg gegen die Französische Revolution 1792–1797*, 2 vols (Vienna, 1905), I, 535.
7. Frederick the Great, *The History of My Own Times* (1746), in *Posthumous Works of Frederic II King of Prussia*, vols I–II (London, 1789), II, 102.
8. See below, pp. 49–55.
9. See below, p. 22.
10. See the excellent map in *Großer historischer Weltatlas*, ed. Josef Engel, 3rd edn (Munich, 1967), p. 117.
11. For a complete list of the full members of the Empire *(Reichsstände)*, see H. Kiesel and P. Münch, *Gesellschaft und Literatur im 18. Jahrhundert* (Munich, 1977), pp. 203–7.
12. Heinrich von Treitschke, *Deutsche Geschichte im 19. Jahrhundert*, 5 vols (Leipzig, 1927), I, 19–20.
13. Rudolf Vierhaus, *Deutschland vor der französischen Revolution* (unpublished Münster Habilitationsschrift, 1961), p. 79.
14. Walter Demel, *Der bayerische Staatsabsolutismus 1806/8–1817* (Munich, 1983), p. 59.
15. Karl Otmar Freiherr von Aretin, *Das Reich. Friedensgarantie und europäisches Gleichgewicht 1648–1806* (Stuttgart, 1986), p. 34; Theodor Schieder, *Friedrich der Große: ein Königtum der Widersprüche* (Frankfurt am Main, Berlin and Vienna, 1983), pp. 157, 264.
16. *Trauerrede auf Joseph den Zweyten* (Vienna, 1790).
17. There are helpful – if greatly simplified – maps showing the ethnic composition of the Habsburg Monarchy in Macartney, *The Habsburg Empire* and Taylor, *Habsburg Monarchy*.
18. Josef Karniel, *Die Toleranzpolitik Kaiser Josephs II.* (Gerlingen, 1986), p. 194.
19. Ibid., p. 133.
20. Ibid., p. 42.

21. Johann Pezzl, *Beschreibung und Grundriß der Haupt- und Residenz-stadt Wien* (Vienna, 1802), p. 238.
22. Ernest Gellner, *Nations and nationalism* (Oxford, 1983), pp. 33–4.
23. James J. Sheehan, *German history 1770–1866* (Oxford, 1989), p.5.
24. See below, pp. 70–2.
25. Handbillets, vol. 51, no. 1158, to Trauttmansdorff, 5 November 1789 fo. 701, (also reprinted in Schlitter, pp. 463–4).
26. Dickson, I, 323.
27. Handbillets, vol. 7 (27), no. 110, fo. 90, to Col. Zechenter in Temesvár, 4 February 1783.
28. Nachum Gross, 'The industrial revolution in the Habsburg Monarchy 1750–1914', in Carlo M. Cipolla (ed.), *The Fontana economic history of Europe*, vol. 4: *The emergence of industrial societies*, pt. 1 (London, 1973), p. 238.
29. David F. Good, *The economic rise of the Habsburg Empire 1750–1914* (Berkeley, 1984), p. 30.
30. R.J.W. Evans, *The Making of the Habsburg Monarchy 1550–1700. An interpretation* (Oxford, 1970), p. xxiii. Despite the dates of the title, this brilliant book is required reading for anyone seeking to understand the Habsburg Monarchy in the eighteenth century and Joseph II in particular. What follows in the next paragraph is based on Evans' argument.
31. Ibid., p. 85.
32. Ibid., p. 93. Dickson, I, 91.
33. Eric Hobsbawm, *The age of revolution. Europe 1789–1848* (London, 1962), p. 15.
34. Dickson, I, 108.
35. Volkmar Braunbehrens, *Mozart in Vienna* (Oxford, 1991), p. 41.
36. Evans, *The making of the Habsburg Monarchy*, p. 73.
37. Ibid., p. 139.
38. Ibid., pp. 401–17.
39. A woman was burned as a witch in Clonmel in 1894, although admittedly the deed was perpetrated by her relations rather than agents of British imperialism – R.E. Hemphill, 'Historical witchcraft and psychiatric illness in western Europe', *Proceedings of the Royal Society of Medicine*, 59 (1966), 892.
40. Evans, *The making of the Habsburg Monarchy*, p. 447.
41. Georg Mühlberger, 'Absolutismus und Freiheitskämpfe', in Joseph Fontana et al., *Geschichte des Landes Tirol*, vol. 2 (Bozen, Innsbruck and Vienna, 1986), p. 385.
42. Confusion can easily arise from the fact that the English word 'estate' is used to translate both *Gut* – landed estate – and *Stand* – Estate of the realm. I have tried to reduce the confusion by using a capital 'E' when the latter sense is meant.

43. Otto Stolz, *Geschichte des Landes Tyrol*, vol. 1 (Innsbruck, Vienna, Munich, 1955), p. 577.
44. Dana Zwitter-Tehovnik, *Wirkungen der Französischen Revolution in Krain* (Salzburg dissertation, 1975), p. 41.
45. Dickson, I, 297.
46. Ibid., I, 297–8. There is an excellent account of the powers of the Estates in Charles Ingrao, *The Habsburg Monarchy 1618–1815* (Cambridge, 1994), p.9.
47. C.A. Macartney (ed.), *The Habsburg and Hohenzollern dynasties in the seventeenth and eighteenth centuries* (New York, 1970), p. 108.
48. H. H. Gerth and C. Wright Mills (eds), *From Max Weber, Essays in sociology*, new edn (London, 1991), pp. 196–8; Anthony Giddens, *Capitalism and modern social theory. An analysis of the writings of Marx, Durkheim and Max Weber* (Cambridge, 1971), p. 158.
49. Hans-Ulrich Wehler, *Modernisierungstheorie und Geschichte* (Göttingen, 1975), *passim*.
50. The fortunes of the Habsburgs during these years are best followed in Charles Ingrao, *The Habsburg Monarchy 1618–1815*, and the international diplomacy in Derek McKay and H.M. Scott, *The rise of the great powers 1648–1815* (London, 1983), ch. 3.
51. Derek McKay, *Prince Eugene of Savoy* (London, 1977), p. 241.

Chapter 2

JOSEPH II, MARIA THERESA AND JOSEPHISM

. . .

FROM EMPIRE TO STATE

In a letter to his brother, Grand Duke Leopold of Tuscany, written in February 1776, Joseph II presented the following indictment of the state of the Habsburg Monarchy after three-and-a-half decades of Maria Theresa's reign:

> I reckon that the best pen is hard put to it to dress it up in such a way as to hide the pitiable condition – of uncertainty and irresolution combined with timidity, weakness and pusillanimity – in which the Monarchy, with all its resources and means, languishes and sinks towards its doom.[1]

As we shall see, Joseph always chafed under the continuing yoke of his mother's sovereignty and was prone to over-excited tirades against her regime. Exaggerated it may have been, but his exasperation reveals his sense of frustration at having to wait so long for total control. With every year that passed, with every measure taken by someone else, his own range of options was narrowed. In other words, his freedom of action was limited not only by geography and history, as analysed in the previous chapter, but also by the reform movement initiated by Maria Theresa. Both in its general orientation and detailed provisions, this had achieved irreversible shape and momentum long before Joseph reached intellectual maturity, let alone began to influence policy. Of course his own programme replicated many of its features, but the overlap was by no means

27

complete, neither in terms of method nor substance. This chapter will identify the forces and conditions which created the Habsburg Monarchy as Joseph found it when he became sole ruler in 1780, by which time he had little room for manoeuvre.

The most powerful agent for change was territorial expansion. Even a cursory comparison between maps of the Habsburg Monarchy in 1680 and 1720 will reveal the dramatic nature of the change. It was a change from a Monarchy which was mainly German-speaking and located within the Holy Roman Empire, to a Monarchy which was as much Hungarian, Balkan and Italian as it was German. This shift in the territorial centre of gravity to the east and the south was bound to transform the Habsburg rulers' sense of priorities. For Ferdinand II (1619–37) or Ferdinand III (1637–57), it was the Holy Roman Empire which was their natural and necessary preoccupation. They were the last to be able to concentrate their attention there. Leopold I (1657–1705) was both obliged and enabled to develop a more continental perspective by his conquest of Hungary and his attempt to conquer the empire vacated by the extinction of his Spanish cousins. Of his two sons, Joseph I (1705–11) consolidated and expanded Habsburg possessions in the Balkans, while Charles VI (1711–40) annexed the Spanish possessions in the Netherlands and Italy, which together made the Habsburg Monarchy an irrevocably international empire.[2] This was a change whose magnitude has not always been appreciated, mainly because of the historical anomaly by which an empire that was essentially German was called 'Holy Roman'.

This did not mean that the Habsburgs lost interest in the Holy Roman Empire. On the contrary, there was something of a revival of imperial patriotism in the early eighteenth century, accompanied by a vigorous initiative by Charles VI to reassert and expand his imperial role.[3] What it did mean was a growing awareness that the Habsburg Monarchy was an entity *separate* from the Holy Roman Empire. This was revealed, for example, in the Pragmatic Sanction, first drafted in 1703, which declared the indivisibility of all Habsburg territories. No longer was the Monarchy to be regarded as a collection of bits of property, owned by the head of the family and his to distribute among his children as he saw fit (as had been the case until very recently). It was a crucial step away from patrimonial dynasticism towards the objectivisation of political authority, or – to put it another way – away from the Habsburg Monarchy as a collection of *Estates* and towards the Habsburg Monarchy as a *state*.

If this seems a little abstract, the process can also be observed in the changing balance of power among institutions of government at Vienna. Throughout the reign of Charles VI there was a struggle for domination between the Imperial Chancellery (*Reichskanzlei*), which dealt with his interests as Holy Roman Emperor, and the Austrian Court Chancellery (*Hofkanzlei*), which dealt with his interests as ruler of the Habsburg Monarchy. The question at stake was: which interests should Charles VI put first? Should he regard himself first and foremost as Holy Roman Emperor, with an obligation to treat all the members of the Empire in an even-handed way? Or should he give priority to those lands he ruled as hereditary sovereign of the Habsburg Monarchy, whose interests often ran counter to – and many of whose territories lay outside – the Holy Roman Empire? In a world of increasingly rapid state-formation, it had to be the second option which proved more compelling.

In other words, the accession of Maria Theresa in 1740 did not mark a sudden break. As the most distinguished modern Austrian historian of the period has stressed, the period straddling the later part of Charles VI's reign and the early years of his daughter's should be regarded as a unity.[4] Even so, the loss of the imperial title for the first time for three centuries certainly concentrated Habsburg minds on their hereditary lands and accelerated the move away from the Holy Roman Empire. In the same way, military defeat was not a new experience for the Habsburgs, especially not after the disasters of the 1730s, but the failure against Prussia in the first two Silesian wars (1740–2 and 1744–5) was an especially brutal reminder of the fragility of the Monarchy's great-power status.

It would be difficult to exaggerate the importance of the loss of Silesia to Prussia which resulted; even the cessions of Naples, Sicily or Serbia extracted from Charles VI paled by comparison. Silesia was populous (about 1,000,000 inhabitants), economically advanced (a flourishing textile industry and excellent water communications) and fiscally productive (yielding about 25 per cent of the total tax revenue of the Austrian and Bohemian lands). To lose all that was bad enough, but the damage did not stop there. As it had formed an integral part of the economies of the neighbouring provinces of Bohemia and Moravia, they too suffered serious and lasting damage.[5] Moreover, the fact that this great asset had passed to Prussia doubled the depth of the wound: if all the various resources of Silesia were added together and expressed by the algebraic symbol 'x', the power-relationship between the Habsburg Monarchy and Prussia changed as a result of its transfer not by 'x' but by two times 'x', for what had been taken away from the one was added to the other.[6] The same applied to its strategic position. In the hands of the Habsburgs, Silesia was a tongue of territory stretching into northern Germany; its loss not only reduced Habsburg influence there, it also put Prussian armies within a hundred miles of Prague and 130 miles of Vienna. The implications were to become painfully obvious in 1790, the year of Joseph's death.

.   .   .

THE DIPLOMATIC REVOLUTION

The loss of the imperial title to the elector of Bavaria and the loss of Silesia to the king of Prussia completed a long-gestating process. It can be summarised best as 'a dual retreat from empire': on the one hand a retreat from the Holy Roman Empire to the Habsburg Monarchy; on the other hand, a retreat from the outlying, 'imperial' parts of that Monarchy to its core. It was a process whose parts were interdependent and complementary. Its motive forces were so strong, so deeply rooted in geopolitics and history, and so intensified by recent events, that sooner or later it must have been articulated and activated. Bismarck once remarked that 'by himself the individual can create nothing; he can only wait until he hears God's footsteps resounding through events and then spring forward to grasp the hem of his mantle – that is all'.[7] On this occasion, the agent of the Almighty proved to be Count Wenzel Anton von Kaunitz.

Kaunitz was well placed to carry out a fundamental reappraisal of Habsburg policy, for he had served in senior diplomatic positions in both Italy and the Netherlands during the 1740s and had served as Austrian representative at the Aachen peace negotiations held in 1748 which brought the war of the Austrian Succession to an end. Direct experience had taught him that neither Italy nor the Austrian Netherlands could be defended successfully against a determined French attack and that in every other respect too their value was greatly inferior to that of the central provinces. Habsburg policy therefore had to be reorientated from periphery to centre and its primary objective had to become the recovery of Silesia. That was easier said than done: the pitiless exposure of the Monarchy's military weakness during the previous two decades made this an impossible task without powerful allies. But where were they to be found? The traditional alliance with the 'maritime powers' – Great Britain and the United Provinces (or 'Dutch Republic') – had proved a broken reed. Preoccupied with hostility to France, the British had helped to force Maria Theresa to abandon Silesia and had positively welcomed the rise of Prussia in Germany. Clearly a spent force by this time, the Dutch had remained neutral throughout the 1740s.

In other words, if the Habsburg Monarchy were to reorientate itself from periphery to centre, from being an empire to being a state, it would have to reorganise its alliance-system. There was the additional consideration that Silesia was landlocked. Even if the maritime powers had been prepared to put their best feet forward, there was little they could have done to have helped Maria Theresa to regain the lost province. A continental target required continental allies. Russia was already an ally, indeed it had been Charles VI's anxiety to preserve the alliance which had prompted him to participate in the disastrous war against the Turks of 1737–9. There was nothing less certain than the quality and quantity of Russian assistance, however, as Maria Theresa had discovered to her cost in 1740 (and as Joseph II was to discover in 1787–90). Immobilised by palace revolution and diverted by Swedish invasion, Russia had played no part in the Silesian wars of 1740–5. So it was essential that the Monarchy should obtain at least the benevolent neutrality and preferably the active assistance of the greatest continental power – France.

This was the analysis presented by Kaunitz to Maria Theresa and her senior ministers in the spring of 1749. Not surprisingly, so radical a proposal aroused scepticism if not hostility. Nevertheless, Kaunitz was sent to France as ambassador in 1750 and allowed to make his case. There is no need to follow the ins and outs of the tortuous diplomacy which followed.[8] Initial rejection by the French was reversed by their impending colonial war with the British and their anger at Prussia's apparent treachery. The result was the 'diplomatic revolution' consummated by the first treaty of Versailles of 1 May 1756, which terminated two-and-a-half centuries of hostility between France and the Habsburgs. It also marked the beginning of what is usually called the Seven Years War but, from the Habsburg standpoint, is better known as 'the third Silesian war'.

.   .   .

THE END OF THE BAROQUE

Presented in this way, the great reorientation of Habsburg policy orchestrated by Kaunitz appears to exemplify the 'primacy of foreign policy' (*Primat der Aussenpolitik*). It was a radical response to a radical change in the European states-system. But it was much more than that. As Grete Klingenstein has stressed, the change in foreign policy was an integral part of a wider programme which embraced complementary domestic reform of similar magnitude.[9] The origins of this dual revolution are not to be sought only in international relations, indeed they were as much cultural as political. In Charles VI, baroque imperial culture had found its last and most splendid representative. Not only did he perpetuate Habsburg traditions, he brought to them an even more pronounced representational character, influenced by the many years he had spent in Spain. A visit to Klosterneuburg, the half-palace half-monastery he built in conscious imitation of the Escorial, can still evoke a culture which was visual, aural, plastic, tactile and olfactory – in a word: sensual.

His daughter (Maria Theresa) and her consort (Francis Stephen of Lorraine), born in 1717 and 1708 respectively, were of quite a different stamp. By 1740 the lavish, elaborate ceremonial and complicated etiquette, which made the Viennese court a paradigm of baroque culture, had come to seem simply out of date. What had carried conviction when Habsburg armies were putting the French and the Turks to flight began to look tired and anachronistic in a period of defeat and contraction. It was a process of cultural transformation similar to that experienced in France during the closing years of Louis XIV.[10] Characteristically, Maria Theresa did not seek to destroy what she had inherited: evasion, exemption and adaptation were her preferred methods. Moreover, on certain occasions she could engage in representational display in a manner distinctly reminiscent of her father.[11] As we shall see, it was left to her son to tear out the old court culture root-and-branch. Nevertheless, her accession did mark a change of generations and the introduction of a new ethos. In music, for example, 1740 did mark a caesura, for it put an end to the great representational baroque operatic festivals favoured by Maria Theresa's predecessors and ushered in the age of the concert.[12]

The self-confidence of the baroque, strident if slightly neurotic, made way for a mood of introspection and doubt. In the second half of the seventeenth century it had been the Catholic powers which had set the pace – France in western and central Europe, the Habsburg Monarchy in the east and Spain in the south and overseas. The conversion to Catholicism of a number of important German princes, led by the elector of Saxony in 1697, the defeat of the forces of Islam in the Balkans and the expulsion of the Protestants from France all signalled the apparently inexorable progress of militant Catholicism. Until 1688 the leading Protestant powers, Great Britain and the Dutch Republic, were enfeebled by persistent civil strife and wars against each other. By 1740 all had changed. It was the British who had found the magic formula which combined prosperity, liberty and power in a mutually supportive triad and it was the Catholic powers which were looking tired, impoverished and backward.

This was not just a question of power and plenty. It was also a victory for open and tolerant societies with their secular and literate cultures. The universities of the Catholic world, dominated almost everywhere by the Jesuits, those embodiments of counter-reformation culture, were by-words for intellectual stagnation. The verdict may have been unjust but it came to be widely held – and not only by Protestants. After a journey through the Habsburg Monarchy and the Holy Roman Empire in the mid-1770s, Carlo Antonio Pilati wrote that neither the sciences nor the humanities were cultivated in the Catholic territories, that any intellectuals to be found there were as full of prejudice as they were devoid of taste and that generally 'Protestant Germans are infinitely more enlightened than the Catholics'. Closer to home, Baron Joseph von Sonnenfels, the leading light of the Austrian enlightenment, lamented that

Saxony, Prussia – indeed every part of Germany which had experienced the Protestant reformation – had gained a cultural lead of several centuries.[13] It was the Prussian university of Halle, the Saxon university of Leipzig or the new Hanoverian university of Göttingen (founded in 1737) which were in the van of modern, progressive scholarship, as the Catholics tacitly recognised by sending their sons there in increasing numbers.

This was no secret in the Habsburg Monarchy. Several of Maria Theresa's advisers were either Protestant converts (Bartenstein, Haugwitz, Zinzendorf) or had studied at Protestant universities (Festetics, Kaunitz). Nor was it any secret that even the officially Catholic parts of the Monarchy were teeming with clandestine Protestants (*Geheimprotestanten*), outwardly conforming to Roman Catholicism, but only to avoid discrimination and persecution. It was estimated that there were at least 40,000 in Upper Austria, Carinthia, Carniola and Styria, that their numbers were growing and that conventional methods such as popular missions were not going to be sufficient for their conversion to the true faith.[14] The logical conclusion to be drawn from all these unflattering comparisons was, of course, that the Habsburgs and all their subjects should become Protestants. That the point can only be made facetiously is indicative of its unreality and points to the dilemma confronting Maria Theresa and her advisers. Unable to abandon the faith which was the core of their regime and indeed their very existence, they had to find a way of emulating Protestant techniques without being tainted by heresy. As we shall see, the search to find a 'Protestant Catholicism' which combined modernisation with the true faith did not prove easy.

· · ·

HAUGWITZ AND DOMESTIC REFORM

These political and cultural forces were fused by the shattering impact of Prussia's seizure of Silesia. The self-confidence of even the most complacent of Austrians could not survive the experience of being raped and robbed by a Protestant vassal with a population five or six times smaller (the population of Prussia in 1740 was only just over 2,000,000). During the long years of war in the 1740s, hand-to-mouth expedients had to be the order of the day, but once a general peace returned in 1748 a longer-term remedy could be attempted. Under the direction of Count Friedrich Wilhelm von Haugwitz, significantly a Silesian convert, both structure and ethos of the Habsburg Monarchy were transformed. The details of the numerous and intricate reforms need not concern us.[15] At the heart of the programme was the intention to change the Monarchy from an aggregate of separate polities, linked only by dynastic accident, into a single state, which recognised provincial diversity but which concentrated power in the hands of the sovereign at the centre.

Maria Theresa's determination to claim a monopoly of legitimate force necessarily involved a confrontation with the magnates, who dominated the provinces through the Estates, and the centre through the chancelleries. Reflecting on the desperate situation in which she found herself in the early 1740s, Maria Theresa wrote in her *Political Testament*:

> Matters got worse and worse, owing to the division between the provinces, none of the ministers was really trying to rescue me and the state from this terrible embarrassment. At first, all proposals which might have inflicted the smallest hardship on any province were immediately rejected by the officials in charge of the province, and everyone cared only for his own interest.[16]

The unreliability of the aristocracy had been dramatised by events in Bohemia in 1741, following the occupation of the province by a Franco-Bavarian army. At a ceremony at Prague on 19 December, the usurper Charles VII, hereditary elector of Bavaria, recently elected Holy Roman Emperor and now self-proclaimed King of Bohemia as well, received the homage of more than four hundred members of the Bohemian Estates. Together with the archbishop of Prague (a Count von Manderscheid), there were representatives from most of the leading aristocratic families of Bohemia present to publicise their desertion of the Habsburgs – Kinsky, Gallas, Königsegg, Kolowrat, Clary and so on.[17]

The reforms of Haugwitz, which began in 1749, concentrated the state's primal function of arranging security in the hands of the sovereign. To support a large standing army (107,000-strong initially), long-term grants of increased taxation were negotiated, or imposed if they could not be negotiated. The old-fashioned, baroque-sounding names of the new central and provincial bodies – the *Directorium in publicis et cameralibus* and *Representations and Chambers (Repraesentationen und Kammer)*, respectively – concealed a fundamental change from control by the Estates to control by the sovereign. The creation of a supreme court for the hereditary lands (*Oberste Justizstelle*) institutionalised the supremacy of royal justice. All this was accomplished by an act of the will from above: in the striking formulation of Peter Dickson, it amounted to a '*coup d'état*'.[18]

But it did not work; or rather, it did not work as intended. By 1756, when the third Silesian war began, the reorganisation of the Monarchy's alliance-system had assembled the mightiest coalition ever seen in Europe: the Habsburg Monarchy, France, Russia, Sweden and the Holy Roman Empire confronted Prussia and Great Britain. Yet despite an overwhelming demographic advantage (the population of the Habsburg Monarchy alone exceeded that of Prussia and Great Britain combined), the war which followed was a failure. After seven years of fighting, the peace of Hubertusburg restored the borders of 1756 (the *status quo ante bellum*, in diplomatic parlance). Even the most optimistic Austrian now had to concede that if Silesia could not be regained with the assistance of most of the European powers, it never would be.

. . .

KAUNITZ AND DOMESTIC REFORM

Just as the reforms associated with the name of Kaunitz had a dual domestic-foreign aspect, so did the failure. It had been his misfortune (or miscalculation) that he had approached France for an alliance just at the time when what had once been the hegemonial power on the continent was slipping towards its terminal plunge into disorder at home and impotence abroad. Military intervention by the French in Germany had been an embarrassment, indeed their rout by Frederick at Rossbach on 5 November 1757 had set the seal on Prussia's great-power status and had thus confirmed the permanence of Austro-Prussian dualism. The pathetic failure by the troops of the Holy Roman Empire at the same battle appeared to advertise with all possible starkness that the future in Germany lay with the idea of the state, not with the Empire. The Russians had demonstrated their habitual volatility and unreliability, failing to deliver the knock-out blow when the opportunity arose (after Frederick's defeat at Kunersdorf in 1759) for the very good reason that it was against their interests to do so. Of course hindsight helps, but – given the understandable tendency among historians to praise Kaunitz for his skill in constructing the great alliance of 1756 – it is legitimate to suggest that he should have paid more attention to the quality of his alliance-system than to its width. The mistake Kaunitz made in putting his eggs in the decaying French basket may be understandable, but it was a mistake all the same. Albion may have been perfidious occasionally, but at least she was also rich.

Nor had the domestic reforms achieved their goals. Certainly both the army and the financial administration performed better during the third Silesian war than during the first two, but that was not saying very much. Once again, it was the Prussian system which proved more efficient and more durable. After only three years of warfare, Austrian coffers were empty and the army was having to be reduced. Long before the death of the Tsarina Elizabeth in January 1762 and the accession of Peter III took Russia out of the coalition and into an alliance with Frederick, the conflict had become a war of attrition between contestants so exhausted that they could barely land a punch on each other. In the last campaign of the war it was Prussia which was still raising money, raising armies and winning battles.[19]

Although Kaunitz can be held mainly responsible for the disastrous wrong-turning taken by the Habsburg Monarchy in 1756, he played no part in the inadequate reforms of the late 1740s and early 1750s. Certainly he always believed that foreign and domestic reconstruction were interdependent, but equally certainly he did not approve of the way in which Haugwitz had set about the latter. This conflict used to be portrayed in terms of a factional struggle for power, but it is now realised that behind the personal rivalry lay a real difference of conception. While Haugwitz represented 'militant absolutism', blaming the Estates for the Monarchy's backwardness and concentrating on the extraction of more direct taxation from their tenacious grasp, the approach of Kaunitz was altogether more subtle and general, as befitted his more devious personality and superior education.[20]

In some ways, the second phase of reforms which Kaunitz directed after 1760 appears less radical than his rival's earlier version, for the centralist-sounding *Directorium in publicis et cameralibus* was abolished and replaced by the more particularist-sounding – and even more clumsily-named – *Vereinigte böhmisch-österreichische Hofkanzlei* ('United Bohemian-Austrian Court Chancellery').[21] But at its heart the Kaunitz programme was much more radical and ambitious. Going beyond the pragmatic, short-term responses to immediate problems favoured by Haugwitz, he sought the reconstruction of the Monarchy from the bottom up. So his approach was broadly economic rather than fiscal: in other words, he sought to increase revenue through the general expansion of the economy rather than in the more efficient exploitation of traditional sources of income. The lynch-pin of the new system was to be a Council of State (*Staatsrat*), established in 1760. Its main function was to provide the general over-view lacking in the past. So its members were not to have administrative responsibilities but were to concentrate on scrutinising and preparing schemes for the reform of every part and aspect of the Monarchy. Of course, Kaunitz's approach was not entirely disinterested: it was through the Council of State that he succeeded in expanding his influence from foreign affairs to every part of government.[22]

The two phases of reform certainly achieved a good deal. If the loss of Silesia had to be conceded, at least the actual survival of the Habsburg Monarchy, which had seemed very much in doubt in the dark days of 1741, was assured and at least it remained a great power. The total strength of the army rose from just over 100,000 in 1740 to 200,000 in 1757 to just over 300,000 in 1779. As essential corollaries, revenue increased by two-and-a-half times during the same period and some progress at least was made towards the formation of a bureaucracy.[23] If these might be regarded as assets for Joseph II, their accomplishment had generated far less appealing side-effects. Kaunitz's diplomatic revolution of 1756 had shackled the Monarchy to a decaying power in the west and an ambitious power in the east, a combination which was to have catastrophic consequences in the late 1780s. At home, the effort to maximise resources had been concentrated on the relatively soft targets of the Austrian and Bohemian lands, with the Italian possessions, Hungary and the Netherlands left virtually untouched. As a result, while the former group 'by 1780 was clearly suffering from long-term tax exhaustion', the latter presented 'a dangerous temptation to Joseph II's standardising inclinations when he ascended his mother's throne'.[24] As Joseph was to discover to his cost, a state which has begun but not yet completed a process of modernisation is a state which has the worst of both worlds.

. . .

EDUCATION

But modernisation involved more than soldiers and taxes. Prussia's victory in the Silesian wars had also been the victory of a superior culture. A suspicion that the Habsburg Monarchy was falling behind Protestant Europe had been gathering strength for many years. The elites of the Habsburg Monarchy, for example, had shown a lack of confidence in their own educational system by sending their children to schools and universities in Protestant Germany. As it was the Jesuits who had dominated secondary and higher education since the early seventeenth century, it was on them that the main weight of criticism fell. At the heart of the reforms which followed military defeat was the belief that education should cease to be part of the Church's domain (an *'ecclesiasticum'*) and become the state's responsibility: 'it is and shall remain for all time a *Politicum'*.[25] A decisive move to implement this principle came in 1753 when financial and administrative control of the university of Vienna was transferred to the *Directorium in publicis et cameralibus*. Academic matters were also withdrawn from church control following the death of archbishop Trautson in 1757.

However, this was no confrontation between Church and state; rather it was a campaign by reformers in both spheres to wrest control from the Jesuits and the old order they personified. If the key figure was Gerhard van Swieten, Maria Theresa's personal physician who dominated cultural policy from his arrival in Vienna from the Netherlands in 1745 to his death in 1772, numerous clerics great and small contributed with enthusiasm. This was shown, for example, by the creation of a proto-ministry of education (*Studienhofkommission*) in 1760 under the chairmanship of none other than Trautson's successor as archbishop, Migazzi. The same cooperation between clergy and laymen can also be found in the simultaneous reduction and eventual abolition of Jesuit influence on censorship.[26] So when Austrians found that they did not have to travel to Saxony or Prussia for a modern education or that they were now allowed to read Montesquieu's *Spirit of the Laws* without fear of prosecution, they could thank Church as well as state.

For all their shortcomings, the reforms of universities and secondary schools undertaken in the 1750s and 1760s marked a watershed in their history: once secularised, they could never be returned to clerical control of the old kind. Primary education proved much less tractable. It was one thing to declare education a *Politicum*, quite another to muster the resources and will-power required to tackle the problem of mass illiteracy. It was not until 1770 that a 'Commission in school matters' was established for Austria and a college of education (*Normalschule*) established. Neither went well, due to the familiar bureaucratic imbalance between an excess of plans and a shortage of funds. The arrival in 1774 of Johann Ignaz Felbiger, an Augustinian from Prussian Silesia and one of the most celebrated pedagogues of his day, gave the process fresh impetus. The general ordinance on schools, which he drafted and Maria Theresa signed in December of that year, established the ideal of a standardised education for all, administered by the state. Resistance was fierce and tenacious, not least from the intended beneficiaries, who believed that the new system was heretical ('Lutheran and bad' as the villagers of Murau put it). They particularly resented losing the labour of their children and having to pay fees and to buy books. In many rural areas there was mass absenteeism, with probably fewer than 25 per cent of children of school age actually attending. Nevertheless, it does seem that significant relative progress was made in the course of the 1770s with perhaps as many as 500 new schools being created in the Austrian and Bohemian lands.[27]

. . .

JANSENISM

It would be a mistake to think of these educational reforms as part of a process of secularisation, except in the sense that they increased state control. Felbiger's primary purpose was religious, to make children 'honest Christians', the two other

objectives – to create 'good citizens, that is faithful and obedi-
ent subjects of the authorities' and 'useful people for the community' – being important but secondary.[28] This exemplifies
the centrality of religion in the Habsburg Monarchy. Educational reform was only one part of a much greater problem
involving the institution apparently responsible for the backwardness of the Habsburg Monarchy – the Catholic church.
The reform movement which followed has become known as
'Josephism', the subject of a fierce and continuing debate
among historians as to its origins, intentions and significance.[29]
Relatively uncontroversial, however, is the observation that the
term is a misnomer, for it was well-established long before
Joseph himself reached intellectual maturity.

Of all the numerous strands which came together to form
Josephism, the strongest and thickest was formed by Jansenism. Named after Cornelius Jansen (1585–1638), bishop of
Ypres in what was then the Spanish Netherlands, its impact on
European religious and political life proved immediate, deep
and durable. In essence it represented a revival within the
Catholic church of Augustinianism, very much under a cloud
since the renegade Augustinian friar Martin Luther had shown
how a particular reading of St Augustine's theology could lead
to heresy and schism. Sooner or later it was bound to revive,
although the clarity and power of Bishop Jansen's *Augustinus*,
published posthumously in 1640, certainly hastened the process. Within just a few years Jansenism won support from prominent Catholics across western Europe, especially in France. It
became fiercely controversial with equal speed and for three
reasons: it was attacked by the Jesuits; it was condemned by the
Pope; and it was supported by many participants in the French
civil war, the *Frondes* (1648–53). At the heart of the controversy
was the age-old argument about the relationship between the
omnipotence of God and the free will of man. Following St
Augustine (and through him St Paul), the Jansenists stressed
that man was so polluted by original sin as a result of the Fall
that he could never achieve salvation by his own efforts. Only a
gift of grace from God could help, but this gift was entirely
gratuitous and was owed by God to no one. Any notion that
God could somehow be induced to bestow his grace by good
works was deemed incompatible with his omnipotence.

From these insoluble theological disputes of the mid-seven-
teenth century to the reforms in the Habsburg Monarchy of the

41

mid-eighteenth is a long and tortuous path, but mercifully it is one we do not need to travel. It must suffice to say that along the way Jansenism developed into a broad movement for the reform of the Catholic church. First and foremost it was against traditional baroque piety. Betraying its origins as a movement of the literate elites, it demanded simplicity instead of display, rigour instead of opulence, austerity instead of indulgence, denial instead of sensuality. While baroque piety stressed all those aspects of doctrine and liturgy which separated Catholicism from Protestantism,[30] the Jansenists were ecumenical: they insisted on the use of the vernacular for at least the Epistle and the Gospel during the Mass; their ideal church was a bare hall, their ideal altar a simple table without relics, crucifix or even candles; if they allowed religious art at all, it was to take the form of biblical scenes only, painted in a sober, realistic fashion; they were against the use of elaborate music in church, but very much in favour of psalm-singing; they rejected rosaries, scapulars and other external badges of piety; they opposed excessive veneration of saints, especially Mariolatry, assigning the Virgin only a modest role as an intercessionary; they were fiercely critical of the cults promoted by the Jesuits, especially the Sacred Heart of Jesus; they downgraded the monasteries and elevated the status of the parish priest.[31] Although Jansenists always insisted on their orthodoxy, it is not difficult to see why their opponents should have likened them to the river Danube: beginning Catholic, becoming Protestant and ending infidel.

It was the opposition from the dominant party within the Church which forced Jansenism into alliances it did not seek. Bishop Jansen himself had been a vigorous supporter of papal supremacy (or 'ultramontanism') and had written to Urban VIII asking for permission to dedicate to him the *Augustinus*. In the event, Urban succumbed to Jesuit pressure and condemned the book without even reading it, thus setting the pattern for sustained papal persecution. So the Jansenists found themselves allying with movements with which essentially they had nothing in common – with Gallicanism, which stressed the rights of the church in France; with conciliarism, which stressed the rights of general councils; with Richerism, which stressed the rights of parish priests; with episcopalism, which stressed the rights of bishops; with Febronianism, which stressed the rights of the prince-bishops of the Holy Roman Empire.

Essentially unpolitical, the attitude of Jansenists towards the state depended entirely on the state's attitude towards them. In France, Louis XIV's association of Jansenism with political opposition as well as heresy led him to seek to extirpate it altogether. He succeeded only in taking the French monarchy into an unnatural alliance with ultramontanism. This allowed the *Parlements* to pick up the Gallican ball he had thrown away and to begin the alienation between state and society which was to culminate in the French Revolution.[32] In the Habsburg Monarchy, fortunately for all concerned, the relationship developed quite differently. This was due largely to the way in which Jansenism belatedly gained access to the Monarchy, towards the end of the seventeenth century. It spread mainly through the medium of aristocrats who had been attracted to Jansenism on their grand tours, such as Count Franz Anton von Sporck, who visited the great Jansenist centre at the abbey of Port Royal and returned to his Bohemian estates to translate and distribute Jansenist tracts, or Prince Karl Theodor von Salm, the tutor of Joseph I, who saw the light during a visit to Paris. Particularly important was Prince Eugene, probably not a Jansenist himself, but sympathetic to their cause and determined to protect them against persecution.[33]

Prince Eugene was important, not only because of his immense prestige but also because he was governor-general of the Netherlands, the home of Bishop Jansen and an enduring centre of Jansenism. The acquisition of the province by the Austrian Habsburgs in 1714 naturally made it easier for Jansenism to reach the centre of the Monarchy. So did the simultaneous spread of reforming influence from another new Habsburg acquisition – Italy. The key figure here was Lodovico Antonio Muratori (1672–1750), not a Jansenist himself in a theological sense but whose influential rejection of baroque piety and call for a modernised form of Catholicism placed him in the same camp. Muratori's influence spread north via many channels: through the Austrian clergy trained at the *Collegium Germanicum* in Rome; through the university of Pavia in the Habsburg duchy of Milan; through the formation of an influential group of his supporters at the university of Salzburg in 1740; through private academies such as the *Academia Taxiana* at Innsbruck and the *Societas incognitorum* at Olmütz; through personal correspondence (he is known to have corresponded with at least seventy-five people in the Habsburg Monarchy); and, above all, through translations of his numerous publications. His most important work – *Della regolata devozione dei cristiani*, described by Peter Hersche as 'a manifesto of enlightened reform-Catholicism' – went through twenty different editions in German translation, eight of them published in Vienna.[34] The Monarchy itself was not simply the passive recipient of foreign influence: especially within the houses of the Benedictine order a native movement for religious change and renewal began to develop during the first half of the eighteenth century.[35]

In short, by the accession of Maria Theresa in 1740 a strong movement for reform had formed within the Catholic church in the Habsburg Monarchy. The break-through from theory to practice came with the appointment of a number of bishops eager to reform the religious life of their dioceses in accordance with the Jansenist programme. Five of them had been members of the Muratori group at Salzburg: Count Joseph Maria von Thun, bishop of Gurk and prince-bishop of Passau; Count Leopold Ernst von Firmian, bishop of Seckau, coadjutor of Trent and prince-bishop of Passau; Count Virgil Maria von Firmian, bishop of Lavant and provost of Salzburg; Count Johann Joseph von Trautson, cardinal-archbishop of Vienna; and Count Johann Karl von Herberstein, archbishop of Laibach. Together with several other reforming prelates, they changed the religious ethos of the Monarchy decisively away from baroque piety.[36]

. . .

CHURCH AND STATE

This account of the origins of religious reform in the Habsburg Monarchy has been necessary to demonstrate that what became known as Josephism did not begin as an attack on the Church by the state. On the contrary, it began as a movement *inside* the Church and *by* the Church to reform itself. On the other hand, the state was certainly involved. In her *Political Testament*, Maria Theresa lamented that over the centuries her predecessors had given away to the Church most of the royal domains. Now that the Church was rich, the Catholic religion flourishing and the clergy well supported, it was necessary to reverse the flow of funds to the impoverished state. In particular it was necessary to trim the self-indulgence of the overblown monasteries which were a heavy burden on the general public and served mainly to support a host of parasites in idle luxury. For all this 'a great remedy' was required.[37]

The link between the reforms of the bishops and the reforms of the state was provided by Count Christoph Anton von Migazzi, a devotee of Muratori who had studied at the *Collegium Germanicum* and succeeded Trautson as archbishop of Vienna in 1757. Eager to cooperate with the secular authorities, the founder of a seminary at Vienna which became a nursery of Jansenism and enjoying the trust of Maria Theresa, Migazzi was one of the most important creators of Josephism; indeed, Peter Hersche has described his role as 'decisive', a verdict all the more striking in view of Migazzi's later opposition to Joseph II.[38] Together with Anton de Haën, a Dutch Jansenist who came to Vienna in 1754 to become professor of medicine and was later appointed Maria Theresa's personal physician; Ignaz Müller, a Jansenist sympathiser who became Maria Theresa's confessor in 1767; and Ambrose Simon Stock, director of the theological faculty of the university of Vienna and the leader of the Jansenists in the capital, Migazzi helped to turn Maria Theresa into a Jansenist in the course of the 1760s.[39] It is quite wrong to suppose that she was a Catholic of the old school, a weak and foolish woman led astray by the devious and cynical Kaunitz, as used to be supposed.[40] The Josephist programme which unfolded in the course of the 1760s and 1770s was a cooperative effort between church and state engendered by conviction and a sense of mutual interest – and that explains its effectiveness.

Kaunitz may not have been Maria Theresa's evil genius, but he was certainly important. As chancellor of state, he was directly responsible for the administration of the Habsburg possessions in Italy and it was there that church reforms were tried out first. The foundation of the reforms was best expressed by the opening sentence of the instructions given to the Habsburg ambassador to the Pope: 'The limits of the power of the Church are determined by its sacred object; this, like its ultimate aim, is purely spiritual and consists in the preaching of Christian teaching on faith and morals, the administration of the sacraments, the conducting of church services and internal church discipline'. Every other function of the Church, it was argued, derived from human institution – and what the secular authorities had given, they could just as properly take away, as they saw fit and the circumstances demanded.[41] In the context of the Habsburg Monarchy in the middle of the eighteenth century, the circumstances demanded above all a proper contribution from the Church to the costs of the state; social and economic modernisation; and a purification of religious life.

The legislative programme introduced first to the Italian provinces and then to the central territories north of the Alps was highly complex, but its main features can be quickly summarised. It involved the taxation of the clergy, a halt to further gifts of land to the Church, and a reduction in the number of monasteries (eighty were secularised in Lombardy during the course of Maria Theresa's reign). It involved making it more difficult for young people to become monks or nuns, and making it more difficult for everyone to avoid useful labour by going on pilgrimages, joining religious confraternities or celebrating religious festivals. It involved reducing the power of the Pope over clerical appointments, reducing clerical influence on the censorship of secular publications and reducing clerical privileges generally. It involved such Jansenist measures as the strict limits imposed on the number of altars, candles, pictures, statues, relics, and church music. The same spirit informed the puritanical legislation against the opening of shops, markets, inns, coffee-houses and theatres on the Sabbath.[42] Perhaps the most important single initiative was the exploitation of the opportunity presented by the dissolution of the Jesuit order in 1773 by Pope Clement XIV. This not only released large resources for the increase in the number of parishes and the improvement of the lot of parish priests but also symbolised the end of an epoch in the cultural life of the Habsburg Monarchy.

The motive forces behind this reform programme have been variously identified as state expropriation (Ferdinand Maass), a defensive reaction to the problem of heresy and atheism (Ernst Wangermann), and an attempt to impose social control (James Van Horn Melton).[43] Other candidates offered by Peter Hersche are demographic pressure, the enlightenment, and 'a new mode of production based on new scientific and technological discoveries'.[44] It is possible that all of these causes were necessary; it is certain that none of them was sufficient. The most satisfactory explanation is that which sees a movement for reform and renewal beginning within the Catholic church and later gaining the cooperation of the state. The decision by the latter to embrace cultural and religious reform stemmed essentially from the changing position of the Habsburg Monarchy within the European states-system, especially from the defeats inflicted by Prussia during the three Silesian wars. If the temptation to be reductionist cannot be resisted, then it is the 'primacy of foreign policy' which deserves pride of place.

. . .

MARIA THERESA

By 1765, when his father died and he became co-regent with his mother, Joseph was confronted by a Habsburg Monarchy set in its ways. That they were new ways did not matter – Joseph's room for manœuvre was now circumscribed by a generation of reform. He inherited an empire which had begun the transition to statehood; a culture which had begun the transition to modernity; and, as a corollary of both, an alliance system based on the *rapprochement* with France. He had also inherited a distinctive political style, deriving partly from Habsburg traditions and partly from the strong and complex personality of his mother. At its centre was a continuing preoccupation with Roman Catholicism of undiminished fervour. Maria Theresa may have become a Jansenist, but that did not signal any move towards pluralism. On the contrary, her vehement aversion to Protestants and Jews was worthy of any counter-reformation saint. To paraphrase Mr Thwackum of *Tom Jones*, when she mentioned religion, she meant the Christian religion; and not only the Christian religion, but the Catholic religion; and not only the Catholic religion, but the Catholic religion as practised by the Church in the Habsburg Monarchy.[45]

To gain an insight into the Catholic frame of reference within which Maria Theresa always worked, one need only consult her *Political Testament*. Through the long, rambling sentences, eccentric syntax and erratic spelling there speaks the voice of a woman who *knows* that walking with her every day is God:

Whose almighty hand singled me out for this position without move or desire of my own and Who would therefore also make me worthy through my conduct, principles, and intentions to fulfil properly the tasks laid on me, and thus to call down and preserve His almighty protection for myself and those He has set under me, which truth I had held daily before my eyes and maturely considered that my duty was not to myself personally but only to the public.[46]

Suddenly finding herself in 1740, at the age of twenty-three, ruler of a huge but weak and vulnerable empire, quickly besieged on all sides by voracious predators, and 'without either money, troops, or counsel', as she put it, her eventual survival with her inheritance more or less intact convinced her that her Catholic God was on her side. It was a debt of gratitude she sought to repay with policy as well as prayer. The 'diplomatic revolution' of 1756 may have stemmed essentially from the need to regain Silesia but it was eased by the consideration that it also created for the first time since the Reformation an alliance of the two great Catholic powers against the heretics. As she herself stated, her determination to regain Silesia owed much to her reluctance to see so many good Catholics passing to Protestant rule. For the same reason she tried to prevent the first partition of Poland in 1772.[47]

Speculation on individual psychology is never conclusive and often unhelpful, but it does seem possible if not likely that Maria Theresa's deeply-felt piety softened her approach to politics. It may have made her uncompromising in the face of heresy, but it may also have made her less ruthless when confronted by a traditional order in which Catholicism and the Church played such an important part. Putting it another way: a radical drive towards state supremacy, which necessarily involves giving pride of place to secular considerations, will always be slowed by greater friction in a Catholic than in a Protestant society, let alone one that is wholly secular. Of course both Protestantism and Catholicism give higher priority to salvation in the next world than in this (or at least they used to), but the Catholic church is by its very nature more international, more independent and, above all, more corporatist. Lutheran clergymen in Prussia were salaried civil servants; Catholic prelates in the Habsburg Monarchy both owned their own estates and sat in the Estates.

So Maria Theresa did not seek to destroy the traditional relationship between sovereign and Church, rather she sought to tilt it more towards the former. The same applies to the nobility in general and the Estates in particular. The hostile language employed in her analysis of her problems in the 1740s was not translated into action of similar radicalism. Haugwitz clearly expressed the religious basis of this restraint when he wrote 'the privileges of the Estates are always to be regarded by a Christian sovereign as high, and sacred'.[48] Once the powers usurped by the Estates over the ages had been reclaimed and a proper contribution to the expenses of the state had been secured, the old mutually supportive relationship could be resumed. Outside the Bohemian and Austrian lands, the old order was left intact. Hungary she wisely left alone after a meeting of its parliament in 1764 revealed the intensity of opposition to change. Her prudence was reinforced by a sense of gratitude for the support she had received from the Magyar gentry in the dark days of 1741. In a letter actually written to her youngest son Max Franz but which should have been directed at Joseph, she advocated a softly-softly approach: 'Anything can be done with this nation if it is treated well and shown affection...You will see this and be astonished at the advantages I have obtained and still obtain from it'. The same pragmatism was revealed in her policy towards another possession which was to give Joseph II so much trouble – Belgium. In the year of her death she wrote to him:

> In the essentials of the constitution and form of government of this province, I do not believe that anything needs changing. It is the only happy province, and it has provided us with so many resources. You know how these peoples value their ancient, even absurd, prejudices. If they are obedient and loyal and contribute more than our impoverished and discontented German lands, what more can one ask of them?.[49]

·   ·   ·

THE CO-REGENCY

Alas, Joseph was not listening. By the time those words were written, on 22 July 1780, he was already middle-aged and seething with frustration. For all his adult life he had been trapped by the accident of inheritance laws. He was Holy

Roman Emperor in his own right, but the kind of authority he exercised in the Empire was too subtle and indirect to suit his 'impatient and perfectionist temperament'.[50] In the Habsburg Monarchy, where real power was to be found, until his mother died he could only be co-regent. Moreover, 'co-regent' proved to be a misnomer, for Maria Theresa always had the last word, usually supported by the third member of the ruling triumvirate, Kaunitz. Although Joseph sometimes got his way, 'junior tri-regent' would have been a more accurate description of his actual status. The bitterness and frequency of the triumvirate's disagreements were dictated by the strength of the personalities involved. Compared with the iron unity of command which ruled in Prussia, Habsburg councils were constantly being disrupted by Maria Theresa threatening to abdicate, Kaunitz threatening to resign or Joseph threatening to withdraw from the co-regency.[51]

Behind the neurotic posturing of three highly-strung individuals could also stand issues of principle. The most important was raised by the discovery of a large group of Protestants in Moravia in 1777. Maria Theresa's wish to unleash the full force of Catholic repression against the heretics was restrained only by the opposition of Kaunitz and Joseph. The latter took the opportunity to deliver a number of resounding statements on toleration, such as: 'politically, differences of religion within a state are an evil only in so far as there is fanaticism, disunion and party spirit. This vanishes automatically when all sectaries are treated with perfect impartiality, and He who directs all hearts is left to do the rest'.[52] If this episode seemed to represent a clash between generations, between reactionary mother and progressive son, then a simultaneous confrontation over serfdom in Bohemia reversed the order. After first showing inconsistency on the central question of forced labour (the '*Robot*') Joseph came out vigorously *against* Maria Theresa's plans to abolish serfdom at once. As Derek Beales has concluded: '[Maria Theresa] unquestionably showed herself the more humane and the more revolutionary of the two in her attitude towards Bohemian serfdom after about 1775'.[53]

As his conservatism in this case was so much at odds with what he had previously written on the subject of serfdom, and so much at odds with what he actually did as sole ruler just a few years later, one must conclude that his opposition to Maria Theresa in this instance was opposition more to the innovator than to the innovation. For most of the co-regency, Joseph's influence was exerted on the side of enlightened reform. Most historians of Josephism have downgraded Joseph's role, stressing instead the influence of a permutation of Jansenist bishops, Maria Theresa, certain of her officials or Kaunitz. As this chapter has sought to show, there is much to be said for preferring 'reform Catholicism' to designate a much longer-term movement than anything that could be associated with Joseph alone. Yet Derek Beales is right to stress that what developed under the co-regency bears the stamp of Joseph: it was his emphatic support for the reform-programme which prevented Maria Theresa from listening to the many conservatives in Church and state who called for its reversal.[54]

The terrible rows between mother and son which erupted so often during the co-regency led Joseph to personalise the nature of political power. Although an intelligent and well-informed observer of conditions in the Habsburg Monarchy, he was always too inclined to overlook the structural nature of his problems and to believe that a change of personnel at the top was what was needed to solve them. Fifteen years of chafing at the bit left him ready to bolt when the reins were dropped. He *knew* what had to be done. He had travelled the length and breadth of the Monarchy several times, so he *knew* just how disorganised, how slack, how incompetent was the existing regime. Once the grim reaper had freed him from his mother's obstructive grasp, he would be able to bang heads together, cut through self-interest, tradition and prejudice, and *make* people do what was right. Until that merciful release, the Monarchy would go on being governed by committee and intrigue, with every proposal for change discussed, opposed, redrafted, modified, watered down, retracted or filibustered *ad infinitum*. That was not to be Joseph's way. Once he was alone on the bridge, only his word of command was to be heard and all hands would have to jump to it. For just that reason, it was an empire that was to be made ungovernable.

. . .

NOTES

1. Beales, p. 354. This magnificent biography is not only the best biography of Joseph II available in any language, it also presents the best account of the reign of Maria Theresa.
2. The Italian ambitions of Joseph I are stressed in Charles W. Ingrao, *In quest and crisis: Emperor Joseph I and the Habsburg Monarchy* (West Lafayette, 1979); see especially ch. 4.
3. Michael Hughes, *Early modern Germany 1477–1806* (London, 1992), pp. 123–38. The arguments advanced here are developed at greater length in Hughes' doctoral dissertation *The Imperial Aulic Council in the reign of Charles VI* (London, 1988); see especially pp. 20–6.
4. Grete Klingenstein, *Staatsverwaltung und kirchliche Autorität im 18. Jahrhundert. Das Problem der Zensur in der theresianischen Reform* (Vienna, 1970), pp. 56–8.
5. Herman Freudenberger, 'Industrialisation in Bohemia and Moravia in the 18th century', *Journal of Central European Affairs*, 19, 4 (1960), 348.
6. In footballing parlance this is known as a 'six-pointer'.
7. Otto Pflanze, *Bismarck and the development of Germany*, vol. 1: *The period of unification 1815–1871* (Princeton, 1963), p. 87.
8. There is a clear and reliable account in the best general history of international relations in the period – Derek McKay and H.M. Scott, *The rise of the great powers 1648–1815* (London, 1983), pp. 181–92.
9. Klingenstein, *Staatsverwaltung und kirchliche Autorität*, p. 51.
10. See the fascinating discussion of a very similar 'crisis of legitimation' in Peter Burke's *The fabrication of Louis XIV* (New Haven and London, 1992), chs 8 and 9 entitled 'Sunset' and 'Crisis of representations' respectively.
11. Beales, pp. 32–4.
12. Kurt Blaukopf, *Musik im Wandel der Gesellschaft. Grundzüge der Musiksoziologie* (Munich and Zürich, 1982), p. 117.
13. Carlo Antonio Pilati, *Voyages en différens pays de l'Europe en 1774, 1775 et 1776*, 2 vols (The Hague, 1777), I, 49–50. Joseph von Sonnenfels, 'Die erste Vorlesung in dem akademischen Jahrgange 1782', in *Gesammelte Schriften*, vol. 8 (Vienna, 1786), p. 109. On the general sense of inferiority shared by all German Catholics, see Richard van Dülmen, 'Antijesuitismus und katholische Aufklärung in Deutschland', *Historisches Jahrbuch*, 89 (1969), 65.
14. Ferdinand Maass, *Der Frühjosephinismus* (Vienna and Munich, 1969), p. 36.

15. There is an excellent and full acount in Dickson, I, pt. 2. There is a good short account in H.M. Scott, 'Reform in the Habsburg Monarchy, 1740–1790', in H.M. Scott (ed.), *Enlightened absolutism. Reform and reformers in later eighteenth-century Europe* (London, 1990), pp. 152–6.

16. C.A. Macartney (ed.), *The Habsburg and Hohenzollern dynasties in the seventeenth and eighteenth centuries* (New York, 1970), p. 103.

17. Alfred Ritter von Arneth, *Geschichte Maria Theresias*, 10 vols (Vienna, 1863–79), I, 344. See also Jörg K. Hoensch, *Geschichte Böhmens. Von der slavischen Landnahme bis ins 20. Jahrhundert* (Munich, 1987), p. 269 and R.J.W. Evans, 'The Habsburg Monarchy and Bohemia, 1526 to 1848', in Mark Greengrass (ed.), *Conquest and coalescence. The shaping of the state in early modern Europe* (London, 1991), p. 147.

18. Dickson, I, 222.

19. Gerd Heinrich, *Geschichte Preußens* (Frankfurt am Main, Berlin and Vienna, 1981), pp. 214–16.

20. Karl-Heinz Osterloh, *Joseph von Sonnenfels und die österreichische Reformbewegung im Zeitalter des aufgeklärten Absolutismus* (Lübeck and Hamburg, 1970), pp. 23–4, 122.

21. Dickson, I, 243.

22. The best account of the Council of State is to be found in Beales, pp. 91–5. Also very useful is Frank A.J. Szabo, 'Haugwitz, Kaunitz and the structure of government in Austria under Maria Theresa, 1745 to 1761', *Historical Communications* (1979), *passim.*

23. By far the fullest and most authoritative account of the financial and military changes is to be found in Dickson, see especially II, chs 1, 2 and 4.

24. Ibid., II, 2.

25. Helmut Engelbrecht, *Geschichte des österreichischen Bildungswesens*, vol. 3 (Vienna, 1984), p. 98. See also Grete Klingenstein, 'Bildungskrise, Gymnasium und Universitäten im Spannungsfeld theresianischer Aufklärung', *Maria Theresia und ihre Zeit. Eine Darstellung der Epoche von 1740–1780 aus Anlaß der 200. Wiederkehr des Todestages der Kaiserin* (Salzburg, 1979) *passim.*

26. Klingenstein, *Staatsverwaltung und kirchliche Autorität*, pp. 148–69. For the view that van Swieten was less important than has been supposed, see Peter Hersche, *Der Spätjansenismus in Österreich* (Vienna, 1977), p. 120.

27. James Van Horn Melton, *Absolutism and the eighteenth-century origins of compulsory schooling in Prussia and Austria* (Cambridge, 1988), pp. 217–22. Beales, p. 459; Engelbrecht, *Geschichte des österreichischen Bildungswesens*, pp. 86–116.

28. Johann Ignaz von Felbiger quoted in T.C.W. Blanning, *Joseph II and enlightened despotism* (London, 1970), p. 123.
29. The best introduction to the subject is to be found in Beales, ch. 14.
30. See above, pp. 16–17.
31. This summary is taken from Hersche, *Der Spätjansenismus*, pp. 29–30, which together with the works by Beales, Dickson, Klingenstein and von Aretin cited earlier is one of the most important modern works on the Habsburg Monarchy. Much of what follows on Jansenism in the Habsburg Monarchy is based on this scholarly, original and distinguished work.
32. 'Parliamentary Jansenism, and with it what d'Argenson called Jansenist nationalism, did more to shake the fabric of French absolutism, in its theory and its practice, then the philosophers' – J.S. Bromley, 'The decline of absolute monarchy', in J. Wallace-Hadrill and J. McManners (eds), *France: government and society*, 2nd edn (London, 1970), p. 144.
33. Hersche, *Der Spätjansenismus*, pp 46–9. Max Braubach, 'Prinz Eugen und der Jansenismus', in Max Braubach, *Diplomatie und geistiges Leben im 17. und 18. Jahrhundert. Gesammelte Abhandlungen*, (Bonn, 1969), pp. 530–45.
34. Adam Wandruszka, 'Die katholische Aufklärung Italiens und ihr Einfluß auf Österreich', in Elisabeth Kovács (ed.), *Katholische Aufklärung und Josephinismus* (Vienna, 1979), p. 64. On Muratori's influence on the Habsburg Monarchy, see also Eduard Winter, *Der Josefinismus. Die Geschichte des österreichischen Reformkatholizismus 1740–1848* (Berlin, 1962), especially pp. 24–7. The most detailed account is to be found in Eleonore Zlabinger, *Lodovico Antonio Muratori und Österreich* (Innsbruck, 1970). As Peter Hersche has pointed out, her conclusion that Muratori did *not* influence Josephism is clearly at odds with the actual findings of her book – Peter Hersche, 'Neuere Literatur zur katholischen Aufklärung in Österreich', *Internationale kirchliche Zeitschrift*, 62, 2 (1972), 122.
35. Richard van Dülmen, 'Antijesuitismus und katholische Aufklärung in Deutschland', *Historisches Jahrbuch*, 89 (1969), 53–5, 64 n. 65; Winter, *Der Josefinismus*, p. 27.
36. Hersche, *Der Spätjansenismus*, pp. 50–64, 170.
37. Macartney (ed.), *The Habsburg and Hohenzollern dynasties*, p. 106.
38. Hersche, *Der Spätjansenismus*, pp. 66–9.
39. Ibid., pp. 66–78, 120–8, 134–58.
40. See especially the introductions to the first two volumes of documents on Josephism edited by Ferdinand Maass S. J. – *Der Josephinismus, Quellen zu seiner Geschichte in Österreich 1760–1790*, vol. 1: *Ursprung und Wesen des Josephinismus, 1760–1769* (Vienna,

1951), vol. 2: *Entfaltung und Krise des Josephinismus 1770–1790* (Vienna, 1953). In his later work – *Der Spätjosephinismus* – Maass revised his opinion, downgrading the role of Kaunitz and enhancing that of Maria Theresa.

41. Blanning, *Joseph II and enlightened despotism,* p. 33.
42. Hersche, *Der Spätjansenismus,* ch. 4, pt. 6.
43. Maass, *Der Josephinismus,* introduction to vols 1 and 2. Wangermann has sought to lend credibility to his assertion by constant repetition; for a representative example, see 'Reform catholicism and political radicalism in the Austrian Enlightenment', in Roy Porter and Mikulas Teich (eds), *The enlightenment in national context* (Cambridge, 1981). Melton, *Absolutism and the eighteenth-century origins of compulsory schooling in Prussia and Austria,* pp. 231–9.
44. Peter Hersche, 'Reformen im "Ancien Régime". Ein Vergleich Österreich-Schweiz', in *Österreich im Europa der Aufklärung,* I, 397.
45. Henry Fielding, *The history of Tom Jones* (1st edn, London, 1749), book 3, ch. 3.
46. Macartney, *The Habsburg and Hohenzollern dynasties,* p. 99.
47. Robert A. Kann, 'Ideengeschichtliche Bezugspunkte der Außenpolitik Maria Theresias und ihrer Söhne', in *Österreich im Europa der Aufklärung,* I, 559–60.
48. Dickson, II, 11.
49. These observations on Hungary and Belgium are quoted in Beales, pp. 484 and 486–7 respectively. See also Dickson, I, 326.
50. Ibid., I, 207.
51. The relationship between Maria Theresa, Joseph and Kaunitz is discussed fully in Beales; see especially pp. 142–7, 192, 205–6, 219–26, 302, 350–1, 354, 398, 404, 426, 452, 488–90.
52. Quoted in Ibid., p. 467.
53. Ibid., p. 357.
54. Ibid., p. 478.

Chapter 3

JOSEPH II AND THE ENLIGHTENED STATE

. . .

THE FIRST SERVANT OF THE STATE

'Everything exists for the state; this word contains everything, so all who live in it should come together to promote its interests'.[1] Taken from Joseph's first political memorandum, written in 1761 shortly after his twentieth birthday, this sentence also contains everything – everything that was essential to Joseph's political thought and practice, for not once during the next twenty-nine years did he waver from this steadfast belief in the paramountcy of the state. It was his proudest boast, expressed in his last will and testament drawn up in 1781, that he had 'lived as a servant of the state'.[2] Only when the intensity of his obsession – no weaker word will suffice – with the state has been appreciated can his policies, methods, problems and failure be properly understood.

Unfortunately for Joseph, the Habsburg Monarchy was not a state; it was a collection of territories whose only unifying characteristic was the accident that they all belonged to the same dynasty. The authority of the Habsburgs was essentially patrimonial, or in other words it was based on ownership, in the same way that a private individual might own a country estate. So power was personal, the subjects swearing allegiance to a specific individual in a direct manner. It was also limited, both by the universal law of God and by the specific laws of each individual territory incorporated in the 'rights, liberties and privileges' (three synonymous concepts) of all who lived there. Within this rich variety of tradition and custom, sovereignty was an alien concept, as was any distinction between public and private authority. The archduke of Austria or duke of Brabant (or whatever the Habsburg ruler's title might happen to be) was only one of many sources of authority within society, sharing power with both individuals and corporate groups. In one word, the Habsburg Monarchy was 'particularist'.[3]

It was also the antipode of the modern state, whose essence lies in its abstraction and its sovereignty. On the one hand, it is 'an apparatus of powers whose existence remains independent of those who may happen to have control of it at any given time', on the other it is 'a monopolist of legitimate force'.[4] This accounts for its immense pretensions. What a single individual can demand only at the cost of being diagnosed as a megalomaniac, the state can command effortlessly. Its theorists had paved the way for its supremacy by stripping political allegiance of its personal associations and attaching it to an abstraction. In other words, the concept of the state was 'objectivised'.[5] Moreover, by enforcing its supremacy and introducing a clear distinction between state and society and between public and private, it can make the individual, now atomised and defenceless, do things and make sacrifices undreamt of during the particularistic old regime. It was this 'conceptual revolution', begun as a reaction to the horrors of the French and English civil wars and completed by Thomas Hobbes (1588–1679), which made the state the 'master noun of political argument' by the middle of the eighteenth century.[6]

Joseph himself believed that the only legitimate methodology was one based on first principles. It was no good looking at things as they were and hoping to arrive at some sort of solution by a process of induction. As he told Grand Duke Paul of Russia: 'My principle has always been to get back to the fundamental origin of everything and to try to see it in its natural state, without pretence or affectation'.[7] Working from an intellectual clean slate necessarily involved disregarding anything whose only source of legitimation appeared to be the fact that it had existed for a very long time. In other words, Joseph had no time for arguments based on prescription: 'If one wants to establish something on secure foundations, then one has to begin with first principles derived from the nature of the object and one must not take into account customs which may be just prejudices, even if they have endured for a century or more'.[8]

The first principles on which Joseph based his political philosophy represented as sharp a break in the political culture of the Habsburg Monarchy as it is possible to imagine. They were radical in two senses of the word – radical because they sought to get to the roots of the problem of political authority and radical because they marked a rejection of the existing system. Joseph was not shy about expounding them; on the contrary, he pressed them on his sceptical officials at every opportunity. Perhaps the most eloquent statement was given in January 1785, as part of a critique of the *status quo* in Hungary. So important is it to appreciate how systematic was Joseph's approach to politics that it needs to be quoted at some length:

No constitution should exist if it is contrary to the principles of natural and social justice; and if such a constitution does exist, then it can be sustained only by force or ignorance. These principles are as follows: 1. Providence and nature have made all men equal and have given them a sense of what is wrong, and thus to be avoided, and what is right, and thus to be actively promoted. 2. Abuse of the natural laws and a failure to observe them obliged men to join together in societies and to pass laws binding on all members. This social assembly of men forms the basis from which all specific forms of government have developed. It is quite certain that in all of them the essential foundation is that every member of a specific community must contribute to the general good in proportion to his property, to his abilities and to the benefit which he himself derives from his membership of that commuity. If it so happens that there are individuals or groups of men who have succeeded in implementing laws which exempt them from this fundamental obligation, then it is simply an abuse and can never be justified by equity or the nature of society.

Forms of government which have developed are merely contingent and have been shaped only by the national character of the physical location, by the need to secure protection against outsiders and by the need to promote material progress. Therefore they can never be determined by the whim of a small number of people but must also be in accordance with the general good of the greatest number.[9]

As the Habsburg Monarchy was riddled with exemptions from top to bottom and from left to right, the implementation of this *credo* would inevitably offend a great number of vested interests. If the essential quality of the old regime was 'particularism', that of the new order envisaged by Joseph II was its antonym – 'standardisation'. Again and again he told his officials that the various provinces must be regarded as a *whole*, the definitive statement coming in his celebrated 'Principles for every servant of the state', often known as the 'Pastoral Letter':

> As the good of the state is always indivisible, namely that which affects the population at large and the greatest number, and as in similar fashion all the provinces of the Monarchy make up one single whole with one common objective, from now on there must be an end to all that jealousy and prejudice which hitherto has so often affected relations between provinces and between national groups, and also between government departments...It must be brought home to everyone that in a body politic, just as in the human body, if one member is unhealthy then all suffer and so all should strive to effect the cure of even the slightest complaint. National or religious differences must not make the slightest difference in all this and all must feel themselves to be brothers in a single monarchy, all striving to be useful to each other.[10]

Shortly after those words were written Joseph demonstrated what they could mean in practice by removing the crown of St Stephen, the supreme symbol of Hungarian kingship, from its traditional home at Pressburg to Vienna. This was a move of great symbolic importance and was interpreted as such by the Hungarians: by refusing to be crowned king of Hungary and by confiscating the actual crown, Joseph demonstrated that Hungary had no special status within the Monarchy but was henceforth to be regarded as just one part of a single unitary state. For the same reason, the crown of St Wenceslas was removed from Prague and the ducal hat of Lower Austria from Klosterneuburg.

This involved nothing less than a total reorientation of loyalties. Whereas in the past most people had felt their primary loyalty to a region, a town, an ethnic group, a religion, a social class or even an individual magnate, now the only loyalty to be permitted was loyalty to the state. The intensity of his own state-patriotism and the fervour with which he tried to instil it in others justifies one in speaking of Joseph's state-religion: 'Love of country, the welfare of the Monarchy, that is genuinely...the only passion I feel, and I would undertake anything for its sake. I am so committed to it that, if I cannot satisfy myself that its condition is good and that the arrangements we are making are beneficial, my mind cannot be at peace nor my body in good health'.[11] *Royauté oblige*: not only did Joseph set a personal example of tireless, selfless devotion to the state, worshipping it like a God and loving it like a mistress, he insisted that the other members of the Habsburg family did likewise. In a letter to Count Colloredo in 1784 he lamented the slow progress of his dim-witted nephew Francis (later the emperor Francis II), whose physical awkwardness made him timid and lethargic. Prescribing a course of vigorous physical training, he added: 'Every person who holds public office and especially we [members of the imperial family] must be ruled first and foremost by the words "commitment" and "duty" and seek to put them into practice in their fullest possible meaning'. So the wretched Francis was not to be permitted to eat, sleep or enjoy himself until he had completed his daily duties.[12]

. . .

AUTOCRACY AND BUREAUCRACY

If Joseph felt obliged to serve the state with every fibre of his being, he also felt obliged to command it. For him (as for Frederick the Great) a belief in the social contract was entirely compatible with a belief in autocracy. Far more than his mother, Joseph ruled as a dictator, allowing only the venerable Kaunitz an independent voice. For the fifteen years of the co-regency Joseph had had to put up with government by bumbling discussion; now that he was his own man he was determined to rule by himself. Three months after the death of Maria Theresa he wrote 'frankly' to his senior ministers to inform them that, with the single exception of judicial matters, all public business was for his decision alone. In a characteristically over-excited, almost manic passage, he called on his ministers to subordinate their wills to his own:

> Every head of department must therefore dedicate himself to business utterly and completely, must make it his sole concern, and must not think, must not hear, must not see anything which does not lead to this end. If he is to be really useful to me in the administration of the department entrusted to him, then his chief occupation must be to provide me with precise information about everything and at the same time he must strive to adopt my way of thinking, my objectives and my perspective on the common good, and to make my principles his own.[13]

As this repetition of the possessive pronoun indicates, Joseph preferred to use his senior civil servants in an executive rather than an advisory capacity. He often took decisions without consulting any of his ministers and even liked to draft his reform proposals himself.[14] Assessing the degree of influence exercised by his senior ministers is a difficult, if not impossible undertaking. As we shall see, Kaunitz continued to direct foreign policy and usually to have his own way when he disagreed with his sovereign,[15] but was now excluded from domestic business, which was where Joseph monopolised decision-making. There was no room for a prime minister, only for specialists in certain fields, although naturally their expertise brought them influence: Kollowrat and Zinzendorf on finance, Kressel on religion, Sonnenfels on education and censorship, Kaschnitz and Holzmeister on the urbarial and tax reforms, Eger on economic policy and Pergen on public order, to name just a few. Although Joseph justifiably prided himself on his long experience and deep knowledge of military matters, he continued to take advice from certain senior military commanders, especially the veteran Field Marshal Count Lacy.[16] Even so, contemporaries were struck by his imperious autocracy: in 1780 an anonymous memorandum asserted that 'nowadays the Austrian *Hofkriegsrat* [ministry of war] exists as an empty form. The Emperor directs everything, and he does with the army exactly what he likes'.[17]

Moreover, his concern to impose his will was not confined to the major issues. To read through his letterbooks for the 1780s is to enter the mind of a man who was obsessed with detail.

Nothing was too petty to attract a sharp directive; for example, after a tour of inspection to Pest in August 1786 he sent a long report to Field Marshal Hadick containing twenty-seven points which required immediate attention, typical of which was: 'Point 20 – I draw to your attention the fact that in the barracks and hospital at Semolin the sewers running to the cesspools must be rebuilt, to prevent the conduits collapsing and offensive odours seeping into the street'. On the same tour he left instructions on the improvement of the botanic garden at Pest University; issued a long memorandum on the institute for the daughters of officers at Herrnals, specifying among many other things that two pianos should be purchased; raged against the 'very obtrusive and useless decoration and wanton expenditure' lavished on the new hospital at Ofen; and so on and so forth.[18] Quite simply, Joseph II was a terrible busy-body who could not mind his own business. To give one petty but typical example: if he happened to notice that some of the street-lights in Vienna had not been ignited, at once he fired off an angry note to the official concerned calling for action.[19]

The temptation to seek a psychological explanation for Joseph's inability to leave things well alone is irresistible when one learns about his deeply unsatisfactory private life. His first wife, Isabella of Parma, was unable to reciprocate his deeply-felt passion (preferring his sister Marie Christine) and died after just three years of marriage in 1763. Their daughter, Maria Theresa, died of smallpox at the age of eight. A second marriage, to Josepha Maria of Bavaria in 1765, proved disastrous. Agreeing to it only with great reluctance, Joseph treated his wife with brutal disdain, describing her as having 'a short, fat figure; no youthfulness; a common face; on it, some little pimples with red spots; bad teeth'.[20] No doubt to their mutual relief, she died after only two years of married misery, leaving Joseph determined to remain single

Never the most relaxed or easy-going of personalities, Joseph emerged from these two scarring experiences an emotional cripple. Denied release for his strong sex-drive, he turned either to prostitutes, who left him feeling soiled, or to masturbation, which left him feeling guilty.[21] With fine hypocrisy he sublimated his loneliness and sense of inadequacy by poking his nose into other people's private lives. Typical was his letter to Field Marshal Hadick in 1788:

Through very reliable channels it has come to my attention that the evil of onanism or self-abuse is very widespread among the boys in the military schools. As it is in every respect a matter of the utmost importance for the state that the boys who are being educated at such great expense to be efficient soldiers should not be allowed to become emaciated skeletons, the men in charge of these institutions are to be told to exercise closer supervision and to give the boys more strenuous physical exercise and not to allow them to sit around so much.[22]

On several occasions Joseph displayed an unhealthy interest in what he called 'raging adolescent passions', insisting – for example – that ordinands should be confined to their seminaries even during the vacations, lest they succumb to the temptations of the world.[23] Whether he was ordering the arrest of an Italian priest who had been unwise enough to offer him some 'extremely indecent' etchings outside St Stephen's Cathedral in Vienna; or ordering the rounding-up of the procuresses who seduced young girls into prostitution; or calling for a full report on an incident at the Leopoldstädter theatre, when a jealous Count Paar seized a Jewess by her hair, dragged her away from his English rival out to the street and threw her into his carriage; or telling his censors to cut the role of Bertha from Schiller's *Fiesko* because she had been raped and banning the same playwright's *Kabale und Liebe* because a mistress appeared in it; or banning ballet from the court theatre because it was 'useless excitement of sensuality by an erotic jumping around the stage'; or enforcing a prohibition on gambling in Belgium, Joseph betrayed a puritanical pedantry which was both pathetic and dangerous.[24]

'Made neither to give nor to receive love', in his own bleak judgment, Joseph lavished all his affection on the state. His first biographer, Lorenz Hübner, identified with sharp insight the source of his single-minded devotion: 'There never was a prince on this earth who was more industrious and more active than Joseph; but equally there never was a common citizen who enjoyed life less than Joseph. Immersed in affairs of state, he seemed to have forgotten every pleasure of life'.[25] To no one was the old saw 'the style is the man' more applicable than to Joseph. If Maria Theresa had moved away from the baroque representation of her predecessors, Joseph turned his back on it. Symbolically, the last great effusion of traditional court display in Vienna was on the occasion of his ill-fated marriage to Isabella of Parma.[26] The style set by Joseph was sober, austere, practical, economical. He closed down and moth-balled the summer palace of Schönbrunn and used the Hofburg (the main imperial palace in the centre of Vienna) as offices, preferring to live in a house he had built for himself at the Augarten 'no bigger, and much plainer and less ostentatious than a Victorian suburban villa'.[27] He delivered the *coup de grâce* to the old etiquette in 1786. Reviewing his reforms of the past few years, he noted with satisfaction that the customs intro-duced to the court from Spain by earlier Habsburgs had been abandoned. Only the special 'court and appartment' dress of the ladies and the practice of bowing the knee to and kissing the hand of the sovereign and other members of the imperial family remained. All that was to cease and the abolition was to be publicised in all parts of the Monarchy 'together with the supplementary order that no one, no matter who he might be, who wishes to petition for something or to submit anything, shall kneel down, because this is not a fitting form of behaviour from one human being to another and should be reserved for God alone'.[28]

The closing words of this instruction to Prince Starhemberg were: 'all this is to be published in the newspapers'. This simple instruction reveals a move from a world in which ruler commu-nicated with his subjects visually, by means of representational display, to one in which the head of state informed his fellow-citizens by means of the written word. Joseph was an autocrat, but he was also a populist. Unlike many of his fellow-sovereigns who paid lip-service to the social contract, he took its implica-tions seriously. His legal code of 1786 marked an epoch in German constitutional history, for the clauses which bound the state to objectives and norms antedating its creation had the status of a constitution.[29] In more concrete terms, as the funda-mental purpose of the state was to promote 'the general good of the greatest number',[30] it was the duty of the ruler to translate principle into practice. This he did repeatedly, for example by issuing detailed instructions on how public entertainment at Brünn was to be improved: 'I also find it necessary that for the amusement of the public (*Publikum*) a place should be provided for public (*öffentlichen*) walks'. He allocated the garden of the old Jesuit college for the purpose, making an annual grant from public funds for the upkeep of the avenues, the replacement of trees and the installation of benches.[31] His grandest gestures were the transformation of the 'Glacis', a large open-space outside the city-walls, by the construction of walk-ways and the planting of 3,000 trees, and the opening of the imperial parks at the Prater in 1766 and the Augarten in 1775, placing over the gate to the latter the motto: 'This place of recreation has been dedicated to the People by one who esteems them'.[32]

Joseph would not be the last autocratic populist (not a contradiction in terms but an oxymoron) to esteem The People but not to like people, nor would he be the last to fail to consider that those he esteemed might be worth consulting. On the contrary, the unitary regime he created was far more authoritarian than anything the Habsburg Monarchy had seen in the past. For him, executive and legislature were inseparable – and vested in himself alone. In particular, he was deeply hostile to the Estates, dismissing their baroque ceremonial as 'peasant dances on an operatic stage' and 'children acting childishly'. Although they survived formally, they lost their remaining control of finance. Only the accounting agencies (*Buchhaltereien*) were retained, to reassure creditors who had more confidence in the Estates than in the government.[33] As the French ambassador, Noailles, reported to Vergennes in 1786: 'In this country the will of a single individual is the supreme law; here there are no consultative assemblies or Estates, nor any kind of official body which might give the crown useful advice'.[34]

That was an exaggeration. There were several central organisations able and willing to offer advice, if Joseph had been prepared to listen. It was characteristic, however, that he should have sought to reduce their number through amalgamation. In 1782 he combined the two main financial departments with the Bohemian-Austrian Court Chancellery to form the 'United Bohemian-Austrian Court Chancellery', while the Illyrian and Transylvanian chancelleries were combined with the Hungarian Chancellery to form a single central authority for the eastern lands. A similar reform was imposed in Lombardy, where a tour of inspection had led Joseph to form a very low opinion of the 'confusion, delay, uncertainty and partiality' of the existing system. The problems derived ultimately, he concluded, from the degenerate national character of his Italian subjects, especially from their incorrigible idleness and hedonism. He had been especially appalled by their habit of carousing late into the night – and rising at a correspondingly late hour the following morning.[35] A burst of radical reforms in 1783–6 abolished all the old institutions which had expressed the hegemony of the local nobility and reduced Lombardy to being just another standardised province of the Habsburg Monarchy.[36] Decision-making was taken away from the locals – and even from the Governor, Joseph's brother the Archduke Ferdinand – and was concentrated in Vienna.

It was symptomatic of the concentration of power which was at the heart of the transformation of the Habsburg Monarchy into a state that the numbers involved in decision-making should have contracted. In 1740 there had been ninety councillors in the central bodies but by 1775 only fifty-three. After 1780 Joseph needed only twenty: five in the Council of State and fifteen in the United Chancellery. As Peter Dickson has observed, this was 'a significant step away from government by extended counsel to government by royal decision'.[37] But also characteristic of the formation of the modern state was the unattractive paradox that legislative activity stands in inverse ratio to the number of decision-makers. The average number of printed decrees issued each year rose from a modest total of thirty-six in the 1740s, to sixty-eight in the 1750s, to 100 in the 1760s, fell back slightly to ninety-six in the 1770s and then exploded to *690* in the 1780s. The total number of decrees issued during Joseph's nine-and-a-quarter years as sole ruler was a staggering 6,206, or more than double the total for 1740–80.

As Joseph knew only too well, it was one thing to draft a reforming decree in his study in Vienna and quite another thing to make it known to the intended beneficiaries – let alone get it implemented. This was the area in which all the various forms of friction discussed in the first chapter slowed the Habsburg state to the pace of its slowest member and more often than not brought it to a complete standstill. As he travelled through such peripheral provinces as Galicia, Transylvania or the Banat of Temesvár, Joseph could see for himself the great divide between central plan and local reality. Complaining to the Hungarian chancellor, Count Esterházy, from Karlstadt (Karlovac) in 1783, he lamented that in many parts of Slavonia and Croatia the inhabitants were simply unaware of what had been ordered.[38] The greatest problem, he concluded, was posed by the officials. In Joseph's eyes, they were usually ignorant, idle, self-seeking and obstructive. They did only as much as was necessary to stave off dismissal and used their intellects only to find fault with government decrees and to invent ways of preventing change.[39]

He tried to overcome this great obstacle in a number of ways. Firstly, he exhorted, mixing criticism of the 'mechanical and servile' fashion in which officials presently went about their business with fervent appeals to join him in renouncing private interest in favour of total dedication to the state, in whose service was perfect freedom. Secondly, he set a personal example of devotion to duty so intensive that it certainly shortened his life by many years. Thirdly, he punished, his tours of inspection usually ending with a list of officials to be disciplined or cashiered. Fourthly, he rewarded, distributing medals, promotions and even patents of nobility to those who had caught his eye.[40] Finally, he tried to turn his servants into bureaucrats by introducing professional training, regular attendance, uniform procedures, a contributory pension scheme and even provision for widows and orphans.[41]

It is impossible to judge what success he had. He himself certainly thought he had failed, still railing on his death-bed with undiminished bitterness against the 'riff-raff' he had to employ *faute de mieux*. Given the slow pace of travel from centre to periphery and given the slow pace of symbolic communication in a largely illiterate society, not even the most dedicated bureaucrats could have achieved very much. But why should they have bothered to exert themselves? Their education was limited, their pay was poor, their status was low and their morale was not improved by constant hectoring from their master. As Count Zinzendorf wrote in his diary about Joseph's Pastoral Letter: 'it looks as though the emperor believes, or would like to make us believe, that he alone loves his country and knows what is right and that all his officials are knaves and fools'.[42]

. . .

EDUCATION

The ambition to make his officials more efficient and his subjects less intractable also inspired Joseph's approach to education. In 1780 he inherited a department of education

(*Studienhofkommission*) which had already done a good deal to modernise and secularise the school system.[43] What he then injected in the course of the 1780s was his own special dedication to the unitary state. A particularly good example was provided by a lengthy document he composed in 1786: 'Observations on the Tyrol for the Governor of Upper Austria Count von Sauer'. After a long and remarkably well-informed account of the region's geography and economy (a tribute to the value of his incessant travelling), he commented that 'in matters of public morality it is backward in many respects'. Both nobility and lower orders, he conceded, had plenty of natural wit, especially in the south, where alas the inhabitants were also vindictive and litigious like the Italians whose language they shared. In the German-speaking regions the nobles were melancholy (*schwermutig*), poor and stuffed with prejudices, the most obtrusive being uncritical devotion to the old order and a corresponding reluctance to cooperate with innovation. So Joseph concluded that 'the education of the next generation is the only sure means to accomplish the gradual enlightenment of this nation'. In the past, he asserted, the government's policy had been utterly misguided: instead of concentrating on rural primary schools, funds had been lavished on the useless university at Innsbruck. It was Sauer's task to set about reversing this order of priorities.[44]

As Joseph stressed repeatedly, he regarded the promotion of mass literacy 'as one of the most important objects of my concern for the general good'.[45] Enraged by reports that less than a third of children of school-age actually attended school and that even in Vienna the figure was only 7,000 out of 17,000, he ordered a vigorous campaign to punish parents of truants with fines or forced labour. To make attendance more attractive, the schools themselves were to be improved. The ideal described in his numerous decrees on the subject called for compulsory education for all children from the age of six to twelve, conducted in every parish by a school-teacher trained at an official college of education, who was properly housed, who enjoyed a salary sufficient to make moonlighting unnecessary, who was paid a pension when he retired, who was respected by the local community, and whose teaching was monitored by state officials. State control was paramount – private schools were prohibited. The necessary funds were to be provided by a combination of contributions from the local lords, fees from female pupils (boys received instruction free) and funds released by the expropriation of the Jesuits and other religious organisations.[46]

The motivation behind this programme was clearly utilitarian. Joseph did not seek to make his subjects literate to improve their quality of life, he did it to make them more useful for the state. In other words, he viewed them as ends not means. They were to learn enough to make themselves useful but no more. He was quite explicit on this score; for example, after one of his tours of inspection in Hungary he complained that the educational system in the frontier region had become too ambitious. Introduced by books to the world beyond their villages, the pupils were no longer content to be peasants and common soldiers but would accept nothing less than NCO status when they left school.[47] So although primary schools were encouraged, numbers attending secondary schools were depressed by the imposition of fees. When pressed to exempt the poor, Joseph replied that he welcomed fees as a means of confining the masses to primary education and the three 'Rs'. The last thing he sought was an excess of over-educated, over-ambitious but under-employed intellectuals.[48] Perhaps because of his limited view of education, he did succeed in accelerating the growth of literacy: it has been estimated that by the end of his reign as many as two-thirds of children of school age in Bohemia were actually attending.[49]

The same argument applied to higher education, except more so. Nothing disqualifies Joseph II more from the ultimate historiographical prize of being classified as a 'liberal reformer' than his contempt for intellectual cultivation for its own sake. In his view, universities existed solely to train state officials:

> Young people must not be taught anything which they will use seldom or never at all for the good of the state, for the essential purpose of study at university is to train state officials and is not to be devoted merely to the education of intellectuals.[50]

Thanks to their over-representation on the commanding heights of any state in any period, universities are the most durable of institutions: it is very rare for any to be closed except as a result of war or revolution. Yet Joseph closed five: at Linz, Brünn, Innsbruck, Graz and Freiburg im Breisgau, converting them into *lycées* and leaving only one for each of the main territorial divisions of the Monarchy: at Vienna, Prague, Louvain, Pest, Padua and a new creation at Lemberg in Galicia. Even the survivors ceased to be universities in the commonly accepted sense of the word. They were no longer *universitates*, but were more like primary schools for adults, with strict state control, prescribed text-books, learning by rote, frequent examinations, shorter periods of study and an academic staff employed to teach and not to engage in anything as pointless as research.[51] The familiar ring this depressing list has for an academic writing in the early 1990s is neither contrived nor accidental: Joseph II may not have been liberal, but he was certainly modern.

. . .

GERMANISATION

The imposition of educational uniformity was accompanied by linguistic standardisation: Joseph had grasped the point that the key to modernisation is to be found in ease of communication. Of the numerous living languages in use in his polyglot empire, only German was a candidate to become *lingua franca*, because more Germans could be found in more provinces than any other national group. This was not a sudden or original move on his part. If the counter-reformation and the baroque had represented the triumph of a Latin culture, the Austrian state spoke in the vernacular.[52] But it was Joseph who sought to make a result out of a trend. In 1784 he decreed that German was to become the official language in all parts of the Monarchy except the Netherlands, Italy and Galicia. In Hungary, where Latin had been the language of law and administration, the German language was to be introduced to the central authorities immediately, to the counties after a year and to other local offices and courts within three years. Any public employee unable to master it within the allotted period would be dismissed. Knowledge of German also became a condition of admission to the Hungarian parliament and the sole language of instruction in schools.[53]

Nothing illustrated better Joseph's approach to political problems in general and the linguistic issue in particular than the reply he sent to the Hungarian chancellor Count Esterházy when the latter protested – in vain – against the proposed

Germanisation decree. Joseph told him curtly that the Hungarians' use of a dead language (Latin) was a terrible reproach to their nation, because it proved that either their native tongue was inadequate or that no one understood how to read or write it. Every civilised country in Europe, he went on, had abandoned the use of Latin – with the exception of the Poles and the Hungarians. If Hungarian-speakers made up a majority of the country's inhabitants, then they could reasonably dictate the official language, but in fact they were outnumbered by those speaking German, Romanian or one of the numerous Slavonic dialects. Joseph now employed what was for him always the decisive argument – unity: 'You can easily work out for yourself just how advantageous it will be when there is only one language for written communications in the Monarchy and how conducive that will be to binding all the different parts to the whole and to creating a sense of fraternity among all the inhabitants. The proof can be seen in the cohesiveness of the French, British and Russian nations'.[54] As impeccably rational as he was tactless, Joseph could not have given more offence to the hypersensitive Hungarians, who especially did not appreciate his condemning them to share a cultural dustbin with the Poles of all people.

Yet Joseph was neither a cultural nationalist nor an imperialist. He did not impose the German language because he believed it to be superior, he did it because it was more convenient. He used the vocabulary of nineteenth-century nationalism but in the sense of the eighteenth century. So when in 1781 he instructed the Council of State to prepare memoranda on how to reawaken the 'national spirit which has died out utterly and completely', he was not referring to any particular ethnic group but to the population of the Monarchy as a whole.[55] In his choice of personnel he never discriminated in favour of Germans; on the contrary he ordered expressly that university teachers, for example, should be selected exclusively on merit 'and without any regard for their nation or religion'.[56] Thanks to his education and travels, he himself was impeccably cosmopolitan, able to converse fluently in all the major languages of his dominions. Joseph did not identify with a nation, he identified with the state. His personal tastes sent no clear national signal. On the one hand, he showed a clear preference for German drama and opera, dismissing the French troupe and founding a 'national theatre' for the performance of work in the

German language. On the other hand, French was the language he preferred to use when corresponding with members of his family or with Kaunitz.[57] Indicative of his essentially practical approach to language was the permission he gave in 1789 to Austrian diplomats to compose their despatches in French rather than German – again on grounds of convenience.[58]

It was all to no avail. By the late eighteenth century, German culture was in the ascendant in Europe, assertively challenging French hegemony. As the minority cultures of the Habsburg Monarchy were also beginning either to revive (in the case of Czech, Polish, Italian and Magyar) or to emerge (in the case of the more 'submerged' Slavonic and Romanian peoples), confrontation between a German centre and a multi-national periphery would be difficult to avoid. With every measure that centralised government in Vienna, which despite its colourful ethnic variety was very much identified as a German city, Joseph made it more likely. The Germanisation decree of 1784 made it certain. As James Sheehan has written: 'a fateful link between Germanisation and centralisation had been forged. Austrian politics would never be the same'.[59]

· · ·

TOLERATION

A more permissive means of promoting the efficiency of the state was through religious toleration. By a series of ordinances beginning in October 1781, Joseph greatly improved the position of Lutherans, Calvinists and Greek Orthodox. In any community where their numbers exceeded 100 families or 500 individuals, they were now allowed to build a church, appoint a clergyman and worship as they pleased. They were also freed from the various forms of secular discrimination which they had suffered in the past, being now permitted to buy property, join guilds, participate in local government, graduate at universities and enter the civil service. Beginning at the same time, but extending over a longer period, another series of decrees brought significant relief to the Jews of the Monarchy. For them, in effect, the ghetto was opened: they could now attend Christian schools and universities, learn and practise a trade, engage in wholesale and retail business, open factories, employ Christian servants, rent houses, stay where they pleased, visit theatres, leave their homes on Christian festivals, and remove the yellow star of David from their clothes.[60]

Joseph's motivation has been fiercely debated. Even if he himself were available for psycho-analysis, it is doubtful whether a satisfactory conclusion could be formed. Of one thing we can be certain: his belief in toleration followed naturally from his basic assumptions about the origins, nature and purpose of the state.[61] The primal contract empowered and obliged the state to protect its citizens, but it did not convey authority to dictate on matters of conscience. This was a conviction of long standing; in his memorandum of 1765, the twenty-four year-old Joseph had written: 'the liberty innate in Man should be accorded to him so far as possible'. The state should only ask an individual to serve, not to believe: 'for the service of God is inseparable from that of the state, and He wishes us to employ those to whom He has given talents and the capacity for business, leaving to His divine mercy the reward of the good souls and the punishment of the bad'.[62]

To principle he added prudence. Persecution was not only wrong, it was harmful. Firstly, it led to civil disorder, most recently in Moravia, where the Protestants had risen in revolt in 1777. Among other things, this episode had demonstrated conclusively that the repressive techniques of the counter-reformation had failed to impose religious uniformity. Joseph's attempts to halt the persecution led to a terrible row with his mother and may well explain why he moved so quickly to introduce the toleration decrees after his mother's death. Secondly, persecution had led in the past to the deportation or emigration of some of the Monarchy's most enterprising and wealthy inhabitants, a self-inflicted wound which had benefited only Protestant neighbours, especially Prussia. In the same way, it had prevented the attraction to the Monarchy of refugees from persecution elsewhere. So when Dutch 'patriots' fled to the Austrian Netherlands after the Prussian invasion in September 1787, Joseph was quick to emphasise that they should be guaranteed full religious toleration, in the hope that they could be persuaded to stay.[63] Finally, toleration was expected to pay dividends for foreign policy, by denying Frederick the Great the chance to play the Protestant card and by making it more difficult for any foreign power to intervene in the domestic affairs of the Habsburg Monarchy. In the event of war, an oppressed minority was a potential fifth column, as

Protestants had demonstrated during the Silesian wars and the Orthodox threatened during any conflict with Russia. On the other hand, toleration would put the boot on the other foot. So the manifesto issued on the outbreak of war in 1787 promised complete toleration to all inhabitants of the Turkish Empire, whether Christian or Moslem.[64]

Although Joseph believed fervently in toleration for both principled and prudential reasons, he was no nineteenth-century liberal, calling for a 'free church in a free state'. His decrees stressed over and over again that Catholicism remained the dominant religion: everyone was to be told that it was his wish and intention that those unfortunate souls who were not at present Catholics as a result of their ignorance or delusion should be converted.[65] Only Catholics were to enjoy the right of public worship and only Catholic churches were to be allowed to display such public signs as towers, bells and public entrances on the street. Toleration was certainly not intended to lead to indifference. On the contrary, he hoped that more generous treatment would lead the heretics to see the error of their ways and guide them back to the True Faith. As he told Maria Theresa at the height of their dispute over the Moravian Protestants: 'God preserve me from thinking that it is a matter of indifference whether subjects become Protestants or remain Catholics, still less whether they believe or at least follow the religion derived from their fathers. I would give all I possess if all the Protestants of your states could become Catholics!'.[66]

It was not long before Joseph discovered that his 'tolerant mission' had failed dismally. Toleration had only encouraged clandestine Protestants to declare themselves and Catholics to convert. In the course of the 1780s the number of Protestants in the non-Hungarian parts of the Habsburg Monarchy more than doubled, from 73,722 with thirty-seven pastors and twenty-eight churches in 1782 to 156,865 with 142 pastors and 154 churches in 1788. In Hungary between 1781 and 1784 more than 1,000 Protestant parishes were created, a number which doubled again by 1790. To staunch this haemorrhage of heretics, Joseph moved quickly to make conversion more difficult. On 15 December 1782 he ordered that with effect from the New Year, anyone wishing to abandon Catholicism would be obliged to attend a six-week refresher course on the old faith, half of the costs of the course to be paid by the aspiring apostate and half by the priest in danger of losing a soul.[67]

He also emphasised that his toleration decrees only applied to those groups specifically mentioned – to Lutherans, Calvinists, Greek Orthodox and Jews. Nonconformists were excluded. Just how far Joseph was removed from the modern conception of toleration can be gathered from the order he issued in March 1783 to Field Marshal Hadick on the subject of the Bohemian 'Deists', a group of modern Anglicans *avant la lettre* who denied the divinity of Christ, rejected the Holy Trinity, venerated God only as the creator of the universe and did not believe in hell. Attempts to make them see the error of their ways having failed, the sixty men and their womenfolk were to be evicted from their homes and property, and were also to be separated from their children, who were to be taken away to be brought up as Catholics. No matter what their age or physical condition, the adults were to be treated as if they were military conscripts, were to be divided into groups of five to six and were to be sent to regiments in the Banat of Temesvár, Transylvania, Galicia or Bukovina. On arrival, the able-bodied were to serve as common soldiers and the old or feeble as medical orderlies. They were never to be given leave.[68] Shortly afterwards Joseph relented, although not before several consignments had been sent off. In future, anyone declaring himself to be a sectarian was to be given twenty-four strokes of the cane and sent home 'not because he is a Deist but because he claims to be something which he cannot know he is'.[69]

Freed from both their own prejudices and the prejudices entertained towards them by the Catholic population, Protestants and Jews were now to make a full contribution to the general good of the state. The utilitarian stress on service for the state was especially pronounced in Joseph's dealings with the Jews. As he informed his ministers, if they thought the object of his decree had been to increase the number of Jews in the Monarchy, they were very much mistaken: in fact, their numbers were to be strictly limited until such time as they could be made 'more useful'. That could only be done through a programme of assimilation. In effect Jews were to cease to be Jews, by adopting German dress, German names, German education, German laws, German occupations and, last but not least, the German language. By abolishing degrading forms of discrimination and by giving them the opportunity to improve their material and cultural standards, Joseph hoped to reduce their prejudices and lead them towards Christianity. But with emancipation went obligation: Jews were now liable for conscription. Not surprisingly, there were many Jews who deeply resented these encroachments on their traditional way of life.[70]

. . .

THE ECONOMY

Once every member of the state was literate, and free to contribute to the general good, a start could be made on exploiting the full potential of the Habsburg Monarchy. Joseph realised that only sustained economic expansion could unlock the resources he needed for his new state; as he wrote in 1779: 'Our provinces are impoverished and cannot afford to maintain the present military establishment. Only the improvement of our agriculture, industry, trade and finance will make possible the upkeep and expansion of our military forces to meet future eventualities'.[71] He was under no illusions as to how difficult this would prove, for his frequent tours of inspection had revealed only too clearly just how backward were most of his possessions.

He found the premise for his economic policy in an analysis of the Habsburg Monarchy's special strengths and weaknesses. As the most important among the former he identified abundant raw materials and a large internal market; the most serious deficiency was the cruel trick of geography which had placed the Monarchy on the periphery of Europe's commercial system, which had condemned it to a permanent trade deficit. So government policy should play to its strengths, Joseph concluded, which meant favouring agriculture and manufacturing at the expense of trade. If there was no prospect of generating large currency reserves through exports or services, then at least the net outflow could be reduced to a minimum.[72]

In other words, what was needed was a protectionist tariff system, which would keep foreign goods out and Austrian money in. This did not mean that all imports were prohibited; rather Joseph devised a sliding scale of acceptability. Utterly useless articles, favoured only because of fashion or prejudice, were to be loaded with dues to such an extent that consumption would soon decline to zero. Less offensive commodities, which had become necessities through habit – such as spices, coffee, cocoa, sugar, dried fish and olive oil – would be discouraged but not eliminated altogether. Only those raw or semi-finished materials to which value would be added inside the Monarchy would be actually welcome.[73] There was an endearing simplicity about Joseph's analysis of economic problems which made up in clarity what it lacked in sophistication. In 1789, for example, he complained to Count Kollowrat that whereas the consumption of sugar in the Habsburg Monarchy amounted to 80,000 Zentner,[74] the total capacity of its four refineries was only 60,000. The shortfall was made up by imports and, as each Zentner cost 20 gulden, no less a sum than 400,000 gulden was lost each year – or 4,000,000 gulden during the previous decade. A total ban should therefore be considered.[75]

He brought the same directness to the question of enforcement. On 6 August 1785, for example, a large quantity of embroidered cloth which had been imported contrary to regulations was burned in public on the city ramparts in Vienna.[76] As usual, he led from the front, making even the most painful sacrifices in the cause of national self-sufficiency and a favourable balance of trade. So when an inventory of all stocks of foreign wine in Vienna was ordered in 1784, following its prohibition, the imperial wine-cellar was not exempted. In future, Joseph ordered, only Hungarian and other national products were to be purchased.[77]

If these measures make Joseph sound like a mercantilist of the kind derided by his contemporary Adam Smith, there were other aspects of his economic policy which were more liberal. As Joseph himself stated, he was an 'atheist' when it came to economic doctrine. Believing that 'everyone should be allowed to earn his living as he sees fit', he strongly disapproved of the restrictive practices enforced by the craft guilds. Although no general reform was introduced, the corrective measures of the previous reign were enforced more rigorously.[78] A number of treaties to liberalise trade were negotiated, although significantly only with countries whose economies were even less developed than that of the Habsburg Monarchy – Morocco (1783), Turkey (1784), and Russia (1785). An Austro-American trading company was founded in 1785.[79]

Joseph himself believed that his pragmatic combination of regulation and deregulation had the desired effect of galvanising the Monarchy's economy. Dismissing the pleas of the merchants, he boasted to Kollowrat in 1786 that his reform of the customs system had led to the expansion of all branches of industry and that only a little fine-tuning was required to achieve perfection.[80] Commerce too had benefited; in the same year he reported to his brother Leopold:

> Shipping on the Danube heading for the Levant and the Crimea is daily increasing. Industry and manufactures are prospering in the absence of the prohibited goods. A large number of people from Nuremberg, Swabia and even from England, who used to make their living by producing in their own country, have recently settled here to carry on manufacture.[81]

It seems clear that Joseph's impression was correct. The Habsburg Monarchy has been the beneficiary of much attention from economic historians in recent years and all are agreed that the 1780s witnessed rapid expansion, especially in manufacturing. In Lower Austria (especially in and around Vienna), in Bohemia (especially in and around Prague) and Moravia (especially in and around Brünn), impressive rates of growth were recorded. From the rich variety of statistics available (and the fact that they *are* available provides a further indication of Joseph's state-building), the following brief sample provides an indication of what was achieved. Between 1779 and 1787 the number of spinners in Bohemia working on flax increased from 122,318 to 229,400, on cotton from 6,410 to 30,901 and on wool from 37,943 to 53,919.[82] In Bohemia the number of 'factories' (by which is meant manufacturing establishments outside guild control and characterised by the division of labour) rose from 24 in 1780 to 34 in 1781 to 40 in 1782 to 63 in 1786 to 86 in 1788 to 95 in 1792.[83] Many of these enterprises, moreover, were really quite substantial, employing hundreds – and in a few cases thousands – of workers.

What is much less clear is just how much credit can be claimed by Joseph in fostering this process. The older historiography, especially when stemming from countries with command economies, stressed the role of the interventionist state in bringing about a new economic order and social relationships to match. Special emphasis was laid on the creation of a single customs area (with the not unimportant exceptions of Hungary and the Tyrol) in 1775, and the abolition of serfdom in 1781, this latter measure being crucial because it allowed surplus labour to move to the new centres of manufacturing.[84] More recent analyses have portrayed expansion occurring in spite of, rather than because of, government policy. The economic modernisation of the Habsburg Monarchy, it is now argued, was a long drawn-out process, beginning in the middle of the eighteenth century.[85] That real progress had occurred since the middle of the century, and at an ever-accelerating pace in the 1780s, seems undeniable. It is doubtful, however, whether all the elements of 'modern economic growth' were in place by 1800, as one arch-revisionist scholar has argued.[86] It was still a 'tale of two economies' in the Habsburg Monarchy–islands of modernity in a sea of rural backwardness whose tides no government could direct. For all Joseph's road-building initiatives, communications were still hobbled by the inability of current technology to overcome natural obstacles. Quantitative expansion had not been matched by qualitative change: the native entrepreneurial class remained weak, and financial services undeveloped.[87] In short, one can borrow François Crouzet's verdict on the French economy at the end of the old regime and conclude: the economy of the Habsburg Monarchy in 1790 was structurally no different from what it had been in 1740 – it was just producing more.[88]

. . .

SOCIAL REFORM

Joseph achieved more success in increasing the number of producers, for at the top of his political agenda was demographic expansion: 'my first priority, on which the political, financial and even military authorities should concentrate all their attention is population, that is to say maintaining and increasing the number of my subjects. It is from the maximum number of subjects that all the benefits of the state derive'.[89] As he told Count Esterházy in 1784: 'It is a proven fact that an increase in population also increases the well-being, the prosperity and the prestige of a state'.[90] For the reasons discussed in a previous chapter,[91] this was an axiom shared by almost all his contemporaries (Thomas Malthus' *Essay on the principle of population* was not published until 1798). If it was an axiom which made ever less sense in overcrowded western Europe, in the Habsburg Monarchy, with its underpopulated frontier regions, it still held good. Joseph was continuing a policy more than a century old when he issued a decree in September 1782 to encourage immigration. Among other things, those prepared to settle in Galicia or the Banat of Temesvár were offered free land, houses, equipment, stock and seed-corn, cash grants, exemption from taxation for ten years, and exemption from conscription for the eldest son of the family. What made Joseph's package of inducements different from those of his predecessors was his ability to offer also religious toleration.[92] This policy certainly had some effect: it has been estimated that about 38,000 immigrants moved to the Habsburg Monarchy during the course of the 1780s.[93]

Concern for population levels also inspired Joseph's programme to improve public health, the most comprehensive yet seen in any European country. Whereas in the past the sick had been lumped together with the poor, the vagrant and other troublesome groups living on the margins of society, now specialised institutions were created to attend to their needs.[94] The show-piece was the great General Hospital, opened in 1784. If the isolation wards, the maternity unit for unmarried mothers, the lunatic asylum and the orphanage are included, it came to have over 2,000 beds by the end of his reign. It was symbolic of the utilitarian nature of his regime that the hospital buildings in the Alser Strasse should become his most important architectural legacy. His attention was not confined to the capital: he decreed that every community should have a state-registered nurse and every Circle (*Kreis*) a doctor employed by the state to supervise public health and hygiene in general.[95]

Joseph's interest in public health was both detailed and continuous, whether he was prohibiting the wearing of corsets on the grounds that it had a detrimental effect on a woman's child-bearing capacity; or sending two surgeons on a tour of thirty-three German, Dutch, English, French and Italian cities to improve their skills; or sending a gynaecologist to study in France, England and Italy; or ordering a mass-raid on brothels and the compulsory treatment of the prostitutes for venereal disease; or establishing an institute for the education of the deaf and dumb; or sending a team of eighteen nuns to improve the medical facilities at Ofen; or devising a twelve-point plan to reduce the mortality rate among foundlings; or establishing a clinic for smallpox vaccinations – just to list a sample of his stream of measures.[96]

. . .

CRIME AND PUNISHMENT

The less appealing side of Joseph's obsession with state service was presented by his approach to the criminal law. Many of the changes he introduced – the standardisation of courts, simplification and acceleration of procedure, the separation of justice from political administration, the abolition of torture, the use of remand prisons, the presumption of innocence until guilt was proven, the redefinition of magic and witchcraft as fraud, and many others in the same vein – were enlightened and humane by any standards. At first sight, so was his effective abolition of the death penalty (although it was still pronounced in court, it was almost always commuted). Yet the punishment which took its place and Joseph's instructions for its implementation were so brutal as to reveal a mind which by any standards was not entirely normal. The punishment in question was the pulling of barges along the Danube in Hungary, which sounds innocuous enough until one discovers how it was enforced. On 7 July 1786 Joseph wrote from Peterwardein to Field Marshal Hadick, complaining that his orders on the conduct of barge-pulling were being ignored and insisting that they be carried out to the letter. As they present a particularly good illustration of the practical consequences of his grim state religion, they are worth summarising:

1. the criminals are to be allowed to retain only the most essential garments; 2. they are not to be permitted knives or any cooking utensils, all bread must be cut in advance and they are to be allowed only spoons for eating; 3. they are not to receive alms or comestibles of any kind; 4. they are to be chained together every night in groups of five by means of a chain through their leg-irons and under no circumstances whatsoever are they to be released before day-break; 5. as the barge-pullers are criminals, they are to be segregated from ordinary soldiers; if they fall ill they are not to be sent to a military hospital but are to be kept in a special place, chained to their beds; 6. as barge-pulling is their punishment, they are to be kept up to their work without pause and without remuneration; 7. care is to be taken that they are sent where they are most needed; 8. they are not to be

allowed to gather in groups of the same religion or nationality, to prevent the hatching of conspiracies.[97]

When combined with this inhuman regime, the physical exertion required to pull the barges and the frequent chest-deep
immersion in the mosquito-infested Danube meant that
reprieve from the death-sentence was only very temporary. Of
the first batch of a hundred haulers sent to Hungary in 1784,
thirty-seven were dead within two months and thirty-eight
more within the year. Over six years, 721 of 1,100 died.[98] Nor
did lesser offenders escape. In Vienna, every prisoner, male or
female, was set to work in chain-gangs repairing and sweeping
the streets, cleaning out sewers and the like, under the supervision of warders equipped with canes. On Joseph's express
orders, their diet was confined to bread and water, their clothing was kept as basic as possible and their heads were shaven,
both to reduce infestation and to make escape more difficult.[99]
Anyone who did try to escape from this nightmarish existence
by suicide was well-advised not to fumble the attempt, for
survivors were confined to a lunatic asylum or prison until they
had convinced themselves that 'self-preservation is a duty to
God, the state and oneself' and that 'the public interest is
damaged if the state is reduced by even one individual'.[100] To
deny the right to suicide on these grounds is to take *raison d'état*
about as far as it can go.

.   .   .

ENLIGHTENED ABSOLUTISM

This brutal assertion of the interests of the state has often
misled historians into denying that Joseph's absolutism was
'enlightened'. A much debated concept, 'enlightened absolutism' can best be defined as 'a regime in which the ruler possess-
es or assumes the right to enact legislation without consent,
exercises the right exclusively and, in doing so, is influenced by
"the Enlightenment"'.[101] It is a definition which fits Joseph's
theory and practice exactly, as this chapter has demonstrated.
He derived from the social contract not only the authority to
command but also the obligation to serve. Moreover, it was to
be service shaped by a belief in reason, equality, toleration and
the rule of law. Of course, the legislation which poured from

Joseph's office was influenced by sources other than this enlightened ideology: by the long traditions of Habsburg reforms, by a cameralist concern to maximise public revenue and by the demands of power politics, to name only three. Of course it would be absurd to suggest that the Enlightenment is a sufficient explanation of Joseph's regime, but it is no more sensible to suggest that it played no part beyond providing a rhetorical fig-leaf to conceal *raison d'état*. If Joseph had been concerned only with the power of his state, he would not have devoted so much time and trouble to its weaker members: not even he could have hoped to transform a deaf and dumb blind crippled lunatic illegitimate unmarried mother into an effective fighting unit.[102]

Nor can his 'enlightened absolutism' be dismissed by reference to the alleged contradiction between 'bourgeois' Enlightenment and 'feudal' absolutism. Now that so much research into both the creators and the consumers of the Enlightenment has demonstrated its social heterogeneity, the notion that it was the ideology of the bourgeoisie can be entertained only by that dwindling band of Marxists whose adamantine faith can be shaken by no amount of evidence. As Robert Darnton has written about France: 'far from rising with the middle class, liberalism descended from a long line of aristocrats, and so did the Enlightenment'.[103] That was doubly true of the Habsburg Monarchy, where the middle classes were so much less numerous and the nobility and clergy so much better integrated in the state. For the same reason, the observation that Joseph was a devout Christian cannot be used to deny him enlightened status. The Enlightenment in German-speaking Europe was concerned to purify the Church and its doctrine from within, with a view to regeneration not destruction.[104]

Joseph never doubted that there was a Catholic God in Heaven – and he never doubted that there was a State God on earth. It was his misfortune that the territories he had inherited neither were nor ever could become a state. By geography, history and ethnic composition, the Habsburg Monarchy could never be anything other than a dynastic empire. By seeking to prove the reverse, Joseph was trying to wash the stripes off the zebra (to adapt Aesop's fable out of respect for late-twentieth century sensitivity). Moreover, he tried to do it in the quickest and most abrasive manner possible. This hurried search for immediate results is, of course, one of the many unattractive features of the modern state, as Joseph's contemporary Lessing spotted with characteristic acumen when he compared modern man to the fanatic: 'he often achieves very accurate insights into the future, but he cannot wait for the future to come. He wants to see the future accelerated, and also wants to do the accelerating himself. For what is there in it for him, if what he sees to be desirable is not brought about in his lifetime?'.[105] Nowhere was Joseph's attempt to hurry history more self-defeating than in his dealings with the privileged orders, to which we now must turn.

. . .

NOTES

1. Arneth, *Maria Theresia und Joseph II.*, I, 10.
2. Quoted in Lorenz Mikoletzky, *Joseph II. Herrscher zwischen den Zeiten* (Göttingen, 1979), p. 94.
3. See above, pp. 10–14.
4. Quentin Skinner, 'The state', in Terence Ball, James Farr and Russell L. Hanson (eds), *Political innovation and conceptual change* (Cambridge, 1989), pp. 102, 107.
5. Hans-Ulrich Wehler, *Deutsche Gesellschaftsgeschichte*, vol. I (Munich, 1987), p. 265.
6. Skinner, 'The state', pp. 122–3.
7. Handbillets, vol. 5 (18), no. 186, 24 February 1781, fo. 143.
8. Ibid., vol. 7 (27), no. 515, to Count Hatzfeld, 30 June 1783, fo. 466.
9. Handbillets, vol. 9 (36), no. 98, 28 January 1785 'Beylage zum Billet, no. 89 wegen der in Hungarn einzuführenden Verbesserung', fos 86–8.
10. The whole text is reprinted in Friedrich Walter, *Die österreichische Zentralverwaltung*, section II, vol. 4 (Vienna, 1950), pp. 123–33, this quotation is on p. 127.
11. To his brother Leopold, 25 July 1768, quoted in Beales, p. 4.
12. Handbillets, vol. 8 (31), no. 735, to Count Colloredo, Brünn, 1 October 1784. See also his later letter to Colonel Marquis de Manfredini of 2 November 1786 about his younger nephews – ibid., vol. 10 (40), no. 833, fos 643–4.
13. Handbillets, vol. 5 (18), unnumbered but situated between nos 275 and 276 and taking up fos 221–5. This is a document entitled simply 'Circulare' and addressed to Prince Schwarzenberg, Field Marshal Hadick, Count Blümegen, Count Kollowrat, Count Esterházy, and Baron Reischach, 21 March 1781.

14. Carl Freiherr von Hock and Ignaz Bidermann, *Der österreich-ische Staatsrath (1760–1848)* (Vienna, 1879), p. 99; Christof Dipper, *Deutsche Geschichte 1648–1789* (Frankfurt am Main, 1991), p. 234.
15. See below, pp. 142, 150–2
16. Karl Gutkas, *Kaiser Joseph II. Eine Biographie* (Vienna and Darmstadt, 1989), pp. 254–8 provides the best concise account of Joseph's ministers.
17. Quoted in Christopher Duffy, *The army of Maria Theresa. The armed forces of imperial Austria 1740–1780* (London, 1977), p. 23. The recent historiographical tendency to downgrade Joseph's role in decision-making has been taken much too far. As Peter Dickson has observed, with reference to ecclesiastical policy: 'Joseph's central role, and characteristically extreme logic, in the formulation of policy, still seem incontestable' – 'Joseph II's reshaping of the Austrian Church', *The Historical Journal*, 36, 1 (1993), 91, n. 4.
18. Handbillets, vol. 10 (40), no. 592, to Field Marshal Hadick, 15 August 1786, fo. 443, no. 596, to Count Niczky, 18 August 1786, fo. 452; no. 876, to Field Marshal Hadick, 14 November 1786, fo. 668; no. 921, to Count Palffy, 25 November 1786, fo. 709.
19. Ibid., vol. 11 (45), no. 661, to Count Pergen, 22 August 1787, fo. 594.
20. Beales, p. 85. This contains by far the fullest and most author-itative account of Joseph's private life.
21. Ibid., pp. 332, 335–6.
22. Handbillets, vol. 12 (47), no. 393, to Field Marshal Hadick, Futack, 8 April 1788, fo. 251.
23. Ibid., vol. 7 (27), no. 643, to Baron Kressel, 18 August 1783 fos 588–9; vol. 8 (31), no. 702, to Baron Kressel, Prague, 19 September 1784, fos 601–2.
24. Ibid., vol. 7 (27), no. 139, to Count Pergen, 13 February 1783, fo. 113; vol. 8 (31), no. 665, to Count Pergen, Hloupetin, 9 September 1784, fos 581–2; vol. 9 (36), no. 865, fos 794–5, to Count Pergen, 15 October 1785; vol. 9 (36), no. 869, fo. 796, to Prince Albert of Saxony, 16 October 1785. Viktor Bibl, *Kaiser Joseph II. Ein Vorkämpfer der großdeutschen Idee* (Vienna and Leipzig, 1943), p. 166. As sub-title and place and date of publication suggest, this book was influenced by Bibl's National Socialist proclivities. However, if one can stomach the preface with its talk of the 'New Order' of Europe, one will find an intelligent, lively and generally well-founded study of Joseph and his regime. Oskar Sashegyi, *Zensur und Geistesfreiheit unter Joseph II. Beitrag zur Kulturgeschichte der habsburgischen Länder,*

(Budapest, 1958), p. 218. Henry E. Strakosch, *The problem of enlightened absolutism* (London and New York, 1970), p. 36.

25. Lorenz Hübner, *Lebensgeschichte Josephs des Zweyten, Kaisers der Deutschen, oder Rosen auf dessen Grab* (Salzburg, n.d. [1790]), p. 543.

26. Fred Hennings, *Das josephinische Wien* (Vienna and Munich, 1966), p. 16.

27. Beales, p. 197.

28. Handbillets, vol. 10 (40), no. 1065, to Prince Starhemberg, 30 December 1786, fo. 837.

29. Werner Ogris, 'Zwischen Absolutismus und Rechtsstaat', in *Österreich im Europa der Aufklärung*, I, 373.

30. See above, p. 59.

31. Handbillets, vol. 3 (41), no. 58, to Count Cavriani, 9 September 1786, fo. 82. At Prague he donated the garden of the Carmelites, its vineyard and farm – ibid., no. 62, to Count Nostitz, fos 101–2.

32. Günter Düriegl, 'Wien – eine Residenzstadt im Uebergang von der adeligen Metropole zur bürgerlichen Urbanität', in *Österreich im Europa der Aufklärung*, I, pp. 313–14.

33. Wolfgang May, *Quellen zu den Reformen Josephs II. in niederoesterreichischen Archiven* (Vienna dissertation, 1981), pp. 122–3; Paul von Mitrofanov, *Joseph II. Seine politische und kulturelle Tätigkeit*, 2 vols (Vienna and Leipzig, 1910), I, 243; Jörg K. Hoensch, *Geschichte Böhmens. Von der slavischen Landnahme bis ins 20. Jahrhundert* (Munich, 1987), p. 282.

34. Quoted in Mitrofanov, *Joseph II.*, I, 236–7.

35. Carlo Capra, 'Il Settecento', in Domenico Sella and Carlo Capra, *Il Ducato di Milano dal 1535 al 1796* (Turin, 1984), p. 514.

36. Dino Carpanetto, 'Le reforme illuministiche in Italia', in Nicola Tranfaglia and Massimo Firpo (eds), *La Storia. I grandi problemi dal Medioevo all'Età Contemporanea* (Turin, 1986), p. 592.

37. Dickson, I, 383.

38. Handbillets, vol. 7 (27), no. 396, to Count Esterházy, Karlstadt, 4 May 1783, fo. 317.

39. Ibid., vol. 10 (40), no. 540, to Kaunitz, Suniow (Galicia), 1 August 1786, fo. 390.

40. See for example his distribution of medals to officials who had distinguished themselves in the difficult business of the tax reform or his ennoblement of police director Okacz at Brünn – Ibid., vol. 10 (40), no. 713, to Count Zinzendorf, Prague, 21 September 1786, fos 531–2 and no. 874 to Count Kollowrat, 13 November 1786, fos 667–8.

41. Hock and Bidermann, *Der österreichische Staatsrath*, pp. 138–9, 149–50.

42. Quoted in ibid., p. 122 and in Bibl, *Kaiser Joseph II.* p. 157.

43. See above, pp. 39–40.

44. Handbillets, vol. 10 (40), no. 941, fos 718–30 'Betrachtungen über Tyrol für den Ober Oesterr. Gouverneur Graf von Sauer', December 1786.

45. Ibid., vol. 11 (45), no. 36, to Count Kollowrat, 12 January 1787, fo. 28.

46. Helmut Engelbrecht, *Geschichte des österreichischen Bildungs-wesens*, vol. 3 (Vienna, 1984), pp. 119–28; Hock and Bider-mann, *Der österreichische Staatsrath*, pp. 527–9. The attendance figure for Vienna is given in Hübner, *Lebensgeschichte Josephs des Zweyten*, p. 213.

47. Handbillets, vol. 10 (40), no. 592, to Field Marshal Hadick, Pest, 15 August 1786, fo. 444.

48. Handbillets, vol. 5 (18), no. 713, to Count Blümegen, 29 November 1781, fos 575–8; Hock and Bidermann, *Der öster-reichische Staatsrath*, p. 527.

49. Ernst Wangermann, 'Joseph II – Fortschritt und Reaktion', in *Österreich im Europa der Aufklärung* I, 39.

50. Quoted in Mitrofanov, *Joseph II.*, II, 808. It has been repeated in many modern acounts, for example in Ernst Wangermann, *Aufklärung und staatsbürgerliche Erziehung: Gottfried van Swieten als Reformator des österreichischen Unterrichtswesens 1781–1787* (Vien-na, 1978), p. 25. The value of this well-researched book is vitiated by the author's obsessive dislike of Joseph and his determination to find a contrast between the 'absolutism' of Joseph and the 'enlightenment' of van Swieten. It is clear from his own account that the contrast is greatly exaggerated, if indeed it exists at all. It is also clear that the credit for the achievements of the *Studienhofkommission* which Wangermann assigns exclusively to van Swieten belongs largely to Joseph.

51. Volkmar Braunbehrens, *Mozart in Vienna* (Oxford, 1991), p. 223.

52. Roger Bauer, 'Kaiser Joseph und die – literarischen – Folgen', in Reinhard Urbach (ed.), *Wien und Europa zwischen den Revolu-tionen (1789–1848)* (Vienna and Munich, 1978), p. 24.

53. C. A. Macartney, *Hungary. A short history* (Edinburgh, 1962), p. 124.

54. Handbillets, vol. 8 (31), no. 284 to Count Esterházy, 26 April 1784, fos 333–6. Part of this document is quoted in Bibl, *Kaiser Joseph II.*, p. 147.

55. Hock and Bidermann, *Der österreichische Staatsrath*, p. 112.

56. Handbillets, vol. 5 (18), no. 713, to Count Blümegen, 29 November 1781, fo. 577.

57. Beales, p. 233.

58. Handbillets, vol. 51, no. 673, to Kaunitz, Laxenburg, 12 June 1789, fos 378–9.
59. James J. Sheehan, *German history 1770–1866* (Oxford, 1989), p. 54.
60. All the edicts relating to toleration are to be found in *Handbuch aller unter der Regierung des Kaisers Josephs des IIten für die k.k. Erbländer ergangenen Verordnungen und Gesetze in einer sistematischen Verbindung*, vol. II (Vienna, 1785), 422–49. See also Mitrofanov, *Joseph II.*, II, 711–27. In a recent lecture – 'Modes of religious tolerance and intolerance in eighteenth century Habsburg politics', published in *Austrian History Yearbook*, 24 (1993), 1–16 – Grete Klingenstein has argued that there was more toleration (both *de facto* and *de jure*) of dissidents in the Habsburg Monarchy before Joseph's decrees than has been realised. She has some good points to make, but her conclusion that 'Joseph's legislation thus only summarised the fundamental changes that had already expanded denominational rights and liberties in the previous decades' (p. 15) is an overstatement at odds with her own evidence. For a more judicious assessment, see Beales, p. 472.
61. See above, pp. 58–9.
62. Quoted in Beales, p. 168.
63. Handbillets, no. 1030, to Count Trauttmansdorff, 24 November 1787, fo., 894. This is reprinted in Schlitter, pp. 16–18.
64. Ibid., vol. 11 (45), no. 806, to Count Cobenzl, 6 October 1787, fo. 735. Josef Karniel, *Die Toleranzpolitik Kaiser Josephs II.* (Gerlingen, 1986), pp. 16, 134–6, 172, 176, 322, 341–2. This is an important book, based on deep and wide research, but its stress on the 'primacy of foreign policy' becomes reductionist.
65. Handbillets, vol. 5 (18), no. 72, to Field Marshal Hadick, 25 January 1782, fos. 60–2.
66. Quoted in Beales, p. 469.
67. Bibl, *Kaiser Joseph II.*, pp. 180–1. Robert A. Horváth, 'L'édit de tolérance en Hongrie: histoire et appréciation critique', in Roland Crahay (ed.), *La Tolérance civile. Colloque internationale organisé á l'université de Mons du 2 au 4 septembre 1981 ál'occasion du deuxième centenaire de l'Édit de Joseph II* (Brussels, 1982), p. 147.
68. Handbillets, vol. 7 (27), no. 208, to Field Marshal Hadick, 8 March 1783, fos 179–81.
69. Bibl, *Kaiser Joseph II.*, p. 181. That some Deists were sent to Hungary can be seen from his instruction concerning seven of them at Temesvár who – not surprisingly – had announced that they would like instruction in the Catholic faith – Handbillets, vol. 7 (27), no. 445, to Field Marshal Lieutenant Zettwitz, Temesvár, 25 May 1783, fo. 381.

70. Karniel, *Die Toleranzpolitik Kaiser Josephs II.*, pp. 381–2, 450, 508–17; Hock and Bidermann, *Der österreichische Staatsrath*, pp. 375–87; Horst Glassl, *Das österreichische Einrichtungswerk in Galizien 1772–1790* (Wiesbaden, 1975), p. 219.

71. Quoted in Ernst Wangermann, *The Austrian Achievement 1700–1800* (London, 1973), p. 90.

72. Hock and Bidermann, *Der österreichische Staatsrath*, pp. 549–50.

73. Handbillets, vol. 7 (27), no. 52, to Count Kollowrat, 14 January 1783, fos 40–4. Cf. his programmatic statement of 1773–Beales, p. 240.

74. A 'Zentner' was approximately a hundredweight.

75. Handbillets, vol. 13 (51), no. 690, to Count Kollowrat, 19 June 1789, fo. 389.

76. Bibl, *Kaiser Joseph II.*, p. 217.

77. Handbillets, vol. 8 (31), no. 732, to Count Rosenberg, 1 October 1784, fo. 630.

78. May, *Quellen zu den Reformen Josephs II.*, p. 418.

79. Hanns Leo Mikoletzky, *Oesterreich–Das große 18. Jahrhundert. Von Leopold I. bis Leopold II.* (Vienna, 1967), p. 338; Karl Uhlirz, *Handbuch der Geschichte Österreichs und seiner Nachbarländer Böhmen und Ungarn*, vol. II, pt. 1 (Graz, Vienna and Leipzig, 1930), p. 390.

80. Handbillets, vol. 10 (40), no. 420, to Count Kollowrat, 2 June 1786, fo. 299.

81. Arneth, *Joseph II und Leopold*, II, 17.

82. James Van Horn Melton, 'Arbeitsprobleme des aufgeklärten Absolutismus in Preußen und Oesterreich', *Mitteilungen des Instituts für österreichische Geschichtsforschung*, 90 (1982) 51.

83. Herbert Hassinger, 'Der Stand der Manufakturen in den deutschen Erbländern der Habsburgermonarchie am Ende des 18. Jahrhunderts', in Friedrich Lütge (ed.), *Die wirtschaftliche Situation in Deutschland und Österreich um die Wende vom 18. zum 19. Jahrhundert* (Stuttgart, 1964), p. 151.

84. See especially the numerous publications of Arnost Klima, for example: 'Industrial development in Bohemia 1648–1781', *Past and Present*, 11 (1957), p. 94, and 'Probleme der Proto-Industrie in Böhmen zur Zeit Maria Theresias', in *Österreich im Europa der Aufklärung*, I 195.

85. Richard Rudolph, 'Economic revolution in Austria? The meaning of 1848 in Austrian economic history', in John Komlos (ed.), *Economic development in the Habsburg Monarchy in the nineteenth century* (New York, 1983), p. 167.

86. David F. Good, *The economic rise of the Habsburg Empire 1750–1914* (Berkeley, 184), p. 15.

87. Dickson, I, 177, 204.

88. François Crouzet, 'England and France in the eighteenth century: a comparative analysis of two economic growths', in R.M. Hartwell (ed.), *The causes of the industrial revolution in England* (London, 1967), p. 155.

89. Quoted in Konrad Schünemann, 'Die Wirtschaftspolitik Josephs II. in der Zeit der Mitregenschaft', *Mitteilungen des österreichischen Instituts für Geschichtsforschung*, 47 (1933), 19.

90. Handbillets, vol. 8 (31), no. 295, to Count Esterházy, 1 May 1784, fo. 349.

91. See above, pp. 4–5.

92. Bibl, *Kaiser Joseph II.*, p. 149.

93. Horst Möller, *Fürstenstaat oder Bürgernation: Deutschland 1763–1815* (Berlin, 1989), p. 82.

94. Günter Düriegl, 'Wien–eine Residenzstadt im Uebergang von der adeligen Metropole zur bürgerlichen Urbanität', in *Österreich im Europa der Aufklärung*, I, 314.

95. May, *Quellen zu den Reformen Josephs II.*, p. 508.

96. Handbillets, vol. 8 (31), no. 665, to Count Pergen, Hloupetin, 9 September 1784, fos 581–2; vol. 9 (36), no. 303, to Count Pergen, 29 March 1785, fos 336–7; vol. 9 (36), no. 792, to Count Palffy, 23 September 1785, fo. 731; vol. 9 (36), no. 1038, to Count Philipp Cobenzl, 9 December 1785, fo. 914; vol. 11 (45), no. 319, to Count Kollowrat, 30 March 1787, fos 226–7; no. 1056, to Doctor Quarin, 3 December 1787, fos 908–12; vol. 12 (47), no. 864, to Prince Starhemberg, Semlin, 13 July 1788, fo. 525; Ignaz de Luca, *Beschreibung der kaiserlichen königlichen Residenzstadt Wien. Ein Versuch*, 2 vols (Vienna, 1785–7) II, 359.

97. Handbillets, vol. 10 (40), no. 498, to Field Marshal Hadick, Peterwardein, 7 July 1786, fos 350–3.

98. Paul P. Bernard, *The limits of enlightenment. Joseph II and the law* (Urbana, 1979), p. 35.

99. Handbillets, vol. 6 (22), no. 583, to Baron Reischach, 14 July 1782, fos 490–1.

100. Quoted in Mitrofanov, *Joseph II.*, II, 528.

101. Derek Beales, 'Was Joseph II an enlightened despot?', *The Austrian Enlightenment and its aftermath*, Austrian Studies 2, ed. Ritchie Robertson and Edward Timms (Edinburgh, 1991), p. 2.

102. This is the only sentence I have consciously taken from my earlier book on Joseph – *Joseph II and enlightened despotism* (London, 1970), p. 72.

103. Robert Darnton, 'In search of enlightenment: recent attempts to create a social history of ideas', *Journal of Modern History*, 43 (1971), 119.

104. T.C.W. Blanning, 'The Enlightenment in Catholic Germany', in Roy Porter and Mikulas Teich (eds), *The enlightenment in national context* (Cambridge, 1981), *passim*.
105. Quoted in Dipper, *Deutsche Geschichte*, p. 225.

Chapter 4

JOSEPH II AND THE PRIVILEGED ORDERS

. . .

THE CHURCH

The state that Joseph built was intended to be essentially unitary, standardised and uniform. No matter what its members' geographic location, social status, ethnic origin or religious denomination might be, they were all required to contribute to the utmost of their ability. No exceptions could be made on the grounds of status, for the same social contract which obliged him to strive tirelessly for the good of the state[1] also obliged him to pay no attention to social conventions. These were mere 'prejudices, which try to make us believe that we have a higher status than other people because we have a count for an ancestor and a piece of parchment in our desk signed by Charles V. In reality, our parents can give us nothing more than physical existence, and for that reason there is not the slightest difference between a king, a count, a burgher or a peasant. It was the Creator who gave us our soul and our mind; and virtues and vices are the result of good or bad education and the example which we see before us'.[2] If certain individuals or groups had secured special treatment over the course of time, they had to justify them on the grounds of utility – simple antiquity was not enough. In other words, for Joseph II 'privilege' was a synonym for 'abuse'.

But the Habsburg Monarchy was as riddled with privilege as it was with particularism. Luckless indeed was the subject who could not claim some sort of special treatment by virtue of birth, vocation, occupation, religion, nationality or location. As

Joseph moved to reduce these fantastic contours to the smooth uniformity favoured by the modern state, it was inevitable that his *Gleichmachung* (equalisation) would have to become *Gleichschaltung* (elimination of opposition). At the top of his list of targets stood the largest, richest and most privileged corporate group in the Monarchy – the Roman Catholic church. As we saw in a previous chapter,[3] much had been done during the previous reign to transfer power and resources from Church to state, but Joseph sought to go much further much faster.

This was as much a difference of style as of substance, as the following episode well illustrates: in 1782 the German reading-public was greatly diverted by the publication in pamphlet form of an exchange of letters between Joseph II and the archbishop-elector of Trier Clemens Wenzeslaus. It had been initiated by the latter's concern for 'the honour of God, the well-being of the Church and the temporal and eternal salvation of Your Imperial Majesty'.[4] In solemn tones, the archbishop admonished the emperor for his anti-papal and secularising policies, reminding him that 'the spiritual power instituted by Jesus Christ is as completely unlimited and autonomous in matters of religion as is the secular power when dealing with the things of this world'.

A public reproach from one of the most senior prelates of the Holy Roman Empire – and Joseph's cousin to boot – was arresting enough. What made it truly sensational was the nature of the reply it provoked. Not only did Joseph reject each complaint, he did so derisively and with biting sarcasm, clearly seeking to cause maximum offence. For example, when defending his decision to ban all discussion of the papal bull condemning Jansenism, he wrote 'Fortunately, my good Austrians and honest Hungarians know nothing of either Molina [the Jesuit theologian] or Jansenius – while I, for my part, did know a Molina once, but he was a greyhound who could course and kill his hare single-handed'. After much more mocking in the same vein, he concluded, 'Finally, to come to the point, I would like to think that both of us can tread the narrow path which leads to our salvation by carrying out the duties of our respective offices, which Providence has allocated to us, and by earning the bread we eat. You eat the bread of the Church and so protest against every innovation; but I eat the bread of the state and so defend and restore its fundamental rights'.

With subtle dignity, Clemens Wenzeslaus replied that Joseph's letter had filled him with joy, for it had allowed him to follow the example of the Apostles in suffering humiliation for the sake of Jesus Christ. Raising his head and voice, he then warned that however confident Joseph's tread might be at present, there would come a time when he would be inconsolable – 'And may that day not be your last!'. In the rejoinder which brought the correspondence to a close, Joseph began in light-hearted vein – 'I see that we are not dancing to the same tune' – but put a sting in the tail: 'You take the form for the substance, whereas I keep strictly to the point in religion, and take action only against the abuses which have crept in to pollute it'.

Joseph campaigned against four kinds of abuses, as he defined them. The first was papal usurpation. As sovereignty was indivisible and as the clergy were just as much his subjects as anyone else, there could be no question of any outside authority encroaching on his jurisdiction. So all official communications from Rome to the Church in the Habsburg Monarchy and *vice versa* were made conditional on secular approval. No longer a state-within-a-state, the Church now became more like a department of state, a change symbolised by the imposition of a new oath on the bishops which obliged them to swear loyalty and obedience to His Imperial Majesty and to promote the interests of the state to the utmost of their power.

The second group of abuses also concerned foreign interference, this time the diocesan rights of the prince-bishops of the Holy Roman Empire which extended into the Habsburg Monarchy, as described in chapter one.[5] That one of Joseph's imperial vassals could exercise jurisdiction over his territories was the clearest possible sign that they did not yet constitute a proper state and was correspondingly repugnant. On hearing in March 1783 that the bishop of Passau was dying, he at once sent instructions to the local official, Count von Thierheim, to get ready. As soon as death was confirmed, Thierheim was to inform the Passau authorities that the writ of their bishop no longer ran in the Habsburg Monarchy and that a new bishopric would be established at Linz to take over his jurisdiction. A necessary corollary, it need hardly be added, was the expropriation of all the Passau estates inside the Monarchy. Within three days, the old bishop was dead, a bishop of Linz had been appointed and the Passau property was safely gathered into the coffers of the Habsburg Monarchy.[6]

This was the most dramatic and flagrantly illegal action by Joseph in this sphere, and – as we shall see later – it was to prove a serious handicap for Habsburg policy in the Holy Roman Empire.[7] However, it was only part of a general campaign to make the territorial and episcopal frontiers of the Monarchy coincide. New bishoprics were also created at Budweis in Bohemia, Leoben in Styria, Tarnów in Galicia and St. Pölten in Lower Austria. Agreement with the foreign powers affected, notably the Pope, Poland and the archbishop of Salzburg, was obtained only after long and arduous negotiations. Further plans to establish another see at Bregenz in the Tyrol and to promote Laibach to archiepiscopal status had to be abandoned in the teeth of fierce opposition.[8] In Lombardy, however, all ties between the Church and Rome which were not purely doctrinal were abolished.[9]

Simultaneously with this two-pronged offensive against external interference, Joseph moved to take control of the Church's assets inside the Monarchy. Their current misuse constituted the third kind of abuse he sought to remedy. He spelled out his reasons in June 1783 in a characteristically radical memorandum to his chief minister in ecclesiastical matters, Baron Kressel. It was the clear duty of the sovereign, he stated, to ensure that there was a Church in his territories with sufficient resources to accomplish its tasks, 'in just the same way that there is an army to defend the state, courts to administer justice and a bureaucracy to deal with political and economic matters'. Unfortunately, he went on, this duty had been neglected by generations of rulers, with the result that material provision for the Church's needs had been abandoned to mere chance. In some places there was a surplus, in others a dearth and so – and now came the most damning of Joseph's rich stock of standard criticisms – 'the totality of the Monarchy is considered by no one'. Bishops only looked to the interests of their own dioceses, monastic orders sought only to increase their own numbers and wealth, and the final say was pronounced by 'a Pope who sits in Rome and who together with his congregation of Italian cardinals has never seen nor knows anything about the country in question'. There were only two ways forward, Joseph concluded: either the state could simply expropriate church property in its entirety, or it could content itself with investigating the current state of ecclesiastical resources and redressing the more flagrant imbalances. For the time being, Joseph preferred the second route but if it proved too slow he reserved the right to move into the fast lane. The detailed instructions which followed for the gathering of information about clerical income were underpinned by the desire for uniformity – the Monarchy was to be regarded as a single whole, with each province doing its share to help each other. He concluded with a familiar exhortation for collective effort: 'no clergyman may live in idleness for himself but must work for his fellow men and for religion'.[10]

To enforce this uniform effort, Joseph took vigorous action to alter the balance within the Church in favour of the 'secular' clergy (priests living in the world and not subject to a rule), especially parish priests, and at the expense of the 'regulars', especially mendicant friars and monks and nuns dedicated to a contemplative life. On 29 November 1781 he ordered the United Chancellery to prepare the dissolution of all religious orders which were 'completely and utterly useless' and therefore could not be pleasing to God. These he defined as those which did not run schools or hospitals or help their fellow-beings in other practical ways. The first charge on the funds released by the expropriation of their property would be pensions for their members, but the large surplus anticipated would be devoted to the promotion of religion and practical charity.[11] By the time of Joseph's death, the imposition of this order had changed the Church in the Habsburg Monarchy radically and irreversibly. While the 25,000 regulars were reduced to 11,000, the 22,000 seculars were increased to 27,000, a net reduction in the clerical population of about a quarter, involving the dissolution of 530 monastic institutions in the central lands (Bohemia, Austria and Hungary) alone.[12] In other words, from constituting 53 per cent of the clergy in 1780, the regulars had sunk to 29 per cent by the end of the decade. The counter-reformation was over.

The final stage in Joseph's creation of a national church to serve the state was the re-education of the clergy. This was the last set of abuses to which he turned his attention. In the past, he believed, the young priests had emerged from the episcopal seminaries and monastic schools equipped to serve neither God, the state nor their fellow-men. What was needed was 'complete uniformity in theological and moral instruction'[13] – and that could only be provided by training organised by the state. In 1783, therefore, he abolished the old institutions and established twelve 'General Seminaries' (at Vienna, Prague, Olmütz, Graz, Innsbruck, Freiburg-im-Breisgau, Lemberg, Pressburg, Pest, Louvain, Luxemburg and Pavia) , where ordinands were to undergo a rigorous six-year course of study. At the heart of the curriculum was the injunction 'that the Church must be useful to the state'. The regime was austere: when Joseph discovered that seminarists at Prague were allowed to go home during vacations, he was horrified. In future, he ordered, only those with completely reliable 'moral characters' were to be permitted to make brief visits to their relations.[14] It was all to no avail, of course: clergymen will be clergymen, and in the last year of his life he was still fulminating about them carousing in the towns, drinking, fornicating and contracting venereal disease.[15]

The nationalisation of the Church by severing foreign ties, the secularisation of a substantial proportion of Church property, the transformation of priests into civil servants and – last, but not least – Joseph's relentlessly erastian rhetoric all suggest a Manichaean struggle between Church and state. It was a confrontation dramatised for contemporaries by Pius VI's journey to Vienna in 1782. How things had changed since the Emperor Henry IV had gone to Canossa in 1077 to wait barefoot in the snow for the summons to do penance before Pope Gregory VII. Writing to his sister, Queen Maria Carolina of Naples, a fortnight before the Pope's arrival, Joseph assured her that he would receive his visitor with all the politeness the Pontiff's position demanded, but also 'with the steadfastness of a man who knows what belongs to him, what he can do and what is required for the welfare of his fatherland. Voltaire wrote that one should kiss the feet of the Pope in order to bind his hands, and I shall follow the spirit if not the letter of this advice'.[16]

Pius VI was in Vienna from 22 March until 22 April 1782. Although he achieved a public relations triumph with the ordinary people of Vienna, attracting more than a hundred thousand to a public blessing, he failed to extract any significant concessions from a Joseph who was determined to remain 'resolute, staunch and unshakeable in his principles', as he put it to his brother Leopold.[17] Although careful to avoid any public rift and at pains to stress the unity between the Roman Pope and the Holy Roman Emperor, Joseph was less restrained in his private correspondence, filling his letters with sarcastic jibes at his guest's expense. He told Grand Duke Paul of Russia, for example, that when he learned that a papal indulgence would be extended not only to those who actually attended Pius' public blessing but also to anyone in earshot of the salute fired to mark the occasion, he ordered his gunners to let off 'a 24-calibre indulgence', so that even people living three leagues away could benefit – if the wind were in the right quarter.[18]

When it was all over and the Pope had moved on to fresh popular triumphs in Bavaria, Joseph reflected: 'I was a good Catholic before his arrival and he had no need to convert me'.[19] He was not being ironic. It would be a great mistake to suppose that because Joseph promoted the state with such enthusiasm he was incapable of serving the Church with equal fervour. Not once in his voluminous correspondence did he ever show the least doubt in the absolute truth of Roman Catholicism – and Joseph was not a man to dissemble. What he did reject was that variety of Roman Catholicism which was ultra-montane in structure and baroque in substance. Although recognising the Pope as the titular head of the Church, he believed that most papal authority was based on usurpation: 'Only the ecumenical councils are authorised to explain the dogma which comes directly from Jesus Christ and it is to them and them alone we owe obedience. It is the same with matters of discipline: abuses can never become laws, and it is by getting back to the fountain-head and the practices of the Church closest to the time of the Apostles that we shall not be found wanting'.[20] Once again, Joseph was showing his liking for first principles.

The obligation to return the Church to a condition in which it was able to perform its original function was one which Joseph felt keenly. It can be seen most clearly in the time and energy he devoted to promoting his subjects' spiritual welfare. Wherever he went on his travels, he sought to promote the true faith, whether it was ordering the reconsecration of a chapel in a Hungarian prison, or ordering the archbishop of Mungacs to go in person to reconvert three villages in the county of Zips which had defected to Greek orthodoxy, or ordering the punishment of two parish priests for leaving the Host unguarded, or ordering the investigation of a report that a young man had been found smoking his pipe in the Piarist church in the Joseph-stadt – just to give a random sample from a single year (1786) of his characteristically detailed attention.[21]

If such instances might be dismissed as further evidence of

compulsive meddling, serious attention must be paid to the use he made of secularised Church property: 'the last thing I want is to employ even the smallest part of it for alien and merely secular purposes, rather I intend to devote it to the creation of a Fund for religion and the parishes'. For the time being, part of the income would have to go to former monks and nuns in the form of pensions, but the remainder would be spent 'solely and exclusively on the advancement of religion'.[22] First and foremost that meant the creation of new parishes: in future no one should be more than one hour's walking-distance from a church. It proved to be unrealisable. Even a reformed Church was not rich enough to support Joseph's ideal of a well-paid, highly qualified and numerous secular clergy. Resources proved too limited to deal with the twin problems of demographic increase and monastic longevity (as Peter Dickson has laconically observed: 'If it had been possible to shoot the ex-monks and nuns, the Fund's problems could have been resolved'[23]). Nevertheless, Joseph's achievement was considerable. In the course of the 1780s, at least 600 new parishes were created and many more received additional curates. This could make a real difference to the religious life of the masses: a report composed in 1789, for example, revealed that in eighteen dioceses in Hungary and Croatia the number of clergy charged with the cure of souls had increased by a third and the ratio between priest and parishioner had halved.[24] Of particular importance for the future religious life of the Monarchy was the creation of forty-seven new parishes in Vienna and its suburbs.

Clergy old and new were subjected to a barrage of instructions on how to conduct the religious life of their flocks. It was indicative of the importance Joseph attached to it that hardly a month went by without some new admonition or prohibition issuing from Vienna. In large measure it was a continuation of the dismantling of baroque piety begun by Maria Theresa,[25] but Joseph brought to the task a new sense of urgency, impatience and radicalism. It would be tedious to recount in any detail the decrees which reduced or abolished the processions, pilgrimages, festivals, confraternities, decorations, relics and all the other traditional practices which were as much social as religious. What is more important is the intense interest Joseph showed in the quality of his subjects' spiritual life. Anything which smacked of superstition, anything which assigned value to externals and anything which seemed 'unnecessary' was to make way for a form of religion which was both inward-looking, in the sense of being willed by the individual, and outward-looking, in the sense of serving one's fellow-man with practical charity. To this end, Joseph was especially keen on comprehensibility, intervening in 1781, for example, to stop conservative bishops impeding the distribution of vernacular bibles.[26]

By the time Joseph had finished his work, the Church and the religious culture of the Habsburg Monarchy had changed fundamentally. Where it had once been international, it was now national; where it had once been a state-within-a-state, it was now a department of state; where it had once given pride of place to the regular clergy, it was now dominated by the seculars; where the lion's shares of its resources had once gone to prelates, it was now the parish priests who were given priority; where the emphasis had once been on worship and ritual, now it was personal salvation and service which were most valued; and finally, where it had once been aristocratic, it was now meritocratic. Joseph made it clear repeatedly that the only avenue to promotion in his Church was ability allied to service – birth counted for nothing. In 1788, for example, he wrote to Baron Kressel asking for suggestions as to whom he should appoint to fill the vacancy at Linz: 'and I must repeat again that when making an appointment we should consider only the best-qualified (*tüchtigsten*) candidate, whether he is to be found among the parish priests, the regular clergy or wherever; and I would always give preference, without any regard for his social status, to someone who had put in good service in the cure of souls'. The choice fell on Canon Gall of Vienna, a commoner who had distinguished himself by sterling work in both parish and school.[27]

Although this recasting of the Church in the Habsburg Monarchy could not help but provoke opposition, there was no simple confrontation between Church and state. There were many clergy, including prelates, who welcomed Joseph's reforms and did their best to implement them. If Cardinal Migazzi of Vienna and Archbishop Edling of Görz protested noisily against the introduction of toleration or the dissolution of monasteries, other members of the hierarchy such as Bishop Herberstein of Laibach, Bishop Hay of Königgrätz or Bishop Kerens of St Pölten composed pastoral letters which might have been written by Joseph himself.[28] The overall docility with which the Church accepted the new order has been well expressed and explained by Peter Dickson:

In France a revolution, in England in the 1830s the threat of one, were needed to procure similar acquiescence. The increase in the power of Austrian secular government since the mid-century, epitomised by Joseph II himself; the penetration of Febronian and Jansenist doctrines, or variants of them, at Court and within the episcopate; the ineffectuality of opposition of those, lay and ecclesiastical, who doubted the emperor's policies; perhaps explain this passivity.[29]

.   .   .

THE NOBILITY

Joseph was not only a meritocrat, he was also an egalitarian. From the time he first began to articulate his political thinking, he showed a deep hostility to the nobility. In his *Rêveries* of 1763 he announced the startling ambition 'to humble and impoverish the grandees, for I do not believe it is very beneficial that there should be little kings and great subjects who live at their ease, not caring what becomes of the state'.[30] It does not seem to have worried him that he himself owed his position solely to the accident of birth, falling back on the convenient fiction that he had been appointed by 'Providence'. Perhaps it was a sense of unease at this logical flaw which drove him to such extremities of effort on behalf of the state and to such a radical programme of levelling everybody else. It was this, more than anything, which separated him from his contemporary Frederick the Great, who wrote in his *Political Testament*: 'a sovereign should regard it as his duty to protect the nobility, who form the finest jewel in his crown and the lustre of his army'.[31]

Frederick was as determined as Joseph to make his nobles work for the state, but he was prudent enough to leave them their social privileges and economic basis in return. This was not Joseph's way. Hard if shallow thinking about the nature of man and the state had convinced him that social differentiation justified only by the fact that it 'had always been like that' was an abuse and should therefore be abolished as quickly as possible. In a dozen different ways, some important and some petty, he brought home to his nobles his determination to destroy their privileged status. In 1783, for example, he abolished the *Theresianum*, the academy established by Maria Theresa for the education of young aristocrats, on the grounds that it had done little or nothing to prepare useful servants of the state. Anyway, he added, he was opposed in principle to the 'segregation of aristocratic youth from other classes', advocating instead state schools 'where young people of all classes can come together in friendship and thus lay the basis for the elimination of all social prejudice, whose baleful influence makes citizens of the same state almost foreigners to each other'. Noble academies in the provinces were thrown open and their foundation places made generally available as public scholarships, so that nobles could sit in class with commoners and see that birth meant nothing.[32] In future young nobles were to be educated for state service in the same way as everyone else, which meant – among many other things – that they were no longer allowed to go off on a grand tour, picking up foreign habits which were expensive and useless.[33]

For contemporaries, the most dramatic illustration of Joseph's egalitarian drive was his abolition of the nobility's legal privileges. This was so important because its implications were immediate, visual and sensational. They were illustrated by the case of the young count who had led a life of dissipation, had been expelled from both the army and the civil service, had been convicted of conspiracy to forge bank-notes and had been sentenced by the courts to imprisonment. Joseph then intervened personally to change the sentence to a period of street-sweeping, followed by the notorious barge-pulling in Hungary, which – predictably – the wretched count survived only briefly. The sight of an aristocrat sweeping the streets of the capital, shackled to a chain-gang of common criminals, his head shaven, wearing a uniform of coarse brown cloth, supervised by warders carrying whips, and watched by a crowd of derisive Viennese represented the humiliation of a whole class.[34]

In view of the behaviour of upper-class radicals in any period, it should not come as a surprise to learn that Joseph combined theoretical egalitarianism with practical snobbery, consorting socially only with the highest of high society. However, he did so only with a small portion of it. His long-standing aversion to anything which smacked of a baroque court[35] was redoubled after he became sole ruler. Although the full paraphernalia could still be unleashed for a grand state occasion, as it was for the visit of the Grand Duke and Duchess of Russia in 1782, in effect the Habsburg Monarchy ceased to have a court. It is impossible to assess what effect this lacuna had on the regime's fortunes. Frederick's Prussia flourished without a court, while Louis XVI's lavish version at Versailles did not save him from the guillotine. On the one hand, it seems reasonable to conclude that Joseph's demonstrative distancing himself from his aristocracy did nothing to foster their sense of loyalty when the crisis came at the end of the 1780s. On the other hand, there were some contemporaries who believed that he had succeeded in instilling a new ethos of service in his nobles:

> In the course of Joseph's reign the nobility in Vienna became steadily more humane, more courteous and more obliging. Before Joseph's day their most common characteristics were dissipation, indebtedness, arrogance and ignorance. But when the monarch set an example by giving priority to service without distinction of birth, by punishing follies and crimes without discrimination, and by showing that it is the lower orders which are the most indispensable and useful members of society and that a state can well do without a nobility, and also by giving a personal example of how well modest frugality becomes a man of high standing – then the nobles had to climb down from their divine pride if they did not want to seem ridiculous by comparison with their sovereign.[36]

This optimistic verdict was echoed by another contemporary, Johann Pezzl, the author of the best-informed account of Vienna in the period, when he observed that whereas in the past the sole function of nobles had been lining a room like wallpaper, now they knew that the only way to attract the attention of their sovereign and the respect of the public was through service of the state.[37]

. . .

THE PEASANTRY

In the past, the Habsburg Monarchy had been governed by an alliance of three roughly equal partners – the dynasty, the Church and the nobility. The reforms of Maria Theresa had elevated the sovereign from being *primus inter pares* to being *primus*, while maintaining the other two in a position elevated above the rest of society. Now Joseph sought to depress them further, in a process of social planing which would reduce all to the same level. It was when this egalitarian programme moved from the realms of law, education or society to attack the economic foundations of noble predominance that the Monarchy began to shake.

Any attempt to explain the tripartite relationship between Joseph II, the nobility and the peasantry is bedeviled by the extreme variety of the last two groups. A great magnate such as Prince Esterházy, with his dozens of castles, thousands of serfs and millions of acres, had nothing in common beyond legal status with a Magyar gentleman farming his own plot single-handed: hence the need to speak not of 'the nobility of the Habsburg Monarchy' but of the nobilities.[38] The same applies to the rural masses. At one end of the scale were the 'slaves' of Bukovina, a group of gypsy origin who could be sold, exchanged or inherited and were legally equivalent to inanimate property, with no rights of any kind and no protection against their owners.[39] At the other end, there were the prosperous farmers of the German-speaking lands, owning their own land or enjoying hereditary tenure, producing for the market and employing agricultural labourers to do the hard work. The rising price of agricultural produce during the latter part of the eighteenth century allowed these rich peasants to get richer, as they proudly demonstrated in the growing size of their splendid houses and their opulent furniture.[40]

Only one generalisation may be made with confidence about the peasantries of the Habsburg Monarchy, namely that any generalisation will be riddled with exceptions and open to all sorts of objections. However, generalisations cannot be avoided if any sort of sense is to be made of what happened under Joseph II. Perhaps the clearest way to explain the pattern of peasant relationships is to think of a peasant as being confronted by four different lords: a lord who controlled his land (*Grundherr* = land-lord), a lord who exercised jurisdiction over him (*Gerichtsherr* = court-lord), a lord who disposed of his person (*Leibherr* = body-lord) and a lord who took a tithe of his produce to support the Church (*Zehntherr* = tithe-lord). In the great majority of cases throughout the Monarchy, the last-named of those was a clergyman and need concern us no further. It was the relationship between the first three which was decisive. Where the three kinds of domination were concentrated in a single lord, we can properly speak of the peasants he controlled as 'serfs' because they were dependent in both a personal and a material sense. But where the functions of *Gerichtsherr* and *Leibherr* were exercised by the sovereign – by a *public* authority – the peasant was essentially free.

With this in mind, an important distinction can be made between the German-speaking lands – Upper and Lower Austria, the Tyrol, Styria, Carinthia etc. – and Bohemia, Moravia, Galicia and Hungary. In the first group, the noble or ecclesiastical landowners leased all or most of their land to peasants, drawing their income in the form of rents and dues. In the northern and eastern provinces, it was more common for the landlords to farm a large domain themselves, making use of the labour dues (known as the *robot* after the Slavonic word for 'work') they were entitled to exact from their serfs. Here the landlord was also *Gerichtsherr* and *Leibherr*. The first system is described by the German phrase '*Grundherrschaft und Grundwirtschaft*', because the exercise of authority (*Herrschaft*) and the economic arrangements (*Wirtschaft*) were based on the land (*Grund*). The second system is described by the German phrase '*Gutsherrschaft und Gutswirtschaft*' because the exercise of authority and the economic arrangements were based on the estate (*Gut*).

The serf of the *Gutsherrschaft und Gutswirtschaft* was dependent on his lord in two ways. The first can be described as 'cultural', for without the permission of his lord he could not leave the estate, could not choose his occupation and could not marry. It was in the lord's court that his civil cases were adjudicated and his misdemeanours punished. In as much as he came into contact with a civilisation beyond the estate, it was the lord who took responsibility, by appointing the priest and – less often – a school-teacher. The other form of dependence was economic. By virtue of having been born on the estate, the serf owed his lord a wide variety of dues and services, the most onerous being the obligation to work for nothing on the lord's domain for a certain number of days per week – usually three and in some places as many as four or five. Particularly strange to modern eyes was '*Gesindedienst*', the practice which obliged a serf's children to work full-time for the lord for three to seven years from the age of fourteen. In addition, the lord was able to exploit his serfs through various monopolies, the most important being brewing and milling. The land which the serf cultivated himself varied enormously in size and security, but where the lord controlled the courts, no tenure could be said to be safe, as the constant complaints about expropriation demonstrated.[41]

Serfdom and the *Gutsherrschaft und Gutswirtschaft* were unacceptable to Joseph II for several reasons. Firstly, the system subjected a large proportion of the population to the authority of the landlords, who for all their wealth and pretensions were nothing more than private individuals. That was repugnant to the modern state's claim to sovereignty. Secondly, the notion of hereditary subservience was incompatible with Joseph's belief in the natural equality of man.[42] Thirdly, the control exercised by the landlords allowed them to expropriate an excessive proportion of the serfs' income, thus denying the state its proper share. Fourthly, the abuse of power permitted by the system led to social disorder, as the serfs resorted to the only weapon at their disposal – insurrection. Fifthly, the restrictions imposed on mobility starved the manufacturing and commercial sectors of labour. Finally, those same restrictions also made it more difficult for the state to recruit soldiers.

These were not original insights on the part of Joseph. Measures to protect serfs against the encroachments of their lords date back to the middle of the sixteenth century, but the very regularity with which the legislation had to be renewed testifies to its lack of effect. For two centuries, any action commanded by the centre was frustrated by the hard-pressed dynasty's need for magnate support and by the landlords' control of local government. It was only when the state began to establish its own network of agents that the theoretical sovereignty of the centre could start to become reality. This proved a mixed blessing for the serfs, for any resources prised from the grasp of their lords were more likely to be diverted to the state than to be left in their own pockets.[43] Increasing demographic pressure on land also led to a deterioration in the peasants' material position.

The eruption of a major peasant revolt in Bohemia in 1775 showed just how little impact the reforms had made. Joseph's own response to the crisis was both weak and inconsistent; at one point he derided plans to regulate labour dues as absurd but shortly afterwards demanded it as essential.[44] Yet when he took charge as sole ruler in 1780, Joseph set in motion a programme of radical reform designed to revolutionise lord-peasant relations. Beginning in 1781, he issued decrees for each province 'abolishing serfdom'. It is necessary to put 'abolishing serfdom' in quotation-marks, for it meant less than might be supposed. The former serf could now marry and move at will, could choose a trade or profession and was no longer obliged to send his children for compulsory domestic service.[45] This certainly represented a major step towards emancipation, but affected neither the lords' jurisdiction nor the system of dues and services – especially the *robot* – which one naturally, if inaccurately, thinks of as being part of 'serfdom'.

Other reforming decrees followed thick and fast. Also in 1781 a new penal code gave peasants better protection against their lords' abuse of their criminal jurisdiction. Among other precautions, it was ordered that punishments exceeding a week's confinement or penal labour had to be confirmed by the local state authorities. If the lords exceeded their powers, they would be punished themselves and obliged to pay compensation to their victims – a method of encouraging a responsible judiciary which might well be resurrected today. Lawyers were appointed by the state to advise peasants about their rights and to assist their protection.[46] Other measures abolished forced labour on crown estates and imposed limits on it elsewhere, improved security of tenure, encouraged the division of domains into peasant holdings, abolished monopolies of milling, brewing and distilling, and introduced a new law on hunting designed to prevent the lords' game damaging peasants' crops. Symbolic of Joseph's replacement of the old style of personal kingship by state service was his decision to close down his hunt, selling the hounds and retraining the hunt-servants as foresters or footmen.[47] Equally characteristic was his order that peasants should no longer have to bow to or kiss the hands of their lords.[48]

Joseph had embarked on an extremely dangerous exercise. On the one hand, his reforms alienated the nobilities, in whose hands lay power in the localities. On the other hand, he gave the oppressed rural masses reason to hope that the hour of their deliverance was at hand. With the state bureaucracy so weak, there was always a danger that conflict between lord and peasant would lead to a breakdown in government. This is what happened in November 1784, with the eruption of a major peasant insurrection in Transylvania. This should have come as no surprise to Joseph. On his first visit to Transylvania in 1773 he wrote home: 'My house is continuously besieged by

Wallachians and peasants giving in memorials, of which, taking only the political, I've already collected more than 7,000'. By the time he left the province, that total had more than doubled.[49] Another visit exactly ten years later taught him that nothing had improved in the meantime: 'everything is just as before: national and religious hatred, confusion and intrigue, magistrates, lords and landowners exploiting the subjects'. He was also well aware of the latters' specific grievances: the infliction of excessive punishments, the extortion of excessive dues and services despite government decrees to the contrary, the expropriation of peasant and communal land and the levying of inequitable and unpredictable taxes. In addition, justice and education were in a deplorable state. With grim prescience, Joseph concluded: 'all these evils can only be eradicated by a cut of the sabre'.[50]

Less than eighteen months later the Romanian serfs took his advice, taking revenge on their Hungarian landlords and their families with terrible brutality, killing, burning, looting and raping. The news could not have come at a worse time for Joseph, just as he was sending his troops off to the Low Countries to prepare for war with the Dutch. But what seems to have upset him most was the revelation that his good intentions had not been enough. He wrote to the governor of Transylvania, Baron Brukenthal: 'I never imagined that such a terrible thing could happen in my day and age and after the advice which I have given so often and so assiduously to promote the general good and general security, and still less that it would spread so far and so intensely. I cannot find the words to say how much this depresses and upsets me'.[51] It was yet another illustration of how counter-productive his reforms could be. He had tried to remove all 'national enmities' and to make all the inhabitants of the province feel that they were all Transylvanians rather than Hungarians, Szekler, Saxons or Romanians. Alas, he had only succeeded in making the separate groups more aware of what divided them from each other.[52]

Joseph now found himself in the unenviable position faced by all rulers who seek to reform in the face of opposition from the local establishment. He knew that the grievances of the Transylvanian serfs were justified, yet he could not allow them to take the law into their own hands. As soon as he received news of the outbreak – ten days after it had happened – he ordered the commander-in-chief in Hungary, General Schack-min, to take immediate repressive action with two cavalry and two infantry regiments, supported by field artillery. Captured ring-leaders were to be executed summarily on the spot.[53] At the same time he organised conciliation, instructing local officials to seek the support of the Greek orthodox clergy in persuading the insurgents to return home. He also appointed a commission of inquiry to investigate grievances, including members who were Greek orthodox by religion, were familiar with the Romanian language and were 'free of prejudice'. Optimistically, he urged the nobles to show mercy to their serfs, as the best way of preventing a recurrence of violence in future.[54] News that in fact they were exacting terrible vengeance, slaughtering sixty prisoners in one place and forty in another, provoked a furious letter to the Hungarian chancellor, ordering immediate military intervention to stop the killing and the granting of a general amnesty.[55]

The investigation of the causes of the outbreak confirmed Joseph's assessment and revealed just how little could be achieved by reforms ordered from Vienna. Enclosing reports from officers on the spot, Joseph concluded:

> It has been well known to me that for many years the serfs on the Szalat estates have presented the most pressing complaints about the oppression and brutality of the public officials as well as of the landlords, and I have called repeatedly for the investigation and redress of grievances, but alas up till now it has all been in vain. Commissions of inquiry have indeed been appointed but all they have been able to achieve is that the serfs have been maltreated even worse than before, the officials have been whitewashed and the abuses have never been attacked at their roots. Certainly the situation can be kept under control by force for a while, but when people are oppressed too much and the bow is strung too tightly, sooner or later it is bound to snap.

Although the serfs' grievances were essentially socio-economic in nature, the situation had been made much worse by ethnic and religious differences.[56]

Although eager to advocate 'justice, love and confidence' to the Hungarian nobles as the best way of averting further trouble, Joseph himself was prepared to authorise the use of brutality with disturbing ruthlessness. Once the revolt was under control, he ordered the parading of the captured ringleaders through the places where the worst atrocities had been committed and their execution 'in an exemplary manner' with maximum publicity, in full view of the greatest possible number of people and in such a way that it was made clear that the executions had been ordered by the Emperor himself.[57] The Transylvanian officials responded with alacrity: on 28 February 1785 the leader of the revolt, Horja, and his chief lieutenant, Gloschka, were broken on the wheel, quartered and displayed in segments on poles alongside the road.[58]

Horja's insurrection had been alarming for several reasons. Firstly, because it was so widespread: a contemporary source estimated that at one point 36,000 insurgents were under arms. Secondly, it was extremely violent: in the county of Hunyad alone, sixty-two villages and 132 noble residences were burned and 4,000 people, most of them nobles and their families, were killed 'in the most horrific manner'.[59] No doubt these estimates were exaggerated, but they demonstrate the impact the episode made on public opinion. Thirdly, and most importantly: Horja claimed to be acting on the authority of the Emperor. When he addressed his first armed band, he wore a brass chain bearing the image of Joseph II, a crucifix and a charter written in gold letters. All these insignia, he told them, had been given to him in Vienna by Joseph himself, together with the mission of liberating the Romanians from the yoke of the Hungarian nobles.[60] It was this, more than anything, which allowed Horja to attract so much support so quickly. When it became clear that the imperial authorities had disowned the revolt, his supporters faded away.

Noble landowners who had warned against any relaxation of the ties which bound serf to lord watched with grim satisfaction as 'the thieving, murdering hordes of peasants' laid waste the Transylvanian countryside. If they hoped that Joseph would have learned his lesson from this episode, they were to be sorely disappointed. The year before Horja's revolt, Joseph had set in motion a comprehensive reform of the Habsburg Monarchy's taxation system which had profound implications for all noble landowners. In a flurry of letters and memoranda he demonstrated yet again his preference for working from simple first principles stridently proclaimed: 'The land and the soil which nature has given to man to support him is the sole source from which everything comes and to which everything returns, and whose existence remains constant through all the vagaries of time. For this reason it is incontestably true that land alone should provide for the needs of the state'. Moreover, 'natural justice' demanded that all land should be treated equally, no matter what the status of the owner. Was it not a 'fatuous prejudice', he asked, to suppose that there had once been a time when there had been only lords and no peasants and that the latter, when they materialised, were allowed the land only on certain conditions? The fact of the matter was that primal equality had made way for privilege and inequality as a result of usurpation. It was high time to strip the abuses away, so that the state and all its members could benefit equally. To this end, he announced the creation of an entirely new system, based on the equal taxation of land. Differences in its value, resulting from variations in type, fertility and location, would be dealt with by taking a ten-year average net return (in other words after the costs of cultivation and the seed had been deducted) based on the market value of threshed corn. All other forms of taxation, whether imposed on trade and industry or consumption, were to be abolished.[61]

This was not just a reform of taxation; it also involved a reconstruction of rural relations. In the past, the wretched peasant was kept chained to the estate and forced to contribute so much to his lord in various dues and services, that there was precious little left for public service or public funds. So long as the rural economy was based on a personal nexus of subservience and dues were paid in kind rather than cash, the mass of the population would remain beyond the reach of the state's agents, whether in the form of tax-collectors or recruiting-sergeants. Joseph ordered therefore that the manifold seigneurial burdens, including the *robot*, should be consolidated into a single cash payment. In this manner, he was convinced, the mighty potential of the Habsburg Monarchy, at present restrained by the bonds of prejudice, could be liberated to serve the state. It was this combination of a reform which was both fiscal and 'urbarial' (i.e. regulating relations between lord and peasant) which made Joseph's programme so radical – and so controversial.[62]

Horja's revolt did nothing to change his mind. Never did Joseph show himself more determined and obstinate than in his imposition of his 'Taxation and Urbarial Regulation'. Not even the bitter opposition from most of his senior bureaucrats made him hesitate. On the contrary, the knowledge that they were all landowners complaining through their pockets spurred him on. In 1785 the great land survey which was a necessary precondition of the new system was begun and driven on with periodic tirades and visitations. By 1789, knowing that he had not long to live and showing all the impatience of Lessing's modern man who wanted the future today,[63] Joseph believed that the time was ripe for implementation. The measure had changed somewhat from earlier drafts: values were now to be based on a six-year average of gross income. The peasant was to keep seventy per cent of his gross produce; of the remaining thirty, 12.5 per cent was to go to the state and 17.5 per cent to the lord. This latter sum included all dues and services, including the ecclesiastical tithe and the *robot*.[64] When countering the criticism of Count Chotek, who refused to sign the law of 10 February 1789 and was dismissed, Joseph stated that if in the past a peasant had been deprived of more than a third of his income, then he had suffered a grievous wrong which must now be corrected.[65]

. . .

HUNGARY AND BELGIUM

It was a good indication of his enthusiasm for the tax decree that, when Joseph made that ringing statement, the Habsburg Monarchy was beginning to fall apart under the dual pressure of foreign war and domestic unrest. Discussion of that crisis, which proved to be final for Joseph and nearly terminal for the Monarchy, must wait until the last chapter. Here it remains to look briefly at what proved to be the two main centres of disaffection. The most serious proved to be Hungary, for two reasons: because it was immediately in the firing-line after the outbreak of the war against the Turks in 1787, and because without its resources the Habsburg Monarchy would have ceased to be a great power. Even when stripped of the Polish, Italian and Belgian provinces, the Monarchy continued to be a major player in the European states-system, but the loss of Hungary in 1918 brought instant regional obscurity from which it emerged only briefly after 1938 as a junior partner of the Third Reich.

As the map on page xi demonstrates, the Kingdom of Hungary, including the Principality of Transylvania, Croatia-Slavonia, the Banat of Temesvár and the Military Frontier Region, was the most diverse part of a diverse empire. With so many mutually hostile groups to manipulate, a policy of 'divide and rule' should have made the task of government from outside relatively easy. Unfortunately for the Habsburgs, there was one group which was deeply entrenched in power and determined to maintain its position. This was the Magyar nobility, itself divided into two groups. At the top were the great magnates such as the Esterházys, Károlyis and Batthyánys, with estates measured in square kilometres and great palaces in Vienna. It used to be thought that the sting of this group – comprising only some fifty families – had been drawn by their inter-marriage with aristocratic families from other parts of the Monarchy and their gradual integration into the court and social life of Vienna during the course of the eighteenth century. Recently, however, Peter Dickson has argued that both propositions are myths: 'the integration of Hungary with the German lands was less advanced at the top of society by 1780 than is commonly asserted, and Joseph II's assault on Hungary [was] likely to arouse a correspondingly greater resentment'.[66]

The most intractable Magyar nobles, however, were the great mass of gentry, some 40,000-strong, often tilling their little farms themselves and distinguishable from peasants only in terms of legal status. These were the men who over three centuries made Hungary ungovernable from Vienna and finally extracted the 'Compromise' (*Ausgleich*) of 1867 which turned the Habsburg Empire into Austria-Hungary. Their fierce sense of separatism stemmed from history, culture, economics and geopolitics. They had sought to dominate the lands of the lower Danube ever since their ancestors first thrust their way over the Carpathians in 896 AD. Even during the worst troughs of the ups and downs of the next millennium, they never forgot that once upon a time they had formed an independent kingdom, nor did they lose the ambition to resurrect it. Whether successful or not, the recurring need to repel invaders – German, Mongol, Turkish – periodically sharpened the sense of struggle which seems to be inseparable from acute nationalism.

Not without reason, the Hungarians believed that the Habsburgs treated them like a colony – as a source of cheap food and raw materials to be exploited, and as a dumping-ground for over-priced manufactured goods from other parts of the Monarchy. This resentment was intensified by the loss of Silesian markets in 1740, the further disruption caused by the first partition of Poland in 1772 and Joseph's imposition of even sharper discrimination against Hungarian goods in 1786.[67] In Vienna, on the other hand, there was a complementary tendency to view the Hungarians as at best ingrates and at worst traitors, never prepared to make a proper contribution to the Monarchy's costs and always inclined to conspire with its enemies. There was something to be said for both accusations. The Hungarians did contribute less in the form of direct taxation and had been left untouched by the fiscal reforms of the 1740s and 1750s which increased the burden in the other provinces.[68] Yet if all forms of contribution were taken into account, especially the fact that a large and increasing proportion of the Habsburg army was stationed in Hungary at Hungarian expense, then it seems that the kingdom did contribute its fair share and possibly more.[69]

Most ethnic groups would have integrated with their neighbours over such a long period. In part, the Magyars were kept apart by linguistic forces. As anyone who has even toyed with the idea of learning Magyar will confirm, it is an exceedingly difficult language, not even Indo-European in origin but Uralic, related only to Estonian and Finnish. Indeed the Magyars themselves did not begin to demand the use of their language until alerted to its merits by their intelligentsia and excited by Joseph's attempts to impose German, preferring until then to conduct their official business in Latin.[70] The Magyar gentry were also kept alienated by religion. Of their two great enemies, the Habsburgs were Roman Catholic and the Turks were Moslem – so most Magyars opted for Protestantism, especially in its Calvinist form. Only in those parts of the country which were not conquered by the Turks after the battle of Mohács in 1526 and which therefore felt the full force of the counter-reformation was Catholicism dominant.[71]

In these respects, the Magyars resembled their Polish neighbours, although it was Catholicism which naturally appealed to Poles sandwiched between Lutheran Prussians and Orthodox Russians. However, what made the Magyars so much tougher when confronted by predators was their capacity for organisation. Since time out of mind, the kingdom of Hungary had been divided into fifty-odd counties (*comitati*), governed by the gentry who met periodically at county assemblies (*congregationes*). It was here that they gained the political experience, organisational skills, self-confidence and *esprit de corps* which again and again frustrated Habsburg policies. The national parliament was easy to ignore – it was not summoned between 1764 and 1790 – but it was only through the *comitati* and their *congregationes* that Hungary could be administered at all.

The roots of the Magyar nobles' separatism went deep – deep into their history, deep into their self-interest and deep into their institutions. So Joseph II's radical attempt to reduce their kingdom to a collection of standardised units forming part of a unified Monarchy was bound to cause shrieks of anger and pain as those roots were torn up. The confrontation between the two parties anticipated the wider conflict between the French Revolution and old regime Europe which was to dominate the next generation. The Magyars took their stand on treaties: during the previous two centuries the Habsburg rulers had confirmed the liberties and privileges of the Hungarian nation on many different occasions. In 1722, for example, the Hungarians had actually made it possible for Joseph II to inherit the throne by agreeing that succession could pass through Charles VI's daughter, Maria Theresa – but they had done so only on the express condition that the integrity of their traditional constitution would be confirmed in perpetuity. These solemn agreements, they argued, could not be broken unilaterally. When opposing Joseph's plans to reorganise Hungary, the Chancellor, Count Esterházy, argued that, although specific laws could be changed as circumstances required, the fundamental laws of a state were immutable. No nation, he stated, would abandon a constitution which was regarded as the guarantee of both liberty and property.[72]

Joseph's reply heralded a new world in which tradition and treaty-rights counted for nothing. For he took his stand on natural law revealed by reason. It was all so obvious, he wrote: if one started from first principles, then one just had to see that everything in the state derived from the social contract. It was this primal agreement which determined that everyone should contribute to the general good in accordance with ability, resources and the benefits derived from the association. If an individual or a group had somehow succeeded in winning special treatment, then that was not a 'right' to be protected, it was an *abuse* to be abolished! A 'constitutional law' which established the rule of a few thousand over millions and which depressed the great mass of the population to being instruments of the elite was not a law at all, because it transgressed that equality which was 'the first article of natural and social law'.[73]

These rationalist principles, expressed with characteristic intemperance, prefaced Joseph's reconstruction of Hungary's administration in 1785–6. The kingdom was divided into ten new districts, without any regard for historical precedent or ethnic distribution. The commissars to run them were, of course, appointed by the centre. With equal predictability, the administration of the *comitati* was also nationalised. The *congregationes* were forbidden to meet, unless choosing deputies for the national parliament (which meant never, as the parliament did not meet).[74] Together with Joseph's refusal to be crowned king of Hungary, his imposition of the German language, his sympathetic treatment of Horja's revolt and preparations for the tax decree,[75] this clean sweep of traditional institutions threatened to turn the Magyar nobility's world upside down.

As their ancestors had resorted to armed resistance for much less cause in the past, it was only a matter of time before insurrection was planned. The first conspiracy to be uncovered came in 1786, although the interrogators of the culprit ceased to take him seriously when he revealed under cross-examination that he had intended to publicise his revolt with the help of proclamations distributed by '100,000 trained dogs'.[76] For the time being Joseph was safe. As the Prussian envoy in Vienna, Baron Jacobi, observed in 1787: despite all the angry noises made by the Magyars, the magnates were tamed, the resentment of the Protestant gentry had been blunted by religious toleration, the peasants worshipped Joseph as their emancipator and the massive military presence would nip any revolt in the bud. However, he added with chilling foresight that the situation would be very different if the Prussians could get an army into Hungary to support the insurgents before Joseph or his successor could strike a deal with them.[77] This was just the scenario which threatened to develop in 1789–90.

Meanwhile, at the other end of the Habsburg Monarchy, a very similar pattern of events was unfolding. The ten provinces which made up the Austrian Netherlands had been part of the Habsburg Monarchy only since the Peace of Rastatt detached them from the Spanish Empire in 1714. For the sake of convenience, they are usually referred to as 'Belgium', as if they constituted a single nation, but they did not. Each 'land' of the Nether*lands* – it is less confusing to use the French formulation: each '*pays*' of the '*Pays Bas*' – had its own constitution, its own institutions, its own culture and its own sense of identity. If the population was almost entirely Catholic, it was divided along linguistic lines between French-speakers ('Walloons') and Flemish-speakers. Blessed by a generation of peace since the Austro-French alliance of 1756, the Austrian Netherlands in 1780 were prosperous, complacent and conservative.

They were the only provinces of the Habsburg Monarchy which Joseph II had *not* visited while co-regent. Partly this was due to his intense dislike of their governor-general – his uncle Prince Charles of Lorraine, who had maintained a lavish court at Brussels, had changed nothing and was correspondingly popular with the local population. On Prince Charles' death in 1780, Maria Theresa kept the post in the family, appointing her son-in-law, Duke Albert of Saxony, and his wife and her daughter, the Arch-Duchess Marie Christine, as joint governors-general. Joseph never intended that they should be anything more than figure-heads. Even before they could move to Brussels, he went there himself, to see what had to be done. It was a most unfortunate visit. According to Belgian contemporaries at least, Joseph spent most of his time with government employees, none of whom dared to contradict him, had no dealings with the all-powerful provincial Estates, barely spoke to the equally formidable ecclesiastical hierarchy, led by the archbishop of Malines, and generally acquired a wholly erroneous notion of the local distribution of political power.[78]

He also came away with the belief that the Austrian Netherlands were decadent in almost every respect. Looking back in unrepentance on his death-bed to his visit in 1781 he recalled that he found an administration which was 'slack and obstructive'; law courts which were in 'a dreadfully ruinous state', slow and corrupt; an educational system which was simply deplorable, exemplified by a university (Louvain) whose academics sought only to line their own pockets; and an all-prevailing nepotism which meant that every aspect of public life was run by an old-boy network.[79] Wherever he turned, he had found evidence of the particularism he hated so much – nothing was done in the same way in more than one place. Joseph would

certainly have endorsed R.R. Palmer's verdict that the Austrian Netherlands constituted 'a museum of late-medieval corporate liberties'.[80]

Joseph's standardising pen was soon at work, issuing decrees
to bring the Belgians into line with the rest of his subjects. In
the early 1780s his main concern was religion, as he introduced
toleration, dissolved 163 monasteries, excluded Roman jurisdiction, abolished confraternities, restricted pilgrimages and
processions, re-organised parishes, replaced episcopal seminaries with a general seminary, and so on. Attention to secular
matters, however, was delayed by the dispute with the Dutch
Republic over the opening of the river Scheldt to international
commerce.[81] He emerged from that experience nursing a deep
sense of grievance. In what can only be described as a hymn of
hate to his Belgian subjects, he told his minister plenipotentiary
at Brussels, Count Belgioioso, that they had done nothing to
help him during the recent dispute with the Dutch – which he
had conducted in the interests of the Belgians. On the contrary,
they had taken every opportunity to exploit him, by lending
money at rates well over the odds, by selling provisions for his
army at inflated prices and by charging excessive fees for
transport: 'that is what is known as making war on the sovereign's purse before turning one's fire on the enemy', he wrote in
disgust. In particular he railed against the provincial Estates,
who had committed the ultimate Josephist crime of seeking to
promote only their sectional interests at the expense of the
'common good'.[82]

In short, Joseph's habitual enthusiasm for standardisation
was given an even sharper edge by his sense of betrayal. So it
was with vindictive resolution that he turned to the *Gleichschaltung* of the Austrian Netherlands when the Dutch dispute
had been settled with the help of French mediation in the
autumn of 1785. He did not begin his blitz with his eyes closed.
On the contrary, as he told Count Belgioioso, he knew that he
would encounter opposition fuelled by greed and prejudice. He
proposed to deal with it in two ways: by introducing his reforms
all at once and by refusing to modify them one jot. That was the
lesson of the crisis of the French monarchy, he observed – by
doing things in dribs and drabs and by making concessions, one
only encouraged one's opponents to ask for more. For him, it
was going to be full-steam ahead with a non-negotiable
package.[83]

It would be wearisome to recount once again the by now familiar reforms. In essence this was another episode in the world-historical clash between reason and history, the state and particularism, modernisation and tradition, abstraction and diversity, artefact and organism, which in the opinion of some began only with the French Revolution. Suffice it to say that Joseph intended to reduce the Austrian Netherlands to being uniform provinces in a unitary state. The ten historic provinces were to be replaced by nine units ruled by bureaucrats. The judicial system was nationalised, while the institutions of the old regime – the provincial Estates, municipal corporations and craft guilds – were marginalised. It was the biggest upheaval in the Netherlands since the revolt against Spain in the sixteenth century. As Henri Pirenne observed, this was less a reform than a *coup d'état*.[84]

It provoked a reaction of corresponding intensity. Moreover, the resistance was more widespread than in Hungary. In the latter, the concentration of privilege in a small group limited both by social status and ethnic origin gave Joseph at least the opportunity to champion the un- or under-privileged and to play one group off against another. In the Austrian Netherlands, the divisions were less acute and privilege went right down to the bottom of society. Neither prelates nor nobles were separated from other groups by language, culture or foreign residence, there were no religious divisions and there was no serfdom. The revolt of this relatively unified society was therefore broader-based than anywhere else in the Habsburg Monarchy – and much more successful. Even so, it is doubtful whether the Belgians could have held out against Joseph's Leviathan, had it not been for the sudden deterioration in the international position of the Monarchy in 1787. So, before the fortunes of this new revolt of the Netherlands can be understood, it is time to return to the primacy of foreign policy.

. . .

NOTES

1. See above, pp. 57–61.
2. Memorandum of 1765, reprinted in Arneth, *Maria Theresia und Joseph II.*, III, 353–4.
3. See above, pp. 44–7.

4. Gottleib Mohnike, 'Briefwechsel zwischen Kaiser Joseph dem Zweiten und Clemens Wenzeslaus, Churfürsten von Trier', *Zeitschrift für die historische Theologie*, 4, 1 (1834), 279. Mohnike reprints the correspondence in full. For confirmation of the authenticity of the letter, see Beales, p. 21 n. 11.

5. See above, pp. 17–18.

6. Handbillets, vol. 7 (27), nos 223 and 237, to Count Kollowrat, 12 March 1783 and 15 March 1783, fos 189, 200.

7. See below, pp. 148–51.

8. Peter Dickson, 'Joseph II's reshaping of the Austrian Church', *The Historical Journal*, 36, 1 (1993), 104–6.

9. Carlo Capra, 'Il Settecento', in Domenico Sella and Carlo Capra, *Il Ducato di Milano dal 1535 al 1796* (Turin, 1984), p. 495.

10. Handbillets, vol. 7 (27), no. 53, to Baron Kressel, 17 June 1783, fos 46–8.

11. Viktor Bibl, *Kaiser Joseph II. Ein Vorkämpfer der großdeutschen Idee* (Vienna and Leipzig, 1943), p. 184.

12. These figures are taken from Dickson, 'Joseph II's reshaping of the Austrian Church', 101, 110.

13. Handbillets, vol. 7 (27), no. 643, to Baron Kressel, 18 August 1783, fo. 588.

14. Ibid., vol. 8 (31), no. 702, to Baron Kressel, Prague, 19 September 1784, fo. 601.

15. Ibid., vol. 13 (51), no. 680, to Count Khevenhüller, Laxenburg, 15 June 1789, fos 381–2.

16. Ibid., vol. 6 (22), no. 210, to the Queen of Naples, 6 March 1782, fo. 192.

17. Ibid., no. 211, to the Grand Duke of Tuscany, 6 March 1782, fo. 193.

18. Ibid., no. 278, to the Grand Duke and Grand Duchess of Russia, 1 April 1782, fos 275–7. The fullest modern account of the papal visit is to be found in Elisabeth Kovács, *Der Pabst in Teutschland. Die Reise Pius VI. im Jahre 1782* (Vienna, 1983), although her account is distorted somewhat by her whistling in the dark to keep ultramontane spirits up.

19. Handbillets, vol. 6 (22), no. 396, to the Grand Duke and Duchess of Russia, 26 April 1782, fo. 370.

20. Ibid., vol. 12 (47), no. 1514, to Count Trauttmansdorff, Buda, 28 November 1788, fo. 852, reprinted in Schlitter, p. 162.

21. Ibid., vol. 10 (40), no. 18, to Count Pergen, 7 January 1786, fo. 13; no. 298, to Baron Woeber, 13 April 1786, fo. 211; no. 501, to Count Pálffy, Szegedin, 10 July 1786, fo. 355; no. 596, to Count Niczy, Pest, 18 August 1786, fos 450–1.

22. Ibid., vol. 6 (22), no. 183, to Count Blümegen, 27 February 1782, fo. 167.

23. Dickson, 'Joseph II's reshaping of the Austrian church', p. 109.
24. Carl Freiherr von Hock and Ignaz Bidermann, *Der österreichische Staatsrath (1760–1848)* (Vienna, 1879), pp. 486–7. On the success of the reforms in Hungary, see Bela K. Király, 'The Hungarian Church', in William J. Callahan and David Higgs (eds), *Church and society in Catholic Europe of the eighteenth century* (Cambridge, 1979), p. 120.
25. See above, pp. 46–7.
26. Oskar Sashegyi, *Zensur und Geistesfreiheit unter Joseph II. Beitrag zur Kulturgeschichte der habsburgischen Länder*, (Budapest, 1958), p. 178.
27. Handbillets, vol. 12 (47), no. 430, to Baron Kressel, Futack, 13 April 1788, fo. 270; no. 500, to Count Kollowrat, Semlin, 3 May 1788, fo. 321.
28. Karl Gutkas, *Kaiser Joseph II. Eine Biographie* (Vienna and Darmstadt, 1989), pp. 320–5.
29. Dickson, 'The reshaping of the Austrian church', pp. 93–4.
30. Beales, p. 98.
31. Quoted in T.C.W. Blanning, 'Frederick the Great and enlightened absolutism', in H.M. Scott (ed.), *Enlightened absolutism. Reform and reformers in later eighteenth-century Europe* (London, 1990), p. 268.
32. Bibl, *Kaiser Joseph II.*, p. 213; Franz Xaver Huber, *Geschichte Josephs II. römischen Kaisers, Königs von Hungarn und Böhmen etc.*, 2 vols (Vienna, 1792), II, 110.
33. Handbillets, vol. 5 (18), no. 333, 22 April 1781, to Counts Blümegen and Esterházy, fo. 258.
34. Huber, *Geschichte Josephs II.*, II, 169–71.
35. See above, p. 63. On Joseph's further reduction of the court, see Beales, 'Court and government', *passim* and Hans Wagner, 'Joseph II, Persönlichkeit und Werk', *Österreich zur Zeit Kaiser Josephs II. Mitregent Maria Theresias und Landesfürst* (Vienna, 1980), p. 14.
36. Lorenz Hübner, *Lebensgeschichte Josephs des Zweyten, Kaisers der Deutschen, oder Rosen auf dessen Grab* (Salzburg, n.d. [1790]), p. 436.
37. Johann Pezzl, *Skizze von Wien* (Vienna and Leipzig, 1787), p. 83.
38. See above, pp. 15–16.
39. Karl Grünberg, *Studien zur österreichischen Agrargeschichte* (Leipzig, 1901), pp. 4–17.
40. Helmuth Feigl, 'Die Auswirkungen der Theresianisch-Josephinischen Reformgesetzgebung auf die ländliche Sozialstruktur Oesterreichs', in *Österreich im Europa der Aufklärung*, I, 56; Roman

Sandgruber, 'Einkommensentwicklung und Einkommensverteilung in der zweiten Hälfte des 18. Jahrhunderts–einige Quellen und Anhaltspunkte', Ibid., I, 262.

41. This summary of the serfs' position is based on Karl Grünberg, *Die Bauernbefreiung und die Auflösung des gutsherrlich-bäuerlichen Verhältnisses in Böhmen, Mähren und Schlesien*, 2 vols (Leipzig, 1894, 1893 [*sic*]), I, 1–91 and Bela K. Király, *Hungary in the late 18th century* (New York, 1969), pp. 59–70.

42. See above, p. 64.

43. Jozef Buszko, 'Theresianisch-josephinische Agrar- und Bauernpolitik in Galizien und ihre Folgen', in *Österreich im Europa der Aufklärung*, I, 71, 81.

44. Beales, p. 357.

45. The decree for Bohemia is published in English translation in T.C.W. Blanning, *Joesph II and enlightened despotism* (London, 1970), pp. 130–1.

46. Bibl, *Kaiser Joseph II.*, p. 200.

47. Handbillets, vol. 12 (47), no. 967, to Prince Dietrichstein, Semlin, 31 July 1788, fo. 579.

48. Roman Rozdolski, *Die große Steuer- und Agrarreform Josefs II. Ein Kapitel zur österreichischen Wirtschaftsgeschichte* (Warsaw, 1961), p. 124.

49. Beales, p. 361.

50. Handbillets, vol. 7 (27), no. 468, to Count Palffy, Hermannstadt, 6 June 1783, fos 405–6.

51. Ibid., vol. 8 (31), no. 936, to Baron Brukenthal, 20 November 1784, fo. 855.

52. Angelika Schaser, *Josephinische Reformen und sozialer Wandel in Siebenbürgen* (Stuttgart, 1989), p. 39.

53. Handbillets, no. 894, to General Schackmin, 15 November 1784. fos 809–11.

54. Ibid, no. 935, to Count Jankovics, 20 November 1784, fos 854–5.

55. Ibid., to Count Esterházy, 22 November 1784, fos 859–61. In fact 'only' thirty-four people had been killed in reprisals – David Prodan, 'Emperor Joseph II and Horea's uprising in Transylvania', in Pompiliu Teodor (ed.), *Enlightenment and Romanian society* (Cluj-Napoca, 1980), p. 110.

56. Handbillets, vol. 8 (31), no. 957, to Count Jankovics, 27 November 1784, fos 869–70; no. 1019, to Count Jankovics, 13 December 1784, fos 937–9.

57. Ibid., no. 29, to Count Jankovics, 10 January 1785, fo. 20.

58. Huber, *Geschichte Josephs II.*, II, 125.

59. *Was war Joseph II. und was wird Leopold II. seyn?* (Prague, 1790), pp. 31–2.

60. Huber, *Geschichte Josephs II.*, II, 121.

61. Handbillets, vol. 7 (27), no. 515, to Count Hatzfeld, Lemberg, 30 June 1783, fos 465–72.
62. Rozdolski, *Die große Steuer- und Agrarreform Josefs II.*, p. 9.
63. See above, p. 84.
64. The precise figures were 12 gulden and 13^1/₃ kreuzers and 17 gulden and 46^2/₃ kreuzers respectively of every hundred gulden. There were sixty kreuzers in a gulden (confusingly abbreviated as 'fl.') – Rozdolski, *Die große Steuer- und Agrarreform Josefs II.*, p. 118.
65. Handbillets, vol. 13 (51), no. 128, 'Antwort über das Votum Separatum des Grafen Chotek in betreff des neuen Steuer Patents den 3ten Feb. [1789]', fos 81–7.
66. Dickson, I, 113.
67. Lorenz Mikoletzky, *Joseph II. Herrscher zwischen den Zeiten* (Göttingen, 1979), p. 61.
68. See above, pp. 138–43.
69. Király, *Hungary in the late 18th century*, pp. 100–4; Macartney, *Hungary*, p. 108.
70. See above, p. 38 and R.J.W. Evans, 'The Habsburgs and the Hungarian problem 1790–1848', *Transactions of the Royal Historical Society*, 5th series, 39 (1989), 44.
71. Király, 'The Hungarian Church', p. 112.
72. Handbillets, vol. 9 (36), no. 98, 'Beylage zum Billet no. 89 wegen der in Hungarn einzuführenden Verbesserung' [28 January 1785], fo. 84.
73. Ibid., fos 87–90.
74. P.G.M. Dickson, 'Joseph II's Hungarian land survey', *English Historical Review* (1992), *passim*.
75. See above, p. 59.
76. Robert Gragger, *Preußen, Weimar und die ungarische Königskrone* (Berlin and Leipzig, 1923), p. 4.
77. Ibid., p. 14.
78. Henri Pirenne, *Histoire de Belgique*, vol. 5 (Brussels, 1920), pp. 391–3.
79. Handbillets, vol. 13 (51), no. 769, 'Réflexions sur les arrangemens à prendre aux Païs Bas pour parvenir à une constitution stable' [22 November 1789], fos 769–70.
80. R.R. Palmer, *The Age of the democratic revolution*, 2 vols (Princeton, 1959, 1964), I, 341.
81. See below, pp. 138–43.
82. Handbillets, vol. 8 (31), no. 1041, to Count Belgioioso, 18 December 1784, fos 976–7.
83. Ibid., vol. 8 (31), no. 317, to Count Belgioioso, 12 May 1784, fos 365–6; vol. 9 (36), no. 630, to Count Belgioioso, 26 July 1785, fo. 579; vol. 9 (36), no. 1087, to Kaunitz, 24 December 1785, fos

952–3; vol. 10 (40), no. 757, to Count Belgioioso, 15 October 1786, fos 578–9; no. 902, to Count Belgioioso, 21 November 1786, fos 689–91.

84.   Pirenne, *Histoire de Belgique*, V, 420.

Chapter 5

JOSEPH II AND THE GREAT POWERS

. . .

THE ARMY AND MILITARISM

One week before he died, Joseph sent a last general order to his army:

> To be a soldier has always been my profession and my favourite occupation. As your comrade-in-arms, it has always been a pleasure to join in everything with you and to share all the dangers as the need arose. Every single individual among you has been precious to me. I would be guilty of base ingratitude if I did not proclaim to the entire army my complete satisfaction with and gratitude for the loyalty, courage and unflagging zeal which every member, without exception, has shown to me on every occasion.[1]

He meant it. Ever since he had first been introduced to the soldier's life as a small child, he had taken to military matters like a duck to water and was never happier than when planning fortifications, reading books on the art of war, drilling troops or going on manœuvres. In 1766 the Venetian ambassador reported that: 'He enjoys talking not only with the officers, but even with the common soldiers. He turns out for the military parade almost every day. He is happy discussing everything to do with the conduct of war, and is careful to keep his body accustomed to exertion and exercise in order to preserve his fitness and so nourish the martial spirit that is showing itself in his character'.[2]

Of all the rulers of the Habsburg Monarchy, Joseph was the most militaristic. Many of his predecessors had been more bellicose – Leopold I had spent forty of the forty-seven years of his reign at war – but none had shown Joseph's single-minded devotion to his army. This was partly the result of the intensive state-building undertaken since the 1740s: as Kurt Peball has argued, it was only during the War of the Austrian Succession that the army finally became Austrian (the army of the Habsburg Monarchy) rather than imperial (the army of the Holy Roman Empire).[3] Moreover, it was not only naturalised, it was also nationalised, as the responsibility for recruiting, training and financing was taken away from the Estates and individual magnates and transferred to the state. The days when a Habsburg ruler such as Ferdinand II had been dependent on a *condottiere* such as Wallenstein and his lawless *soldateska* were gone for ever.

Now that the army was theirs to command, Maria Theresa and her ministers set about reforming it. In the course of her long reign it was transformed both qualitatively and quantitatively. By the time of the War of the Bavarian Succession, the demoralised, disorganised and depleted rabble of 1740 had become a modern army second only to the Russian in terms of numbers and second to none in terms of quality.[4] In this process Joseph played a crucial role. On the death of his father in 1765, he had been made 'coregent' by his mother, but in reality she retained control of decision-making.[5] Only in military matters was he given some measure of independent control. Although this certainly did not amount to the total command sometimes ascribed to him in the past, it did allow him to give full rein to his military enthusiasm. If the actual reforms which improved training, equipment and weaponry, which standardised drill, uniforms and regulations and which provided social security for soldiers' dependants were largely the work of the Military Council (*Hofkriegsrat*) and its president Field Marshal Count Lacy, Joseph had an important part to play in raising the prestige of the military profession and in making sure that its needs were placed high on the government's list of priorities.

At no time was this more important than when conscription was being introduced after 1770. By a series of measures beginning in 1770 and continuing through the following decade, the Habsburg Monarchy was divided into uniform districts, each of which was allocated to a regiment for the supply of manpower. In principle, all adult males were liable to serve between the ages of seventeen and forty, but in practice the numerous social and occupational exemptions confined recruitment to small-holders, labourers, vagrants, the unemployed, and petty criminals (a set of categories capacious enough). As in Prussia, which provided the model, in peace-time most conscripts were sent on leave after training and were recalled to the colours only for a short period each year or on the outbreak of war. The full-time core of the army was provided by foreign volunteers, who made up three-eighths of the total manpower and were mainly enrolled from the principalities of the Holy Roman Empire.[6] The efficiency of these arrangements was shown by the ability of the Monarchy to mobilise 250,000 troops for the war of 1778.[7]

But the significance of conscription went far beyond the supply of soldiers. It is no exaggeration to say that it was with this reform that the Austrian state came of age. As one of Joseph's earlier biographers observed: 'It can be said that with this institution Austria won a new and higher status among the states of Europe, for [the introduction of conscription] meant that it had achieved the transition from barbarism to civ-ilisation'.[8] If that smacks of over-statement, it should be borne in mind that the immediate result of conscription was a massive and unprecedented increase in state interference in the lives of ordinary people. Everywhere, lists of those eligible had to be compiled, houses had to be numbered, local authorities had to be organised – and even draught animals had to be mustered. For the first time, the authorities acquired some sort of idea of how many subjects they had to govern and where they all were.[9]

In this process Joseph played a decisive role, working with Lacy to ensure that the military took first place in the queue for scarce resources.[10] He insisted that the Monarchy both needed and could afford a large army:

The military estate consists of several thousand people orga-nised and trained for the service of the state. What little they receive in the form of wages they spend inside the country and so thus become consumers. Virtually everything which the state provides for them in kind – namely, victuals and uniforms – is also produced or manufactured at home. More-over, the system of granting leave allows them to contribute their labour to agriculture and manufacturing, while the ease with which permission to marry can be obtained also makes them procreators.[11]

More important still, he went out of his way to raise the prestige of the military calling by showing that he thought of himself as a soldier first and foremost. He did this in the most visual way possible – by always wearing a military uniform, either the white and red of his infantry regiment or the green and red of his regiment of light horse.[12] All Habsburg rulers in the past had presented themselves as mighty warriors when the occasion demanded, but their courts had remained civilian: boots, spurs and sabres were left in camp. It was Joseph who made the uniform presentable at court – *hoffähig* – and, indeed, in the cemetery, for he was buried in his field-marshal's uniform.

If militarism means the primacy of military needs and values, then Joseph was incontestably a militarist. That was certainly how contemporaries viewed him. They could hardly miss, for example, the transformation of Vienna into a garrison, with fine new barracks surrounding the city 'like a laurel-wreath'.[13] Sir Nathaniel Wraxall was not the only visitor to be struck by the Emperor's military enthusiasms:

> All the qualities and passions of the Emperor are, however, either subservient to, or swallowed up in his ambition. Hence his affection for the soldiery, his inspection of their barracks, his affectation of wearing, like Frederic, no other dress than a uniform, his solicitous attention to the sick and wounded; in a word, his anxiety to acquire the confidence of the troops, and to shew them that in him they will find a father and a leader, no less than a Sovereign.[14]

Knowing as we do that Joseph's attempt to turn the Habsburg Monarchy into a unitary state ended in tears, it is easy to underestimate the alarm which this process of militarisation aroused in contemporaries. What they saw was a vast empire stretching from the North Sea to the Adriatic, from the Carpathians to the Appenines, and now being given what threatened soon to become the largest and best army in Europe. Memories of Charles V began to stir, with fateful consequences for the conduct of Austrian foreign policy. Just one year after

Joseph became Holy Roman Emperor, the Austrian ambassador at Versailles, Count Mercy, lamented in a report to Kaunitz that their enemies had persuaded the French ministry, court and public opinion that Joseph was anti-French: 'The trouble he takes over the army is seen as evidence of a very marked penchant for the military profession. His interest in the affairs of the Holy Roman Empire is interpreted as a plan for the re-establishment of the power which emperors used to enjoy and for the resurrection of their former rights'.[15]

. . .

THE CO-REGENCY

A reputation for militarism could only be a handicap for the conduct of the Habsburg Monarchy's foreign policy, especially after the great upheaval in the affairs of Eastern Europe which began in 1768. The outbreak of war between the Ottoman Empire and Russia in that year posed the great 'Eastern Question' which has remained unresolved until the present day. The scale of Russian victories, which included the astonishing feat of sending a fleet from the Baltic to the Mediterranean to destroy the Turkish fleet at Chesme in June 1770 (a battle to compare with Lepanto or Trafalgar), raised the possibility of a Russian conquest of the entire Balkan peninsula and the expulsion of the Turks from Europe.

That was a threat the Habsburg Monarchy was obliged to counter, especially because Russia had been allied to Prussia since 1764. With every Turkish defeat, military intervention to prevent a total Russian victory became more likely. To no one was this more unwelcome than Frederick the Great, who had no real interests at stake in the Balkans and was still preoccupied with the reconstruction of Prussia after the devastation of the Seven Years War. It was to avoid being dragged into the war that he came up with what Hamish Scott has called his 'diplomatic masterpiece'.[16] This was the proposal that the three great powers of Eastern Europe should settle their differences at the expense of Poland. In return for moderating her demands against the Turks, Catherine the Great of Russia was awarded a huge slice (92,000 square kilometres) of Eastern Poland. Frederick took little more than a third of that, but for him it was very much a question of 'never mind the width – feel the quality'. By linking East Prussia to the central core of the Hohenzollern territories and by gaining control of the lower reaches of the river Vistula, this acquisition brought to Prussia colossal strategic, economic and fiscal advantages.

For the Austrians, the advantages were much less obvious. The province of Galicia which they obtained was four times as populous (2,650,000 inhabitants) as the Prussian share and almost as extensive (83,000 square kilometres) as the Russian, but its value was certainly far less than that of either. Strategically, Galicia was a liability, lying to the north of the Carpathian mountains which formed the natural frontier of the Monarchy in the north-east. Economically and socially, it was primitive, destined to become a burden rather than an asset. When he visited Galicia for the last time, in 1787, Joseph lamented that not all the vast sums lavished on the province had made it a going concern.[17] Politically, it posed a constant irredentist threat, as the Polish nobles never ceased to look for an opportunity to achieve reunion with Poland. As the events of 1789–90 were to show, this could prove to be a serious problem. In any case, it is difficult to appreciate what benefit accrued to the Habsburgs from the expropriation of a Catholic country which was traditionally pro-Austrian, mainly to the benefit of Protestant Prussia and Orthodox Russia. It had been a Polish king – John Sobieski – who had led the army which relieved the siege of Vienna in 1683.

In other words, the first partition of Poland had tilted the balance of power away from the Habsburg Monarchy. Perhaps equally serious was the 'image-problem' it created. The brutal cynicism displayed by the three partitioning powers could do little harm to Prussia or Russia, whose very *raison d'être* was predatory expansion, but it cut at the roots of that respect for law which was the Habsburg Monarchy's legitimation. If a country ruled by the Holy Roman Emperor could seize territory in peace-time without any justification other than convenience, then no one could feel secure. The rule of brute force had been established. The acquisitive drive which now fuelled Habsburg policy was paraded again soon afterwards, in 1775, when a slice of Turkish territory – 'the Bukovina' – was annexed on the grounds that it had been a dependency of Podolia, which the Habsburg Monarchy had acquired in the partition of 1772.[18]

Within the ruling triumvirate of the Habsburg Monarchy, there had been considerable disagreement about the partition. Maria Theresa had been the most reluctant to participate, not only restrained by considerations of religion, morality and international law but also instinctively averse to anything proposed by the detested Frederick and Catherine. 'She wept – but she took' was Frederick's laconic dismissal of her agonising. By far the most aggressive was Kaunitz, who grasped Galicia with both hands, pausing only to try to increase the Austrian share. Joseph found himself in the middle, disagreeing with Kaunitz about Galicia's value and clearly feeling some moral scruples, but concluding in the end that the Monarchy must benefit from what could not be prevented.[19] Fifteen years later, in 1787, he tried to explain to a sceptical German prince that it had all been the fault of the Prussians. Without Frederick the Great's unique combination of malevolence and cunning, he argued, the partition would not have happened. The only alternative policy for Austria had been war against Russia, which very likely would have ended in disaster and most certainly would have involved ruinous expense.[20]

Joseph's reservations, which were genuine, could not be made public at the time. The result was that he gained a reputation for restless aggression which should have been pinned to Kaunitz. It is not difficult to understand why. A young ruler, with a well-publicised taste for the military and a harsh, uncompromising manner, provided Prussian propagandists with a heaven-sent opportunity for spreading gloom and despondency. This became especially serious towards the end of the 1770s when two succession problems in the Holy Roman Empire became acute. The most serious concerned Bavaria, where the ruling Wittelsbach dynasty was about to die out with the current elector, Maximilian III. The natural heir was the head of the senior Wittelsbach line, the Elector Karl Theodor of the Palatinate, also elderly by the standards of the day and also without a male heir. His own heir-apparent was yet another scion of the once prolific but now failing Wittelsbachs, the duke of Zweibrücken. For the Habsburg Monarchy, this raised the unappealing prospect of a new and rival power bloc being formed in southern Germany consisting of the three Wittelsbach territories united under a single ruler. Our knowledge that these fears proved groundless should not be allowed to obscure an appreciation of Habsburg anxiety. Everyone conversant with Austrian history knew about the terrible time at the beginning of the Thirty Years War when Emperor Ferdinand II had been largely dependent on the military assistance of Maximilian I of Bavaria. In the more recent past, it had been from Bavaria that invasions of Austria had been launched during both the War of the Spanish and of the Austrian Succession.

These anxieties were increased by the simultaneous problems experienced by the Margrave of Ansbach and Bayreuth in fathering a legitimate male heir. The accepted successor to these two substantial and strategically important principalities, located to the north-west and north of Bavaria respectively, was none other than Frederick the Great of Prussia. There was a real danger, therefore, that a greatly strengthened Bavaria, together with a Prussia now established territorially in southern Germany, would combine to drive the Habsburgs from the Holy Roman Empire.[21] This was an anxiety intensified by the recent change of dynasty in the strategically crucial principality of Baden, where the pro-Prussian Protestant Baden-Durlach line had succeeded to the inheritance of their Baden-Baden cousins, who had been pro-Austrian and Catholic.[22]

It was perfectly natural, therefore, that Maria Theresa, Joseph and Kaunitz should take a keen interest in events adjacent to their western frontier. It was not long before rumours began to circulate that a pre-emptive strike was being planned to deal with the problem by the simple expedient of annexing Bavaria to the Habsburg Monarchy. No one supposed that this could be done without conflict, but it was generally believed that what the great powers had done to Poland they could do again to the even softer target of the Holy Roman Empire. In 1776 the British envoy at Munich, Hugh Elliot, predicted that if the Bavarian succession could not be settled at the Imperial Diet (a most unlikely contingency!), then 'the Courts of Vienna and Berlin will either prosecute their separate claims by the sword and involve Germany in war, or they will even extend the same system of partition into the Empire that proved so irresistible in Poland'.[23] At the beginning of January 1777, the British government passed on to their envoy in Munich an intelligence report they had received, to the effect that when the ailing Elector eventually died, most of the Austrian Netherlands would be offered to his heir in exchange for Bavaria, with French acquiescence being bought by the cession of Luxemburg.[24] This flesh-creeping rumour was only one of many circulating about Austrian plans long before the crisis actually erupted.

Neither rumour proved to be correct. Opposition from Maria Theresa, who believed the Austrian Netherlands to be much richer than Bavaria (a very reasonable assumption at that time) and preferred her Belgian subjects to the 'stupid Bavarians' (a more debatable choice) as well as opposition from the French, ruled out an exchange – at least for the time being.[25] In the event, Austrian diplomats secured an agreement with the new Elector Karl Theodor which ceded a substantial part of Bavaria to the Habsburg Monarchy in return for uncontested succession to the remainder.[26] Military occupation quickly followed.

Hopes that this *fait accompli* would attract only verbal protests were soon dashed. Frederick the Great did indeed organise a brilliant propaganda campaign, but he also supported it with a more compelling argument in the shape of an invasion of Bohemia. The war which followed – the grandly named War of the Bavarian Succession – is always described in dismissive or derisive terms, and understandably so. As the last major encounter between two great powers before the French Revolution, it was appropriately the apotheosis (or perhaps caricature) of old regime warfare. There were no battles, only sedate manœuvring at a safe distance, while diplomats hurried to find a peaceful solution. What they found was undeniably a defeat for the Habsburg Monarchy. All Bavaria had to be abandoned, apart from a modest strip of territory on the river Inn. Moreover, the Prussian right of succession to Ansbach and Bayreuth had to be formally acknowledged.

With the advantage of hindsight, we can also see that the treaty of Teschen (13 May 1779), which brought the Bavarian war to an end, was an important step in the downward path of the Holy Roman Empire and therefore of the Habsburg Monarchy. For the first – but not the last – time, Russia had a decisive say in German affairs. Not only had the Russian threat to enter the war on the Prussian side played a major part in forcing Joseph and Kaunitz to abandon their forward position, it was Russian mediation which shaped the peace settlement. The reward of Catherine the Great was to become a guarantor of the *status quo* in the Holy Roman Empire and thus to achieve parity with France.[27] One more foreign power had thus been added to the list of those entitled to intervene in German affairs.

Once again, it was not the policy of Joseph but the policy of Kaunitz which had set the pace in Vienna and it is he who must shoulder much of the blame for its failure. In the crushing verdict of Derek Beales: 'As each of Kaunitz's calculations proved false, he embraced new error'.[28] But it was Joseph whom everyone associated with Austrian policy, especially as it soon became known that the ageing Maria Theresa had deeply disapproved of the forward policy being pursued and had done her best to sabotage it.

In short, the experience of the co-regency persuaded the other European powers that Joseph was an aggressive militarist, constantly looking for opportunities for expansion. At the time of the Bavarian crisis, the French ambassador to Vienna, the baron de Breteuil, predicted that Joseph would also soon turn his attention to Italy and the annexation of Venice, summarising the Emperor's approach to international relations with the hostile comment: 'Anything he thinks easy he will also think just'.[29] It was this apparent contempt for international law which so alarmed and outraged contemporaries. Just one amoral predator was all that was needed to tear apart the delicate web of prescriptive right and treaty obligations which kept the weaker states of Europe in being. No polity was more at risk than the Holy Roman Empire, as the British secretary of state, the earl of Suffolk, noted in a rare moment of perception: 'the hasty conduct of the Court of Vienna must at first sight be extremely alarming if claims of Inheritance of obsolete date are in the instant to be decided by law of arms. There can be no security for the weaker members of the Empire whose territories may be unfortunately situated in the Neighbourhood of powerful Princes'.[30]

.   .   .

JOSEPH II AND THE RUSSIAN ALLIANCE

Joseph learned the wrong lesson from the events of the 1770s. What (relative) success in the first partition of Poland and (relative) failure in the Bavarian imbroglio seemed to show was that it was Russia which held the ring. When the Russians cooperated, the Habsburg Monarchy had acquired the huge province of Galicia; when the Russians opposed, the Habsburg Monarchy had been obliged to hand back Bavaria. As Joseph told his man in St Petersburg: 'Russia with us, and we with Russia, can achieve anything we like, but without each other we find it very difficult to achieve anything important and worthwhile'.[31]

Those words were written less than a month after his mother's death. While Maria Theresa had been alive, there had been no prospect of an Austro-Russian alliance, although Joseph had been allowed to visit Catherine the Great earlier in 1780. Now that the apron-strings had been severed, Joseph could initiate a closer relationship. In a nauseating 'ostensible instruction', written in the knowledge that it would be intercepted, opened and copied by the Russians, Joseph laid on the flattery with a trowel: 'I am not just saying it for the sake of appearances when I declare that if anyone has gained by this event [the death of his mother] then it is the Tsarina of Russia. Although she may not care about it, the fact is that I now dedicate to her truly and sincerely a large measure of that infinite devotion and especially the admiration which I had for my august mother'.[32] It was just as well that Catherine did not intercept another letter sent a few days later in which Joseph described her as a pathologically selfish woman who cared no more for Russia than she did for him and 'whose idol is her vanity'.[33]

Unfortunately for the Habsburg Monarchy, Catherine was in a receptive mood. The limited gains she had made in the war against the Turks of 1768–74, despite overwhelming military and naval supremacy, had convinced her that the expansion she sought so avidly around the Black Sea, on the Danube and in the Balkans could not be achieved in the face of Austrian opposition. By 1780 she had been persuaded by her ambitious ex-lover and favourite adviser Potemkin, that the best way forward was in alliance with the Austrians. With both partners so eager, consummation was not long delayed: by an exchange of letters in May 1781 the alliance was sealed. The most important provision obliged the two powers to come to each other's aid with equal forces – but only if the attack came from the Turks. Any other aggressor required only modest assistance: 10,000 infantry, 2,000 cavalry plus appropriate artillery, or a cash subsidy of 400,000 roubles if the theatre of operations was too remote for direct intervention. The Italian and Asiatic possessions were excluded altogether.[34]

No great acumen is needed to spot that Russia had got by far the better of this bargain. All Catherine's ambitions were now concentrated on extending her southern frontier, so the guarantee of a full Austrian war-effort, should the Turks launch a preemptive strike, was invaluable. For Joseph, however, it was Prussia which was still very much the main enemy, yet for any conflict in that quarter he could expect only token support from his new ally. The use Catherine proposed to make of her new alliance was soon revealed when she sent to Joseph an outline of her famous 'Greek plan'. This envisaged nothing less than a partition of the European provinces of the Ottoman empire. Russia's own share would be relatively modest – more land to the north-west of the Black Sea and 'one or two islands' in the Aegean. However, Catherine also proposed the creation of two new states, both of which would be Russian puppets: a new 'Kingdom of Dacia', comprising Moldavia, Wallachia and Bessarabia, to be ruled by a Christian prince (Potemkin was not mentioned by name but he was the most likely candidate); and a new Byzantine kingdom with its capital at Constantinople, to be ruled by the younger of Catherine's two grandsons, who had been equipped at birth with the auspicious name of Constantine (the elder was christened 'Alexander'). Two could play at that game. In his equally visionary reply, Joseph proposed buying off France with Egypt, and the annexation of parts of the Republic of Venice and vast tracts of the Balkans. He was also careful to point out that opposition from the other European powers, notably France and Prussia, made the scheme impracticable.[35]

This kind of armchair map-making was not taken seriously in Vienna: Joseph clearly had his tongue in his cheek when he composed his reply. But Catherine was in deadly earnest, if not about the full version of the Greek project then certainly about pushing the Turks back towards Asia. Shortly afterwards she struck again, not with a project this time but with action: in April 1783 she announced the annexation of the Crimea, an acquisition of colossal strategic and economic importance for Russia. In Vienna this move provoked consternation and confusion. Kaunitz was anxious for the Habsburg Monarchy to grab its own slice by the immediate occupation of the Danubian principalities of Moldavia and Wallachia, which would have had the additional benefit of demonstrating that the Austro-Russian alliance was an equal partnership. Joseph had a more realistic appreciation of the difficulties involved and vetoed the proposal. Although he toyed with the idea of extorting Turkish consent for a 'frontier adjustment', in the end he contented himself with a diplomatic offensive to persuade the Turks to accept the Russian annexation of the Crimea as a *fait accompli*.[36]

No other power was more outraged by this latest act of international piracy than was France. For two-and-a-half centuries the French had regarded the Ottoman Turks as their natural allies in eastern Europe and were horrified by the Russian seizure, which seemed to herald the end of Turkey as a European power. Having just concluded a ruinously expensive war against the British, they were in no position to intervene militarily, but they did launch a diplomatic offensive. In this, they demanded – and had every right to expect – the assistance of their Austrian ally, and so were suitably angry when they discovered that not only was Joseph doing everything he could to *support* Catherine but that he had been secretly allied to her for the past two years. No wonder that the unfortunate Austrian ambassador at Versailles, Count Mercy, was subjected to several 'lively exchanges' with the French foreign minister, Vergennes.[37]

Yet this sense of grievance was shared with equal intensity by Joseph. As he saw it, he had supported the French through thick and thin during the American war – in his own words '*Je suis Français de cœur*'[38] – but had received nothing in return. The French had reneged on their treaty obligations during the Bavarian war, had secretly supported the anti-Austrian party in the Holy Roman Empire and had even evaded the offer of Austrian mediation to end the war against the British. As he complained to his sister, Queen Marie Antoinette, the French had reduced the alliance to mere 'promises, compliments and rhetoric'.[39] Not without reason, Joseph suspected that the French were more alarmed about possible Austrian acquisitions in the Balkans than they were about Russian expansion.

. . .

JOSEPH II AND THE DUTCH

The timing of this mutual alienation proved especially unfortunate, because Joseph was preparing an initiative which crucially depended on French cooperation. This was the opening of the river Scheldt, the most important waterway in the Austrian Netherlands. Until the late sixteenth century, the Scheldt had been the artery which made Antwerp the richest port in northern Europe. In the course of their revolt against Spain, however, the Dutch had conquered the mouth of the river and had promptly closed it to seaborne traffic. Choked off from international trade, Antwerp sank into provincial obscurity, now eclipsed by its Dutch rival, Amsterdam. The closure was given the status of international law when it was incorporated in the treaty of Westphalia in 1648.[40]

It is probable that Joseph would have turned his attention to this anomaly sooner or later anyway, but in the event the initiative came from a third party – from the British. In the summer of 1780 they tried to enlist the support of Joseph in their impending war with the Dutch Republic by offering their support in opening the Scheldt – 'a project in every way worthy of the greatness of the Emperor's views'.[41] Joseph was attracted by the idea, but was soon brought down to earth by a grimly negative critique from Kaunitz. Such a move would be contrary to the treaty of Westphalia, he argued, and would bring down on the Habsburg Monarchy the combined forces of the Dutch Republic, Prussia and France. In return for helping a few fat burghers of Antwerp, the Austrians would be risking their very existence. He added for good measure that the proposal was motivated by a British desire to spite the Dutch, destroy the Austro-French alliance and reimpose the '*ancien esclavage*' under which the Habsburg Monarchy had laboured for so long before 1756.[42]

In the following year Joseph travelled to the Austrian Netherlands for what proved to be his first and last visit. There he formed a very low opinion of the natives, dismissing them contemptuously as provincial dullards governed by women and monks.[43] The only means to rouse them from their clerical torpor was economic modernisation – and that required the maximisation of commercial assets, which in turn depended on reopening what was potentially the Monarchy's greatest port to international traffic. For the moment, the time was not ripe but the project was never far from Joseph's mind and popped up every now and again in his febrile correspondence, itself always brimful with bright ideas.

As Joseph began to articulate his desire to reopen the Scheldt, the most important motive proved to be not so much a desire to right an injustice or to promote the prosperity of his Belgian subjects as an intense feeling that a restriction imposed by a foreign power was incompatible with the dignity of his state. In a particularly revealing letter to Count Mercy written in September 1782, he proclaimed that his plan to liberate the Scheldt was entirely in keeping with the 'great principles of liberty and of trade'. By demanding recognition of the independence of his state and the removal of an offensive and humiliating restriction on its sovereignty, he was doing nothing more than the French had done already over Dunkirk, the Spanish wished to do over Gibraltar and the Russians sought to do everywhere.[44] So when finally launching the diplomatic initiative, at the end of 1783, he stressed to his chief official in the Austrian Netherlands, Count Belgioioso, that 'for the sake of appearances and especially for esteem, this impertinent closure of the Scheldt is too shameful for a power such as mine'.[45]

It was characteristic that Joseph should choose libertarian rhetoric to justify his policy – but should think only in terms of the liberty of the state. It was also characteristic, alas, that he should have underestimated the obstacles which make even the simplest political objective so difficult to achieve. It turned out that he had made three fatal miscalculations. Firstly, he had misread the situation inside the Dutch Republic. In 1782 he had revoked unilaterally the 'Barrier treaty' of 1715, which had given the Dutch the right to garrison a number of forts on the Franco-Belgian border. On this occasion his timing was impeccable, for the Dutch were at war with the British and so could expect no assistance from that quarter. On the other hand, as the Barrier treaty had been aimed squarely against the French, they too would not oppose the Austrian *démarche*. So the Dutch troops were withdrawn and the forts were demolished.[46] Encouraged by this capitulation and by the knowledge that the Dutch war against the British was proving a disaster (a definitive peace was not signed until May 1784), Joseph expected an equal degree of compliance over the Scheldt. He was rudely disabused. When vital commercial interests were deemed to be at stake, the Dutch (or rather the merchants of Amsterdam who determined policy) could be just as obstinate as any monarch. Rather than allow Antwerp to revive, they would risk anything – including war.

They were encouraged to do so by their knowledge that they enjoyed French support. And that was Joseph's second miscalculation. Despite early and urgent warnings from his man at Versailles, Joseph believed that his French ally could be made to help.[47] In reality, nothing could have been less welcome to the French than a dispute between their existing ally, Austria, and their potential ally, the Dutch Republic. Although the French and the Dutch had been fighting together against the British on the same side since 1780, they were not yet formally linked. It was imperative, however, that they should be so – if the French were to capitalise on the advantage they had gained in the American War. If Dutch possessions at the Cape of Good Hope and in Ceylon could be combined with French bases in the Indian Ocean, then – it was generally believed – the French could do to the British in Asia what they had just done in America and thus complete the reversal of the Seven Years War.[48]

With nothing less than the future of the world at stake, the French were not inclined to listen to Joseph's requests for help against the Dutch. They had already been alienated by the discovery of his secret alliance with the Tsarina and the support he had given to her annexation of the Crimea. In the twilight of the *ancien régime*, there was now a last sunburst of decisive action. In November 1784, when the crisis reached its peak, Louis XVI asked each member of his Council of State for his opinion. They all agreed that if France had to choose between the Habsburg Monarchy and the Dutch Republic, it was the latter which should be preferred. Indeed, as the minister of finance, Calonne, told Mercy, the very dissolution of the Austrian alliance had been discussed. All had agreed that if it could be used to maintain peace on the continent, the alliance was still valuable, but that 'under a monarch as volatile as the Emperor, there would often arise the danger of being involved in very ticklish business [*des affaires fort épineuses*]'. Calonne also revealed the horrifying news that an approach had been made to Prussia for joint action in support of the Dutch.[49] Joseph's expansionist reputation had returned to plague him, for none of the French decision-makers believed that the opening of Scheldt represented the limit of Joseph's ambitions. On the contrary, that specific initiative was thought to be the prelude to the dismemberment of the Dutch Republic and the annexation of its most flourishing provinces.[50] Exception was also taken to the 'proud contempt' which characterised the Austrian diplomatic communications.[51] So Joseph was informed that, in the French view, the Dutch were in the right over the Scheldt, and was threatened with French military intervention if he persevered with his own preparations for war.

Those preparations were not going well – and this was Joseph's third miscalculation. All the military reforms of the past two decades had failed to provide him with an instrument capable of coercing the Dutch. In eighteenth-century conditions, moving troops from their bases in the central core of the Habsburg Monarchy (the majority were stationed in Hungary during peace-time) to the periphery was a slow, arduous and expensive business. It soon became apparent – even to Joseph – that there was a gross discrepancy between the potential value of the objective and the cost of the means required. As he lamented to Count Belgioioso, the exercise was bound to cost at least 8,000,000 gulden and probably more.[52] At the beginning of October 1784 he had given the order to force the passage of the Scheldt by sending a ship down to the sea from Antwerp. The bluff was promptly called, as the Dutch gunners fired on the ship and forced it to retreat. There proved to be nothing that Joseph could do by way of retaliation. When he began hostile manœuvres, the Dutch responded in time-honoured fashion by opening their sluices and flooding thousands of acres of Belgian farmland.

Confronted by Dutch determination, French hostility and military impotence, Joseph began to retreat. On the day – 20 November 1784 – that he accepted Louis XVI's offer of mediation, he also signalled the beginning of the end of the affair.[53] Ten months were to pass before agreement was reached. During that time, Joseph often blew hot again, threatening war to support his demands for the cession of Maastricht and financial reparations, but the pass had been sold. In the end, he had to settle for a public apology from the Dutch for firing on his ship and compensation of 10,000,000 gulden (which the French paid). It was a dismal, enervating experience for him: he could only unload his frustration by writing violent attacks on the ingratitude of his Belgian subjects and the perfidy of his French 'ally'. From his many anguished letters on the subject of the latter, his sense of humiliation and injured pride come through loud and clear. In a pathetic letter to Kaunitz of 26 August 1785, written at a time when it seemed that the negotiations might fail altogether, he lamented: 'I know that the game is not worth the candle, that the advantages which we might draw will not justify the expense; and that there is risk involved; and that the political situation is anything but favourable: but there are occasions when one should consult only one's courage; and this aura of reputation must take priority over every other consideration'.[54]

Kaunitz was not in a sympathetic mood. Back in 1781 he had advised Joseph against trying to open Scheldt[55] and he never changed his mind. He had no liking for the Dutch – 'these insolent cheese merchants' he called them – but he did have a sense of political realism. In a remarkably candid letter to Mercy, written just after the Dutch had apparently made war inevitable by firing on the Austrian ship, he wrote that the exercise was going to prove hideously expensive, adding 'You know me too well not to be certain that I shall assist the Emperor with the same zeal and enthusiasm I would have brought to the business if all that is being done (and all that is not being done) had been on my advice'.[56] But the two men were equally culpable in misreading completely the balance of power in Europe after the American War. Both believed that Great Britain was finished as a great power: 'England's position beggars belief', wrote Joseph in the spring of 1783 with characteristic *Schadenfreude*, 'it shows just how much this nation has degenerated. If France had gained nothing from the late war beyond her demonstration to the rest of Europe of the desperate and pitiable condition of her rival she would still have achieved a great deal'.[57] In this failure of understanding they betrayed both prejudice and ignorance, believing that Great Britain was fundamentally unstable because of her parliamentary politics and commercial economy. France, for all her present problems, was the kind of country they felt at home with – an absolute monarchy with a good solid agricultural base – and so was always to be preferred to the meretricious British.

It was a fateful error, for it was just at this time that the British were not only about to embark on an era of unprecedented prosperity and stability but were also more eager than ever before for a restoration of the 'old alliance' with Austria: 'no difficulty ought...ever to deter us from the steady and determined pursuit of the great and important Object this Country should ever keep in view, I mean, the detaching of the Emperor from France', wrote the new foreign secretary, the marquis of Carmarthen.[58] Although it was by no means certain that the British could have secured the opening of the Scheldt, or any other of Joseph's objectives, at least they would have put their best foot forward. Joseph and Kaunitz preferred to stay chained to the rotting corpse that was old regime France.[59]

. . .

BAVARIA AGAIN

It was a corpse which could still act as a succubus, draining the life from any Austrian initiative. That capacity was demonstrated by the fate of another of Joseph's bright ideas, which he tried to realise at the same time as the Scheldt affair. This was the revival of the attempt to secure Bavaria. After Austrian support had helped Catherine the Great to wrest the Crimea from the Turks without having to fight a war (yet!), a suitably grateful Tsarina had offered Joseph what was in effect a blank cheque promising Russian support for any project he cared to name. As soon as it became clear that the Turks had given in – in January 1784 – Joseph and Kaunitz considered their options. Given French hostility to any expansion in the Balkans, the obvious target was Bavaria, to be secured this time by means of an exchange with the Austrian Netherlands. In a memorandum strongly reminiscent of the policy documents he had prepared in the 1740s,[60] Kaunitz argued that the Belgian provinces could never be defended against France and so would always be a manacle shackling Austria to French policy. The substitution of this negative asset for Bavaria, on the other hand, would give the Monarchy the edge against Prussia in Germany. This was especially desirable in view of Prussia's impending inheritance of Ansbach and Bayreuth.[61] On 1 April 1784 Joseph instructed his man in Munich, Baron Lehrbach, to conduct a survey of all Bavarian assets and to review the prospects for an exchange.[62]

There is no need to follow the highly complex diplomacy which followed.[63] The most striking characteristic of the episode was Joseph's extraordinary manner of conducting foreign policy. In its early stages, his project was quite simple – a straight swap between two rulers, himself and the elector of Bavaria. In this form it won the enthusiastic support even of Kaunitz, (although he soon began to backpedal when he considered the possible obstacles).[64] But Joseph just could not leave well alone. Before long he was wondering whether the opportunity might not also be taken to acquire the archbishopric of Salzburg and the associated priory of Berchtesgaden which formed such irritating enclaves in the Habsburg Monarchy.[65] The archbishop would be compensated with two provinces – the duchy of Luxemburg and the county of Namur – to be detached from the rest of the Austrian Netherlands. But then it occurred to him that the archbishop would be without a see. Never mind, it so happened that there was a vacancy in the prince-bishopric of Liège, whose substantial territory bisected the Habsburg possessions. Could not the archbishop of Salzburg be elected there instead? Then he would only have to be given Luxemburg and the small duchy of Limburg, leaving Namur in the hands of the elector of Bavaria. In return, however, the latter would be expected to take with him to Brussels a larger share of the Bavarian national debt. Then it occurred to Joseph that there would be a problem over the cathedral chapter of Salzburg – what would happen to them? A moment's thought solved the problem without difficulty: some of the canons would be sent off to Liège, and some would be retained to support the new archbishop, who would of course be appointed by the new ruler – Joseph II![66]

This visionary farrago of high improbability and sheer impossibility was meant to be taken seriously. In Joseph's defence, it has to be said that the current elector of Bavaria, Karl Theodor, was sure to be responsive. His mother came from one of the great aristocratic dynasties of the Netherlands (the Arenbergs), he had been born in Brussels and had spent much of his youth there, and he did not like Munich. More understandably, he had no desire to return to his previous residence at Mannheim and his estranged wife. He also liked the idea of the royal title and status Joseph had promised to him. On the other hand he did not like the constant chopping and changing of his share of the exchange, nor did he like Joseph's insistence that the best Belgian regiments would remain in the Austrian army and that Austrian recruiting sergeants should continue to operate as before.[67] On balance, he was inclined to accept and if the only parties involved had been Joseph and the Elector Karl Theodor, a deal could have been struck.

It was not to be. The familiar Wittelsbach problem of procreation intervened again to frustrate Joseph's plans. Although blessed with several illegitimate offspring (one reason for accepting the exchange was his wish to provide for them), Karl Theodor was without an heir. The heir-apparent was his cousin, Karl August duke of Zweibrücken, whose only son died in September 1784, leaving his brother Maximilian Joseph in line to succeed eventually to both Wittelsbach possessions. In other words, consent to the exchange had to be won from the two Zweibrücken brothers as well. This was where the real problem started. Karl August was a profligate princeling of the old school, kept solvent only by regular loans from the French. As his sense of obligation was strengthened further by strong cultural preference and geographical proximity, he was certain to follow the instructions of his paymasters. With Mercy warning that the only chance of dealing with French opposition was to gain the consent of *all* parties involved before the news of the plan leaked out, the prospects were bleak.[68]

Joseph did not despair. In addition to his habitual conviction that anything he planned was right, rational and therefore practicable, he believed that his crucial asset was Russian support. At the very outset, the Tsarina had given an assurance of all possible help, adding that her envoy at Frankfurt, Count Rumyantsev, would spare no effort in persuading the duke of Zweibrücken to accept the exchange.[69] Given Russia's new status in the Holy Roman Empire as a guarantor of the treaty of Teschen, this reinforcement was very welcome. Joseph also believed that his simultaneous Dutch initiative could be made to interact profitably. He knew just how eager were the French to secure an alliance with the Dutch and how embarrassed they were by his dispute with the latter. So he proposed that French support for the Bavarian exchange should be bought by concessions to the Dutch.[70] After French ministerial opinion had been primed by a despatch sent *en clair* through the ordinary post (in the sure knowledge that it would be opened and read), a formal approach was made in the middle of November.[71]

It was all to no avail. Alerted by the news that the Austrians were trying to woo the duke of Zweibrücken by offers of loans, the French had moved swiftly to increase their own.[72] There was never any prospect, as Joseph had hoped, that they themselves would conclude that a Bavarian exchange was in the interests of France. Any increase in influence in the Low Countries would be more than counter-balanced by the prospect of Habsburg hegemony in Germany. Moreover, they were suitably angered by the sudden news in December 1784 that Joseph had changed the small print of the exchange yet again. To make it all 'more simple', as he put it with disarming naïvety, he now announced that he would drop the plan to include Salzburg and Berchtesgaden and would keep Luxemburg and Namur after all. As Vergennes tartly pointed out, that move annulled at a stroke Joseph's argument that France would benefit from the exchange by the removal of an Austrian presence on her Northern frontier.[73]

So when Louis XVI consulted his ministers on the Austrian proposal, the result was a foregone conclusion. Under intense pressure from the Queen, who more than ever before was acting as her brother's agent at Versailles, Vergennes was obliged to dissemble, but he could do so secure in the knowledge that his colleagues would vote the right way. And so they did; every one voted firmly against.[74] Duly primed by his paymasters, on 3 January 1785 Karl August of Zweibrücken turned down the plan presented to him by Rumyantsev, adding insult to injury by doing so in a letter which an enraged Joseph described as *'insolente et ridicule'*.[75] As Joseph recognised at once, with that brusque rejection, the Bavarian project was dead and buried. A year's intense diplomacy had come to nothing.[76] But Joseph's problems were only just beginning. Rumours about the proposed exchange had been circulating for some time; now that they were confirmed, his enemies could organise. The result was a collapse of Austrian influence in the Holy Roman Empire. As this proved to be such a fateful episode in German history – a major milestone on the road which led to 1866 and a *kleindeutsch* Germany without Austria – this is an appropriate moment for a consideration of Joseph's relations with the Empire.

. . .

THE HOLY ROMAN EMPIRE

When Joseph succeeded his father in 1765, his imperial inheritance was meagre indeed. Twenty years of vigorous exploitation of the office to serve the interests of the Austrian state rather than the Holy Roman Empire had alienated many traditional supporters among the German princes. In particular, the French alliance of 1756 had proved a disaster in the Empire, for this formation of a Catholic bloc in Europe – for the first time – had given a much more pronounced denominational character to the imperial office. It was an association which the Austrians themselves made all the more obvious by describing the rival Anglo-Prussian alliance as a 'Protestant league'. This 'reconfessionalisation' of imperial politics after 1756 led to a contraction of imperial influence. Of course, everyone knew that the Habsburg Emperor was a Roman Catholic but, in his imperial capacity, and especially when acting as imperial judge, he was expected to adopt a neutral stance between the two religious parties.[77]

When the Seven Years War ended with Prussian influence in the Empire actually expanded, despite Frederick the Great's unprovoked invasion of Saxony in 1756, there was a major reconsideration of policy in Vienna. The old policy of confrontation and aggression made way for a defensive strategy based on strict legality and impartiality, in the hope that the confidence of the Emperor's former supporters could be regained. At first, the new Emperor played his part conscientiously and convincingly. Although he had found his coronation as King of the Romans 'disagreeable and useless', he took his duties seriously. In 1766 he commissioned reports on the benefits of the imperial connection from Kaunitz, the imperial vice-chancellor Prince Colloredo and Count Pergen; in 1767 he founded a Council of Imperial Affairs, whose weekly meetings he often chaired in person; and he began the reform of the two main imperial courts – the Aulic Council (*Reichshofrat*) and Cameral Tribunal (*Reichskammergericht*).[78]

It all ended in disappointment. Some progress was made with the *Reichshofrat*, which was located in Vienna and was under direct imperial control, but the *Reichskammergericht* proved more intractable. The latter became the touchstone of

147

the new policy. After several years of onerous, enervating toil, it became clear that the Holy Roman Empire's legendary forces of inertia were stifling every initiative for change. It would have taxed the patience of a much less impulsive man than Joseph II. This dismal experience of the late 1760s convinced him that there was nothing to be gained from a policy of pandering to imperial prejudice, and so he turned back to great-power politics and a pursuit of Austrian interests even more ruthless than in the past.[79] Indeed, by 1778 he was beginning to wonder whether it would not be desirable to sever his links with the Holy Roman Empire altogether, by abdication of the imperial title. During the second Bavarian episode, in 1784, he held out the prospect of a transplanted Elector becoming Holy Roman Emperor instead of him.[80]

Joseph was not a man of half-measures. Once he had abandoned his attempt to make the Holy Roman Empire work, he turned against it with vehemence, making no secret of his contempt for its institutions and its members. The imperial office was 'a ghost of an honorific power', its business was 'loathsome', the imperial constitution was 'vicious', the princes were spineless ignoramuses, putty in the hands of their pedantic and venal ministers.[81] Of the senior dignitary of the Holy Roman Empire, the Elector-Archbishop of Mainz, he wrote to Count Trauttmansdorff, his envoy at Mainz: 'As I have just come from making my Easter confession on Good Friday and have forgiven all those who trespass against me, I cannot harbour any thoughts of revenge, only contempt for an arrant shit who is bursting with pride, although he is simply being taken for a ride by his women'.[82]

Even while Maria Theresa had been still alive, the first partition of Poland and the war of the Bavarian Succession had alerted the German princes to the danger from an expansionist Emperor. In the last year of her life the warning signals were well and truly posted when the youngest of Joseph's brothers, the archduke Max Franz, was elected 'coadjutor' of the Elector-Archbishop of Cologne and Prince-Bishop of Münster. This meant that on the death of the present incumbent (the two bishoprics were held in plurality by the same man), a Habsburg archduke would succeed automatically to two large, prosperous and strategically important principalities in north-west Germany. Indeed, their territory surrounded the western provinces of Prussia – Cleves, Mark and Geldern. As a response to the impending Prussian intrusion into southern Germany through the inheritance of Ansbach and Bayreuth this could hardly be bettered. Moreover, with schemes of secularisation in the air, who was to say that the Habsburg presence in the region would not prove permanent? Such was the enthusiasm in Vienna for the election of Max Franz that over a million gulden were expended in buying the votes of the canons of Cologne and Münster ('making sure of the inspiration of the Holy Ghost' was the cynical euphemism offered by Frederick the Great).[83] As Max Franz was already Grand Master of the Order of Teutonic Knights, he was set fair to become the most powerful ecclesiastical prince ever seen in the Holy Roman Empire. Moreover, throughout the 1780s there were rumours constantly making the rounds that he was going to add several other prince-bishoprics – probably Hildesheim, perhaps even the archbishopric of Salzburg – to his pluralistic haul. It was also believed that Joseph intended to provide for his large brood of nephews by the acquisition of other ecclesiastical states as they fell vacant.[84]

It came as no surprise, therefore, that Joseph's reign as sole ruler was marked by a more aggressive imperial policy. It would be tedious to recount all of his initiatives. A brief summary of two episodes must suffice to demonstrate his apparent determination to alienate as many German princes as possible. At the beginning of 1782 Joseph cancelled all payments made to ministers and other public officials throughout the Holy Roman Empire. Although these 'pensions' were thinly disguised bribes, they had been a vital lubricant oiling the cogs of Habsburg influence at the various German courts. At a stroke, therefore, Joseph had turned the most influential political figures in the Empire from friends into enemies and had cut off a vital source of information – and all for the sake of a modest economy.[85] In the following year he came up with the bright idea of reviving the ancient custom of issuing 'letters of maintenance' (*Panisbriefe*) to monastic foundations, requiring them to pay for the upkeep of imperial officials. The fact that the practice had not been employed since the Reformation, that Joseph tried to introduce them to Protestant territories and that he intended to use the money for Austrian (not imperial) officials, did nothing to enhance their popularity. He was also foolish enough to select as his first target the convent of Adersleben in the Prussian territory of Halberstadt, thus inviting –

and getting – an immediate rebuff. As he had no means with which to enforce the policy, he succeeded only in causing more irritation and anxiety for no return.[86]

Together with the campaign to eliminate the diocesan juris-diction of the prince-bishops from the Habsburg Monarchy discussed earlier,[87] incidents such as these convinced even those members of the Empire bound to the Habsburg Emperor by history and self-interest[88] that the ground was moving be-neath their feet. Help was at hand in the unlikely shape of Frederick the Great. Now that the Austrian game-keeper had turned poacher, the Prussian poacher could – indeed *had to* – turn game-keeper. Frederick was able to grasp that plenty could be achieved through the archaic structure of the Empire – *but only if the* status quo *was accepted and impartiality between the religious parties was observed.* After 1763, and especially after 1778, Frederick was at pains to present himself as a neutral arbiter, distancing himself from the Protestants and broadening his appeal to include Catholics.[89]

His reward came in 1785 with the formation of the League of Princes (*Fürstenbund*). This was an association aimed squarely against Joseph's imperial policies, especially the attempt to exchange Bavaria for the Austrian Netherlands. Frederick's ability to enlist two of the most important princes (the electors of Hanover and Saxony) and many more of the second rank (Saxony-Weimar, Saxony-Gotha, Zweibrücken, Brunswick, Baden, Hessen-Kassel, the Anhalts, Osnabrück, Ansbach, Pfalz-Birkenfeld, the Mecklenburgs, and Hessen-Darmstadt) demonstrated the collapse of Austrian influence in the Empire.[90] Perhaps the greatest catch was the Archbishop-Elec-tor of Mainz, the senior prelate of the Church in Germany and the arch-chancellor of the Holy Roman Empire, whose defec-tion was of great symbolic importance – and was recognised as such by contemporaries.[91] The formation of the League also had important international ramifications, arresting a British initiative for an Austrian alliance, rescuing Frederick from diplomatic isolation and bringing Catherine the Great's influ-ence on German affairs to an abrupt halt.[92]

Joseph proved quite irrepressible, continuing on his anti-imperial course undeterred by the increasingly blunt criticisms from Kaunitz. The latter had sought to construct a pro-Aus-trian party in the Empire after 1780 and was suitably dismayed when Joseph's single-minded pursuit of Austrian interests sabotaged all his efforts. In the spring of 1787, when Joseph's resumption of his diocesan campaign foiled a promising bid to win over the new coadjutor of Mainz, an exasperated Kaunitz exclaimed: 'It will be up to him and not me to justify the results of his actions before God and man'.[93]

. . .

JOSEPH II AND THE GREAT POWERS

This wilful destruction of Austrian influence in the Holy Roman Empire would have made more sense if it had brought corresponding benefits in the great-power arena, but it did not. Joseph was under no illusions about his international position. As he told his envoy in Russia, Count Ludwig Cobenzl, in the immediate aftermath of French perfidy over the Scheldt and Bavaria, to have a nominal ally who is in reality a secret enemy is to have the worst of all worlds.[94] Yet if he could grasp that fundamental weakness of his position, he could not see the solution. He made two fundamental miscalculations. Firstly, he consistently underestimated the British. All their enthusiastic attempts to secure an alliance he dismissed with that contempt which came so easily to him 'in view of the wretched condition and decline of England, and especially its execrable ministry and government'.[95] As he wrote those words, the British economy was booming as never before, the debt incurred during the American war was being brought quickly under control and William Pitt was settling in for almost two decades in office. Secondly, he consistently overestimated France, still in his view the most powerful state in Europe and capable of causing the Habsburg Monarchy insuperable problems in half-a-dozen different theatres.[96] This was a less excusable error of judgment because he was receiving regular and accurate reports on the decadence of France from Count Mercy.

The only way out of this impasse which Joseph was prepared to consider was a *rapprochement* with Prussia. After the death of Frederick the Great (on 17 August 1786) he wrote a memorandum arguing that if only they could bury the hatchet, Austria and Prussia could save enormous sums on armaments, liberate themselves from their grasping allies and give the law to Europe. After the seizure of Silesia, he conceded, hostility between Frederick the Great and Maria Theresa had been unavoidable but now that two new monarchs were in place, a new era of cooperation might be opened.[97] But this was a weak opinion weakly held. Two days later he told his ambassador at Berlin, Prince Reuss, that extreme caution had to be exercised where Frederick William II was concerned, because of his patent inability to make up his mind which policy to follow. Indeed, he dismissed the new king of Prussia as a credulous cretin who believed in such masonic idiocies as conjuring up the spirit of Julius Caesar and persuading it to talk.[98] So when Kaunitz promptly vetoed any approach to Prussia, Joseph meekly agreed.[99]

Joseph was intelligent enough to spot the structural weakness in the Habsburg Monarchy's international position: with Austro-Prussian antagonism the central axiom of central European politics, Russia was always going to be in the enviable position of being able to play one side off against the other, or – as he put it himself – maintain *'un certain équilibre de jalousie'*.[100] Catherine had deftly exploited her favourable position to win Prussian support for placing her puppet on the Polish throne in 1764 and then to win Austrian support for her annexation of the Crimea in 1783. What Joseph was unable to appreciate was that he himself could have played that pivotal role by playing off Russia against Prussia in Poland, Russia against Turkey in the Balkans and France against Great Britain overseas. By taking advantage of the central geographical position of the Monarchy and by taking advantage of his imperial role, he could have imposed a *pax Austriaca* on Europe. He would certainly have enjoyed the support of both the British and the French in maintaining the *status quo* on the continent. But that required one essential precondition: the abandoning of any ambition to expand territorially. Only a satiated power, only a polity which took as its fundamental legitimation a respect for law and looked for no selfish advantage could hope to play one predator off against another.

It was a precondition which Joseph could not accept, because it would have involved denying the very basis of his political philosophy – the belief in the state. Like Frederick the Great and Catherine the Great, he believed that the mark of a successful state was expansion. As the French ambassador, Breteuil, wrote in 1784: 'the emperor believes that for history, as for contemporaries, the greatest prince will always be he who gains the most territory'.[101] To have changed from a strategy based on the maximisation of resources for the purposes of conquest would have been to recognise that the whole programme of modernisation undertaken since 1740 had been a terrible mistake and had been based on a mistaken assessment of the Habsburg Monarchy's geopolitical position. It would have meant abandoning the idea of the state (*Staatsidee*) and going back to the idea of empire (*Reichsidee*). It would have meant a recognition that the relationship between the Holy Roman Empire and the Habsburg Monarchy was symbiotic. It would have meant protecting the weak against the strong, supporting the imperial knights, the free imperial cities, the ecclesiastical states and the smaller secular princes against those over-mighty princes who aspired to sovereignty, expansion and to statehood. It could have been done – but not by Joseph II.[102]

The dangers of Joseph's doomed attempt to turn an empire into a state – to scrub the stripes off the zebra – became suddenly apparent in 1787. Up till now, his clumsy initiatives had brought no worse penalty than a sense of frustration and humiliation. But now the very existence of his state was to be put at risk. On 22 February 1787 the French 'pre-revolution' began with the convocation of the Assembly of Notables. The process by which France turned from nominal ally into avowed enemy had begun. In May 1787 Joseph went to meet Catherine the Great in the Crimea. There he found her 'dying with desire to begin again against the Turks' and deaf to pleas for peace.[103] In the event, it did not matter, for on 17 August the Russian ambassador in Constantinople was arrested and imprisoned in the Seven Towers of the Topkapi Palace – the traditional Turkish way of declaring war.

This pre-emptive strike by the Turks activated the defensive alliance between Catherine and Joseph concluded in 1781. Although Joseph recognised his obligation at once – the *casus fœderis* in diplomatic parlance – he did so with a heavy heart. As he lamented to his brother Leopold, 'these damned Turks' had forced him to wage war in regions where plague and famine were endemic and all for the prospect of very little gain.[104] Kaunitz was much more enthusiastic, stating that Austria was going to war not only to honour the treaty but also because 'our power has been consolidated and an unconditional desire for the maintenance of peace is no longer our main priority'.[105] As events were to show, Joseph's gloomy appraisal was the more realistic.

Almost immediately the disastrous consequences of the Turkish war made themselves apparent. With Austria tied down in the Balkans for the forseeable future, the Prussians felt able to intervene militarily in the Dutch Republic to restore Frederick William II's brother-in-law, the Stadholder William V, to all the powers stripped from him by the pro-French party during the past few years. Invading on 13 September 1787, it took them only a few weeks to conquer the entire country and thus to achieve what had been denied Philip II of Spain, Louis XIV of France – and Joseph II of Austria. The result was a triple alliance between a suitably purged Dutch Republic, a resurgent Great Britain and a triumphalist Prussia to form a menacing axis stretching across northern Europe. Given Joseph's growing problems inside the Habsburg Monarchy, especially in the Belgian provinces where an open insurrection had been narrowly averted in the spring of 1787,[106] the future was bleak. Now both the domestic and foreign implications of his state-building began to fuse. It was not only France which appeared to be entering a terminal crisis.

. . .

NOTES

1. Viktor Bibl, *Kaiser Joseph II. Ein Vorkämpfer der großdeutschen Idee* (Vienna and Leipzig, 1943), p. 290.
2. Beales, pp. 66, 185.
3. Kurt Peball, 'Aspekte der Forschung zum Kriegswesen der Zeit Maria Theresias und Josephs II., in *Österreich im Europa der Aufklärung*, I, 610.
4. In the view of Christopher Duffy, the War of the Bavarian Succession was 'a defensive triumph' for the Austrians – Christopher Duffy, *The army of Maria Theresa. The armed forces of imperial Austria 1740–1780* (London, 1977), p. 213.
5. See above, pp. 50–1.
6. Wolfgang May, *Quellen zu den Reformen Josephs II. in niederoester-reichischen Archiven* (Vienna dissertation, 1981), pp. 225–8.
7. Beales, p. 404.

8. [Anton Johann Gross-Hoffinger], *Lebens- und Regierungs-geschichte Josephs des Zweiten*, 4 vols (2nd edn, Stuttgart, 1842), I, 203.

9. Joseph Christoph Allmayer-Beck, 'Das Heerwesen unter Joseph II.', *Österreich zur Zeit Josephs II. Mitregent Maria Theresias und Landesfürst* (Vienna, 1980), pp. 40–3.

10. Beales, p. 222.

11. Joseph II, 'Grundsätze für jeden diener des staats (Hirtenbrief) 1783', in Friedrich Walter, *Die österreichische Zentralverwaltung*, section II, vol. 4 (Vienna, 1950), p. 128.

12. Lorenz Hübner, *Lebensgeschichte Josephs des Zweyten, Kaisers der Deutschen, oder Rosen auf dessen Grab* (Salzburg, n.d. [1790]), pp. 538–9.

13. Felix Czeike, *Geschichte der Stadt Wien* (Vienna, 1981), p. 152.

14. N.W. Wraxall, *Memoirs of the Courts of Berlin, Dresden, Warsaw and Vienna in the years 1777, 1778 and 1779*, 2 vols (London, 1799), vol. II, p. 449.

15. Arneth and Flammermont *Correspondance secrète*, II, 322.

16. Derek McKay and H.M. Scott, *The rise of the great powers 1648–1815* (London, 1983), p. 228.

17. Horst Glassl, *Das österreichische Einrichtungswerk in Galizien 1772–1790* (Wiesbaden, 1975), p. 12.

18. Gaston Zeller, *Histoire des relations internationales. Les temps modernes*, vol. 2: *De Louis XIV à 1789* (Paris, 1955), p. 288.

19. Beales, pp. 280–302 provides the most authoritative account of this episode.

20. Handbillets, vol. 11 (45), no. 536, to Count Trauttmansdorff, 18 July 1787, fos 482–6. This is also reprinted in Schlitter, pp. 2–5.

21. Karl Otmar Freiherr von Aretin, *Heiliges Römisches Reich*, 2 vols (Wiesbaden, 1967), I, 110.

22. Gabriele Haug-Moritz, *Württembergischer Ständekonflikt und deutscher Dualismus* (Stuttgart, 1992), p. 221.

23. H.W.V. Temperley, *Frederic the Great and Kaiser Joseph. An episode of war and diplomacy in the eighteenth century* (London, 1915, reprinted 1968), p. 63.

24. PRO SP/81/112 no. 1 The earl of Suffolk to Morton Eden, 17 January 1777.

25. Paul P. Bernard, *Joseph II and Bavaria: Two eighteenth-century attempts at German unification* (The Hague, 1965), p. 79.

26. The Bavarian succession is best followed in Beales, ch. 13.

27. Karl Otmar Freiherr von Aretin, 'Russia as a guarantor power of the imperial constitution under Catherine II', *Journal of Modern History*, 58, Supplement (1986).

28. Beales, p. 401.

29. Albert Sorel, *Europe and the French Revolution,* vol. I: *The political traditions of the old régime,* ed. Alfred Cobban and J.W. Hunt (London, 1969), p. 480.
30. PRO SP/105/43 no. 6 The earl of Suffolk to Morton Eden, 16 April 1778. For other comments by contemporaries on Joseph's expansionism, see Beales, pp. 302–5.
31. Joseph to Count Ludwig Cobenzl, 23 December 1780, Beer, *Joseph II., Leopold II. und Kaunitz,* p. 26.
32. Ibid., p. 25.
33. Arneth, *Joseph II. und Katharina,* p. 35 n.
34. The letters are reprinted in ibid., pp. 73–84. There is a good account of the negotiations in Karl A. Roider, *Austria's eastern question 1700–1790* (Princeton, 1982), pp. 159–62. See also Isabel de Madariaga, 'The secret Austro-Russian treaty of 1781', *The Slavonic and East European Review,* 38 (1959).
35. Catherine's letter to Joseph of 10 September 1782 can be found in Arneth, *Joseph II. und Katharina,* pp. 143–56, together with Joseph's reply. For the Russian dimension, see Isabel de Madariaga, *Russia in the age of Catherine the Great* (London, 1981), pp. 383–4, 387–8.
36. Joseph II to Kaunitz, 5 July 1783, Beer, *Joseph II., Leopold II. und Kaunitz,* pp. 134–6; Roider, *Austria's eastern question,* pp. 165–7.
37. The French reaction is best followed in Arneth and Flammermont, especially I, 185 n. 2, 188–9.
38. Joseph to Mercy, 4 March 1780, ibid., II, 550.
39. Joseph to Marie Antoinette, 9 September 1783, Arneth, *Marie Antoinette, Joseph II. und Leopold II.,* p. 31.
40. On the history of the Scheldt as an international issue, see S.T. Bindoff, *The Scheldt question* (London, 1945).
41. BL Add. MSS 35,519, Lord Stormont to Sir Robert Murray Keith, 8 August 1780, fo. 158.
42. Kaunitz to Joseph, 20 January 1781, Beer, p. 32.
43. Handbillets, vol. 11 (45), no. 953, 'Points d'instruction pour le Général Commandant aux Païs-Bas Feldzeugmeister Comte d'Alton' [November 1787], fo. 843.
44. Joseph to Mercy, 23 September 1782, Arneth and Flammermont, I, 128.
45. Handbillets, vol. 7 (27), no. 974, to Count Belgioioso, 3 December 1783, fos 859–60.
46. Paul von Mitrofanov, *Joseph II. seine politische und kulturelle Tätigkeit,* 2 vols (Vienna and Leipzig, 1910), I, 119; Leopold von Ranke, *Die deutschen Mächte und der Fürstenbund,* 2 vols (Leipzig, 1871–2), I, 188–9.

47. For Mercy's warnings to Joseph, see especially his letters of 9 October 1782 and 28 December 1782, Arneth and Flammermont, I, 134, 145.

48. Haus-, Hof- und Staatsarchiv, Staatskanzlei, England, Berichte, Kart. 124, no. 2, Count Kageneck to Kaunitz, London, 7 January 1785.

49. Arneth and Flammermont, I, 342 n. 1. A. Tratchevsky, *La France et l'Allemagne sous Louis XVI*, 2 vols (Paris, 1880), I, 50–2.

50. Mercy to Joseph, 6 November 1784, Arneth and Flammermont, I, 325–6.

51. Ibid., p. 346 n. 1.

52. Handbillets, vol. 8 (31), no. 912, to Count Belgioioso, 20 November 1784 fo. 828.

53. Joseph to Louis XVI, 20 November 1784, Arneth, *Marie Antoinette, Joseph II. und Leopold II.*, p. 49.

54. Beer, p. 215.

55. See above, p. 138.

56. Kaunitz to Mercy, 21 October 1784, Arneth and Flammermont, I, 310. See also his letter to Joseph of 17 July 1785 reprinted in Beer, pp. 207–10.

57. Joseph to Mercy, 31 March 1783, Arneth and Flammermont, I, 175.

58. BL Add. MSS 35,532, Carmarthen to Sir Robert Murray Keith, 17 August 1784, fo. 201. Parts of this despatch are also quoted in T.C.W. Blanning, '"That horrid electorate" or *"Ma patrie germanique"?* George III, Hanover and the *Fürstenbund* of 1785', *The Historical Journal*, 20, 2 (1977), pp. 318–19, where other examples of British wooing of Austria are given and discussed. See also Jeremy Black, 'British policy towards Austria, 1780–93', *Mitteilungen des österreichischen Staatsarchivs*, 42 (1992), 199.

59. For a good example of Kaunitz's obdurate loyalty to the alliance he had negotiated in 1756, see his letter to Joseph of 28 September 1785 reprinted in Beer, p. 224.

60. See above, pp. 30–2.

61. Ranke, *Die deutschen Mächte und der Fürstenbund*, I, 163–4. On Ansbach and Bayreuth see above, pp. 132–3.

62. Handbillets, vol. 8 (31), no. 157, Joseph to Baron Lehrbach, 1 April 1784, fos 249–50.

63. For a detailed account, although not accurate in every detail, see the closing chapters of Bernard, *Joseph II and Bavaria*.

64. Kaunitz to Joseph, 4 April 1784 and 4 May 1784, Beer, pp. 168–9, 173.

65. See the map on p. xi.

66. Joseph to Kaunitz, 14 May 1784, Beer, pp. 174–6.

67. Ranke, *Die deutschen Mächte und der Fürstenbund*, I, 173, 177–81.

68. Mercy to Kaunitz, 16 August 1784, Arneth and Flammermont, I, 287.
69. Catherine the Great to Joseph, 23 May 1784, Arneth, *Joseph II. und Katharina*, p. 231. The name of the Count has been transliterated in many different ways – 'Romanzow', 'Romantzoff', 'Roumantsiev' and so on. I have preferred the version used by Isabel de Madariaga in her *Russia in the age of Catherine the Great.*
70. Joseph to Kaunitz, 4 July 1784, Joseph to Mercy, 29 October 1784, Joseph to his brother Leopold, 31 October 1784, Beer, p. 180; Arneth and Flammermont, p. 321; Arneth, *Joseph II. und Leopold*, I, 228.
71. Joseph to Marie Antoinette, 19 November 1784, Arneth, *Marie Antoinette, Joseph II. und Leopold II.*, p. 47. On the despatch sent *en clair*, see Arneth and Flammermont I, p. 306.
72. Bernard, *Joseph II and Bavaria*, p. 184.
73. Arneth and Flammermont I, p. 365 n. 2.
74. Tratchevsky, *La France et l'Allemagne*, I, 70–2, II, 51ff.
75. Joseph to Leopold, 13 January 1785, Arneth, *Joseph II. und Leopold*, I, 261.
76. Joseph to Mercy, 18 January 1785, Arneth and Flammermont, I, 375.
77. This paragraph is based on Haug-Moritz, *Württembergischer Ständekonflikt und deutscher Dualismus,* especially ch. II, pt. 1, pp. 135–71. This remarkable monograph, which began life as a dissertation supervised by Volker Press, is one of the most original contributions to the political history of the Holy Roman Empire in the eighteenth century to be published in recent years.
78. Ibid., pp. 288–93; Beales *Joseph II*, ch. 5.
79. Haug-Moritz, *Württembergischer Ständekonflikt*, pp. 294–6.
80. Aretin, *Heiliges Römisches Reich*, I, 13.
81. Joseph to Catherine the Great, 6 March 1781, Arneth, *Joseph II. und Katharina*, p. 54; Breteuil to Vergennes, 26 May 1779, quoted in Mitrofanov, *Joseph II.*, I, 131, n. 1; Handbillets, vol. 7 (27), no 758, Joseph to Prince Khevenhüller, 7 October 1783, fo. 688; ibid., vol. 9 (36), no. 168, to Prince Albert of Saxony, 21 February 1785, fo. 174.
82. Ibid., vol. 10 (40), no. 299, Joseph to Trauttmansdorff at Mainz, 14 April 1786, fo. 212. 'The women' refer to the Elector of Mainz's well-known penchant for female company.
83. Max Braubach, *Maria Theresias jüngster Sohn. Max Franz, Letzter Kurfürst von Köln und Fürstbischof von Münster* (Vienna and Munich, 1961), pp. 51–64. Max Franz succeeded in 1784.
84. Ranke, *Die deutschen Mächte und der Fürstenbund*, I, 94–5.

85. Aretin, *Heiliges Römisches Reich*, I, 15–16.
86. Ibid, p. 16.
87. See above, pp. 94–5.
88. See above, pp. 7–9.
89. Aretin, *Heiliges Römisches Reich*, I, 54, 155.
90. For the dates on which the various princes joined, see Alfred Kohler, 'Das Reich im Spannungsfeld des preußisch-österreichischen Gegensatzes. Die Fürstenbundbestrebungen 1783–1785', in Friedrich Engel-Janosi, Grete Klingenstein and Heinrich Lutz (eds), *Fürst, Bürger, Mensch* (Vienna, 1975), p. 92.
91. T.C.W. Blanning, *Reform and revolution in Mainz 1743–1803* (Cambridge, 1974), ch. 6, *passim*.
92. Blanning, '"That horrid electorate" or *"Ma patrie germanique"?'*, pp. 332–3.
93. Aretin, *Heiliges Römisches Reich*, I, 202.
94. Handbillets, vol. 9 (36), no. 73, Joseph to Cobenzl, 22 January 1785, fo. 67.
95. Ibid., no. 626, Joseph to Cobenzl, 26 July 1785, fo. 566.
96. Ibid., no. 812, Joseph to Cobenzl, 30 September 1785, fo. 763.
97. Ibid., vol. 10 (40) no. 954, 'Réflexions sur les avantages d'une alliance entre les maisons d'Autriche et de Brandebourg. ce 6 xbre 1786. envoyées au P. Kaunitz', fos 747–9 This document is summarised in Ranke, *Die deutschen Mächte und der Fürstenbund*, I, 297–9.
98. Handbillets, vol. 11 (45), no. 969, Joseph to Prince Reuss, 8 December 1786, fo. 761 and vol. 11 (45), no. 2, Joseph to Mercy, 2 January 1787, fo. 1.
99. Ranke, *Die deutschen Mächte und der Fürstenbund*, I, 300–2.
100. Handbillets, vol. 9 (36), no. 73, Joseph to Cobenzl, 22 January 1785, fo. 67.
101. Aretin, *Heiliges Römisches Reich*, I, 24.
102. As will be clear from this paragraph and other comments in this book, I disgree with the central tenet of Aretin's *Heiliges Römisches Reich* – that the Holy Roman Empire was doomed to collapse because it was not a state.
103. Joseph to Kaunitz, Cherson, 25 May 1787, Arneth, *Joseph II und Katharina*, p. 292 n.; Beer, p. 261.
104. Handbillets, vol. 11 (45), no. 681, Joseph to Cobenzl, 30 August 1787, fo. 610; Joseph to Leopold, 30 August 1787; Arneth, *Joseph II. und Leopold*, II, 115.
105. Quoted in Hellmuth Rössler, *Graf Johann Philipp Stadion. Napoleons deutscher Gegenspieler*, 2 vols (Vienna and Munich, 1966), I, 137. Kaunitz clearly believed the time was ripe to settle accounts with the Turks once and for all: 'provided that the

bombs must go off sooner or later, it appears that the present political situation in which they have exploded, is more favourable than unfavourable' – quoted in Karl A. Roider, 'Kaunitz, Joseph II and the Turkish war', *Slavonic and East European Review*, 54, 4, (1976), 544.

106. See above, pp. 116–19 and below, pp. 171–5.

Chapter 6

JOSEPH II AND THE CRISIS OF THE HABSBURG MONARCHY

·   ·   ·

CENSORSHIP

> Criticisms, if they are not slanderous, are not to be prohib-
> ited, no matter who their targets might be, whether the
> humblest or the highest, including the sovereign, especially
> if the author appends his name as a guarantee of validity, for
> every lover of truth must rejoice to be told the truth, even if it
> is conveyed to him via the uncomfortable route of criticism.[1]

This is the unmistakable voice of Joseph II – direct, crisp,
uncompromising and egalitarian. On this occasion he was
introducing new censorship regulations in 1781 – and they
caused a sensation throughout the German-speaking world.
Although *de facto* freedom of expression was common in the
Holy Roman Empire, thanks to its political fragmentation and
cultural pluralism, never before had a ruler announced in
public that his subjects could write what they liked about what
they liked.

Or could they? Many contemporaries, deluded by Joseph's
libertarian tone, chose to believe that censorship had simply
been abolished in the Habsburg Monarchy. As events soon
demonstrated, they had mistaken his purpose. He was not
concerned with encouraging intellectual activity *per se* but with
the promotion of the interests of his state. The liberation of the
literate from the last vestiges of clerical control, he believed,
would allow them to contribute more effectively to the public

good by propagating enlightenment. Freedom to do good, not anarchic self-indulgence, was his objective. So there were still censors, and there were still prohibitions, although far fewer than in the past: perfect freedom was available only to those who sought it in the service of the state. Significantly, censorship for the clergy actually became more rigorous, for now all religious publications – even the shortest prayers – were subject to approval by the secular authorities. Complaints from Cardinal Migazzi, the archbishop of Vienna, about the disregard of episcopal rights which the new arrangements entailed were not even favoured by a reply.[2]

The new system was thus a characteristically Josephist mixture of liberalism and autocracy. On the one hand, Joseph intervened personally to permit the publication of some works his censors sought to ban, such as Eybel's notorious pamphlet *What is the Pope?* or Goethe's best-selling novel *The Sufferings of Young Werther*.[3] On occasions, he used these interventions to make ideological points. In 1783, for example, an abusive pamphlet was nailed to the new Calvinist church, situated in a recently secularised convent. Part of its contents ran as follows: 'This temple was established long ago by the pious rulers of Austria and was the dwelling-place of godly virgins. But now its sacred treasures have been plundered by Martin Luther's faithful disciple and successor Joseph II, that notorious iconoclast'. Joseph had the offending document reprinted at his own expense, sold at six kreuzers a copy – and the proceeds sent to the Protestant community.[4] As this episode suggests, he was particularly indulgent to personal attacks on himself:

> If anyone should be so shamelessly impertinent as to attack us with frivolous and arrogant slanders, or should seek to denigrate our policies, then such impropriety should be countered not by punishment but by disdain. If the slanders derive from arrogance, the author deserves contempt; if they derive from mental deficiency, he deserves pity; and if simple ill-will is the cause – then we forgive the idiot.[5]

On the other hand, Joseph also took executive action to stop the publication of works he deemed offensive. Pornography was still proscribed (especially when his sister Marie Antoinette featured in the erotic fantasies, which was often), as was radical anti-clericalism, including the complete works of Voltaire in translation.[6] When the newspapers published 'all sorts of non-sense' about Horja's revolt in Transylvania, he was quick to impose silence – and to fine those who broke it.[7] In the following year – 1785 – he stopped a planned performance of Beaumarchais' *The Marriage of Figaro* because it contained 'much that is offensive', only letting through the opera of the same name when assured by the librettist Lorenzo Da Ponte that the text had been sanitised and that Mozart's music was wonderful.[8]

When problems began to accumulate in the second half of the decade, Joseph's interventions became more severe and more general. Until then the prevailing atmosphere was undeniably permissive. The clearest evidence was the sudden and massive increase in publishing unleashed by the new regulations of 1781. Between April 1781 and September 1782 no fewer than 1,172 pamphlets appeared in Vienna, not counting reprints of foreign publications.[9] This was the '*Broschürenflut*' – the 'pamphlet-flood' – which swept Vienna from book-trade backwater to mainstream status in just a few months. Pamphlets appeared about every conceivable subject, political, social, cultural and especially religious, as anyone with a bee in his bonnet hurried to let it buzz in public. As the more controversial provoked replies and then counter-replies, a real public debate on the great and not-so-great issues of the day was opened up.

.   .   .

THE PUBLIC SPHERE

It was just at this time, indeed, that the very concept of 'the public' was becoming established. Throughout Europe, access to the printed word had increased appreciably in the eighteenth century, as part of a wider process of modernisation involving higher rates of literacy, greater prosperity, improved communications, urbanisation and secularisation. As a result, a 'literary market' had formed, both creating and responding to a growing demand for publications of every kind. For the first time, it became possible for fortunes to be made from books – and by writers as well as publishers, as the dazzling careers of Alexander Pope and Voltaire demonstrated. It was a development which exemplified a more general shift from a culture which was 'representational' to a culture which was public, in other words from a culture serving the prince, the aristocracy or the Church to a culture which served the anonymous public. If the essence of the former was a passive relationship between the person, institution or value being represented and those observing (as at a coronation, for example), then the latter was distinguished by an interaction between creator and audience which can be termed 'critical'.[10]

The development of the periodical press (very much an eighteenth-century phenomenon) and the topical pamphlet helped to create a 'public sphere' in which private citizens could apply their rational, critical faculties to the great issues of the day. Only in such odd polities as Great Britain or the free imperial cities of the Holy Roman Empire could they do so in a political forum, but everywhere they found institutional modes of expression in voluntary associations (also very much an eighteenth-century phenomenon). The most ubiquitous and important of the latter were the lodges of Freemasonry which spread like wild-fire across the entire continent in the course of the century. The first lodge in Vienna was founded in 1742, under the patronage of the prince-bishop of Breslau and the secret protection of Maria Theresa's husband Francis Stephen, himself a mason since 1731.[11] Although condemned by the Pope and discouraged by the Empress, Freemasonry flourished in the Habsburg Monarchy. By 1780 there were thirteen lodges operating in the capital with a combined membership of about 700.[12]

In other words, the 'pamphlet-flood' unleashed by Joseph's relaxation of censorship and the popularity of Freemasonry showed that by the mid-1780s a public sphere had formed independent of the state. That this was a relatively recent development is shown by the rather self-conscious way in which contemporary writers used the concept, as in the pamphlet given the epigraph 'To the public outside Austria', whose author began his preface with the words: 'It has now become the custom to begin publicly with a compliment for the public'.[13] Joseph himself often used the term, as when he told Count Cavriani in 1786 that he had been considering ways of making the theatre at Brünn more satisfactory for 'the public'.[14] However he emphatically did not share the kind of enthusiasm for it which some contemporary writers such as Schiller ('the public is my preoccupation, my sovereign and my friend') liked to parade. On the contrary, he made no secret of his profound contempt for the public and its tastes, as in his well-publicised reply to a protest from the archbishop of Trier:[15] 'The relaxation of censorship in Vienna seems to make you uneasy. I would feel just the same if I did not know people well enough to be sure that there are few who read, even fewer who understand what they read and very few who derive any benefit from or can remember what they have read'. And he could not resist the temptation to add the following gratuitous insult to the already sorely-tried prelate: 'I even know some people who do not know what they are writing'.[16]

Not surprisingly, therefore, Joseph observed the burgeoning public sphere in the Habsburg Monarchy with deep mistrust. At the end of 1785 he moved to bring Freemasonry under his control: 'I know nothing about the secrets of the so-called Freemasonry societies, and have never experienced any curiosity about their mumbo-jumbo, but they are now multiplying and spreading to all towns, even the smallest, and to all regiments too'. Although aware that they had done a good deal for charitable causes, especially poor-relief and education, Joseph believed that if they were left to their own devices, they could become prejudicial to 'religion, public order and morality'. He proposed therefore to place them under the care and protection of the state. In future, only one lodge could be formed in each provincial capital or army corps. If one lodge proved inadequate, up to two branches could be added, but no more – any private masonic initiative was strictly prohibited. The police were to be kept informed about the time and place of meetings and membership rolls were to be updated each quarter.[17]

There is more than a whiff of totalitarianism about this revealing instruction, which was sent to his four most senior ministers. It is clear that Joseph just could not bear the thought of anything happening outside the control of the state, especially not in secret societies: 'because any association which is socially disparate cannot be left to its own devices but must be placed under the direction and supervision of men of experience'.[18] Not surprisingly, this determination to place the Freemasons (and the public sphere in general) under the tutelage of the state caused resentment. Shortly after his death, Count Rottenhahn wrote candidly to Leopold II: 'The late Emperor, who – if I may be so bold – did not know much about human nature, believed that his sarcastic letter [of December 1785] had destroyed the whole masonic movement, but in reality all he had achieved was to make himself hated by the great mass of intellectuals who were members of the Order'.[19] This unpopularity was not confined to masons. As his earliest biographer recorded, Joseph's equation of intellectual activity with any common trade and, more specifically, his contemptuous comparison of the book-trade with the cheese-trade had alienated those who should have been his most loyal allies.[20]

. . .

ABSOLUTISM AND ENLIGHTENMENT

Remarks such as these have prompted some historians to postulate a necessary contradiction between Joseph's absolutism and the enlightenment of his educated subjects. Although finding overt expression in the political clash between autocracy and liberalism, they argue, this contradiction derived most fundamentally from a social clash between a state which was essentially feudal and an opposition which was essentially bourgeois. According to this scenario, Joseph released the brakes on public opinion in 1781 but became increasingly alarmed as it began to veer off to the left from the narrow road he had marked out for it. Growing in confidence and ambition with every stride, public opinion took hold of the bit so firmly that all attempts to rein it in were in vain. Or, to employ another metaphor of motion, Joseph was 'overtaken' by an increasing number of his subjects no longer content with the passive role he had allocated to them.

It is undeniably correct that a number of intellectuals believed that Joseph's reforms did not go far enough and wished to proceed to a liberal, constitutional state. What is much less certain is just how many of them there were and what sort of threat they posed to the regime. Once all the necessary qualifications have been logged, the problem recedes to vanishing-point. The first that needs to be made is perhaps the most important: this was not a social confrontation between an aristocratic old regime and a bourgeois opposition. On the one hand, no one could have been less 'aristocratic' than Joseph II, whose egalitarianism put him at loggerheads with the nobility;[21] on the other hand, the public sphere which formed in

Vienna (and elsewhere in the Habsburg Monarchy) lacked any single social identity, drawing its members from all three estates, with nobles, army officers and clergymen all heavily represented.

This heterogeneity can be seen most clearly in the composition of the masonic lodges, the subject of a recent detailed statistical survey. Of the 700-odd members of the Viennese lodges between 1780 and 1785, no fewer than 42 per cent were nobles, with 14 per cent coming from the high nobility. The largest occupational groups were provided by army officers and civil servants, with about 22 per cent each. Trade and industry were conspicuously under-represented with just 8 per cent.[22] Whatever else it may have been, the masonic culture of Vienna was patently not 'bourgeois'. The same applies to writers. A contemporary survey revealed 226 authors active in the capital in the mid 1780s, of whom 61 (27 per cent) were nobles, 125 (55 per cent) were in some form of state employment and 54 (24 per cent) were clergy (and 21 of these were former Jesuits).[23]

In other words, the enlightened culture which developed in the public sphere of the Habsburg Monarchy was the creation of an intelligentsia – ideologically united but mixed in terms of social origin. It is just what one would expect from a society at this stage of its development and the description of this process as 'the emergence of bourgeois culture'[24] can be sustained only by giving the word 'bourgeois' such elastic parameters as to render it meaningless. It leads to such absurdities as presenting as 'the chief protagonist of bourgeois culture in Austria' none other than Joseph Baron von Sonnenfels, a second-generation noble![25] This distortion arises from the necessity imposed by the Marxist-Leninist straitjacket of postulating a contradiction between the state and public sphere. In reality, the relationship was as close, as amicable – and as problematic – as one would expect between parent and child.

This leads one naturally to another qualification. The opposition to Joseph II which developed in the course of the 1780s has been both exaggerated and misunderstood. That many pamphlets critical of the regime were published is certain; that they were representative even of the intelligentsia, let alone the broad mass of the population, is highly questionable. In the first place, as the indignant native Viennese were quick to point out, many of the radical journalists were not native-born Austrians but were opportunists who had flocked in from all over

Germany to take advantage of the new censorship regulations. Georg Philipp Wucherer and Johann Jakob Fezer were from Swabia, Joseph Milbiller was from Bavaria, Franz Wilhelm von Meynern was from Erlangen, Joseph Friedrich von Keppler was from Stralsund, Johann Pezzl was from Bavaria (via Switzerland) and Paul Weidmann was from Würzburg – just to mention some of the more prominent immigrants.[26]

Secondly, for every publication criticising Joseph, there were many more which eulogised him. A pamphlet entitled *Why is Joseph II not loved by his people?*, published in 1787, for example, provoked a flurry of replies. None of them denied that some people had grumbled about some of the reforms but all denied emphatically that discontent was either general or serious: it was like saying that a child did not love its parents if it threw a tantrum whenever failing to receive everything it wanted, as one put it.[27] They pointed to the fact that everyone rushed to greet him whenever he rode out, that he was able to move around the city and suburbs without an escort, that his portrait could be found in practically every dwelling, that so many children were named after him, and so on.[28] Among his measures they singled out for special praise were freedom of the press, toleration, abolition of serfdom, and judicial reform. In other words, this was a defence of Joseph mounted not by conservative defenders of the *status quo* but by progressive supporters of his reform programme.[29]

Unlike some later historians, the enlightened intelligentsia could appreciate that the best chance of progress lay in an alliance with the enlightened state against the vested interests. They were encouraged in this belief, of course, by the fact that so many of them were employed by the state. This was especially true in Bohemia and Hungary, where – it has been argued – the intelligentsia was largely Joseph II's creation.[30] One needs to look beyond the rhetoric employed by opponents of the regime to what was actually demanded. The Magyar gentry of Hungary, for example, used the terminology of the French enlightenment to justify their opposition but, as Peter Sugar has shown, 'the concept owed nothing to Rousseau but its name. It was limited only to the rights of the nobility and served as a slogan for these gentlemen in their fight for their own particularistic interests'. In the same way, the same bourgeois who should have been Joseph's class enemies (according to the Marxist script, at least) appreciated that 'only a strong king, like Joseph II, could win for them their battle with the nobility. So the burghers, like the nobles, adapted French ideas to their own aims and used them to demand not only the abolition of the nobility but also a return to absolute monarchy'.[31] All over the Habsburg Monarchy there were many intellectuals who were affronted by Joseph's many sins of commission and omission, but they were able to see past the venial blemishes to the essence of his programme and thus to realise that he and his state represented the best – the only – way forward. As we shall see later, the situation was quite different from that which prevailed in contemporary France.

Joseph's own alienation from the process of liberalisation he had initiated had several sources. One was certainly a feeling that some of the radical pamphleteers had gone too far, especially in their attacks on religion – for example, the anonymous assailant of clerical celibacy who blamed it for the priesthood's notorious addiction to onanism, sodomy and fornication.[32] And Joseph certainly did take steps to protect the Church. More potent, however, was his deep disillusionment with the quality of the publications which his relaxation of censorship had unleashed, a feeling which was shared by his senior ministers.[33] Anyone who has worked through the flotsam and jetsam washed in by the 'pamphlet-flood' of the 1780s can only sympathise. More specifically, these feeble but strident effusions brought it home to him just how profoundly conservative were the subjects he was trying to enlighten. Their rejection of his attempts to improve public hygiene by persuading them to bury their dead in linen sacks, and to accelerate decomposition with quick-lime, seems to have been a crucial moment which prompted him to throw up his hands in despair.[34]

More potent still was the realisation that the liberty of the press was not being used to propagate enlightenment, as he had hoped, but rather to incite *conservative* resistance to his reforms. As so often before and since, it was the reactionaries which proved the more adept at exploiting the written word, not least because their arguments struck a much more responsive chord than those of their progressive opponents. It is worth recalling what historians with a teleological vision of social change are inclined to forget: the public sphere was a neutral vessel, as receptive to effusions from the right as from the left. What worried Joseph most were not the marginal rantings of radical atheists, who represented few apart from themselves, but the attacks instigated by dissident nobles who were quick to take advantage of the new media.[35] It was they – and they alone – who had the social muscle to generate real problems for his state.

Joseph's relationship with Freemasonry was also more problematic than appears at first sight. On the one hand, the movement was far from being in opposition to the regime – how could it be when so many of its members were high-ranking ministers and the Grand Master of the Austrian National Lodge, Prince Josef Dietrichstein, was a close friend of the Emperor? The oath of initiation stressed that 'nothing is undertaken against state, sovereign, religion and public decency'.[36] Moreover, although masonry had a Deist tinge, it was not thought to be incompatible with Roman Catholicism. Many clergymen were members, including two successive abbots of Melk, whose masonic aprons were buried with them.[37] In any case, it would be a great mistake to think of Freemasonry as an unequivocally rationalist and progressive movement. A large part of its allure lay in the arcane ritual which was such a prominent feature of its assemblies. Many historians now like to draw a distinction between 'enlightened' Freemasonry and 'superstitious' Rosicrucianism, but the distinction was not at all clear to the many who joined both.[38] It was certainly not clear to Joseph II, who lumped the two together, describing King Frederick William II of Prussia, who in fact was a Rosicrucian of a particularly credulous kind, as a member of the *Illuminati*, who were definitely at the progressive end of the masonic spectrum.[39] Indeed, it is entirely possible that, far from being a defensive reaction against an organisation that was becoming too radical, Joseph's move to control Freemasonry in 1785 was designed to guard it against further infiltration by sects of the Rosicrucian variety.[40]

In short, there was no threat to the stability of Joseph's regime from the educated elites, however much they may have grumbled about this or that. It was not until the decade or so before 1848 – the *Vormärz* period – that alienation between state and intelligentsia in the Habsburg Monarchy became so intense as to create a revolutionary potential. The great danger in the 1780s came from the opposite direction, from the conservative vested interests whose ascendancy was threatened by Joseph's levelling reforms. In 1787, they got their chance to move from passive to active resistance when the outbreak of war sent most of the armed forces to the Balkans to meet the Turkish threat. Within less than three years, Joseph's reform programme was shipwrecked and the very existence of the Habsburg Monarchy placed in jeopardy.

. . .

BELGIUM

Joseph's relations with his subjects in the Austrian Netherlands had always been unfortunate. His only visit, in 1781, had been marked by mutual incomprehension; his clumsy attempt to open the Scheldt, in 1784–5, had ended in failure, convincing Joseph that the Belgians were not worth helping and the Belgians that Joseph was incompetent; his simultaneous bid to use the province as a bargaining-counter in the equally ill-fated Bavarian exchange project completed the process of alienation.[41] However, it was his radical reform programme which took the Belgians from hostility to revolt. The announcement on 1 January 1787 of a fundamental change in the political, administrative and judicial structure led, first to protests and then to a tax-strike by the Estates of Brabant, the most important of the Belgian provinces.[42]

The governors-general – Joseph's sister, the archduchess Marie Christine, and her husband, Duke Albert of Saxony-Teschen – were in a most unenviable position, lacking adequate means of coercion but only too familiar with their employer's inflexibility. It was the immediate rather than the distant threat which proved the more compelling, so in April and May 1787 they made a series of concessions which left precious little of the reform programme intact. Joseph was in the Crimea with Catherine the Great[43] when the news of this débâcle eventually reached him. When he realised the extent of the concessions made, he was incandescent with rage ('in all my life I have never felt such justifiable indignation', he told Kaunitz), firing off intemperate letters in all directions, recalling the governors-general and the chief minister (Count Belgioioso) to Vienna, summoning a deputation from the various Belgian Estates, ordering the despatch of extra troops, and promising 'cost what it may, to use my last soldier and my last shilling in reconquering these provinces, if it proves necessary'.[44]

If Joseph had been able to swamp Belgium with soldiers – and he was sharp enough to realise that it was German-speakers who were needed[45] – he might have been able to make his reforms stick long enough for his ungrateful subjects to appreciate their very real potential benefits. (The validity of this hypothesis was demonstrated during the long French occupation from 1792 until 1814, especially under Napoleon.) But Joseph could not; it was just at this time that the Turkish war had to take priority. Consequently, all his vindictive rhetoric could be ignored by its targets with impunity. In September 1787 the commander-in-chief, General Murray, who was running the province in the continuing absence of the disgraced governors-general, was obliged to concede the final abrogation of the January edicts. He was promptly dismissed and a new team consisting of General d'Alton, as commander-in-chief, and Ferdinand Count Trauttmansdorff, as chief minister, was despatched.

There is no need to follow the course of the next two years in any detail.[46] The government tried to claw back the concessions of 1787 with the same tenacity as the Estates resisted any encroachment on the *status quo*. Another tax strike in November 1788 by the Estates of Brabant and Hainaut was countered by Joseph's declaration that he regarded their privileges as abolished, their constitutions null and void and their people outlaws. Inflamed by another singularly ill-timed burst of reforms in the spring and early summer of 1789, and encouraged by the revolutionary examples set by adjacent France and Liège, the dissidents took up arms. After a false start in October 1789, they returned in November, quickly expelled the remaining Austrian soldiers and took possession of all provinces except Luxemburg by the end of the year. On 11 January 1790 the combined Estates proclaimed the independence of the 'United States of Belgium'. This dreadful news was brought to poor Joseph as he lay on his death-bed.

It was all the more galling for being unexpected. For someone so prone to misanthropy, Joseph was always remarkably optimistic about prospects for success in Belgium. In the autumn of 1786, just before he began his major reforms, he told Belgioioso that he was certain of success: 'I believe that the most sensible section of the public will be pleased with what I propose, especially when the judicial reforms are added'.[47] Not all the reports from his various luckless agents on the ground could persuade him otherwise; he was convinced that their dire predictions of disaster were alarmist, designed to provide an alibi for their own shortcomings. As darkness deepened in the summer of 1789, he was still whistling vigorously, not only to keep his spirits up but also because he really still believed that everything would turn out alright in the end. He breezily told General d'Alton in August that his agents' reports of insurrection were just the 'tittle-tattle of drunks and braggarts'.[48] There was no danger that the plans for an armed rising would succeed, he opined, because the rebels were divided among themselves, had no leaders, no money, no prospects of subverting the Austrian forces and no support from abroad.[49] Just as the rebels were giving the lie to those predictions, he told d'Alton that 'provided that we can gain some time, that we hold firm and that we hit back hard at the first opportunity, I believe that we can still avoid a major disaster'.[50]

This fatal optimism was not the result of ignorance. There were plenty of well-informed observers, in both Vienna and Brussels, to tell him about the true state of affairs. Rather it was Joseph's inability to listen – *he knew better*. Not only had he been to Belgium to see for himself, he had worked out his reform programme rationally from first principles and so it was obviously, demonstratively, absolutely right. Only a fool or a knave could fail to appreciate that. Alas, by this token it turned out that his Belgian provinces were populated almost entirely with fools and knaves, but Joseph could never bring himself to admit that. Certainly he often expressed his contempt and loathing for the 'fanatics' and their 'ignorance and stupidity', especially the Flemish-speakers among them who were notoriously 'narrow-minded...obstinate...lunatics...idiots'.[51] On the other hand, he constantly deluded himself that they were just sheep, more sinned against than sinning. As he told Count Trauttmansdorff in the autumn of 1787, after the first burst of agitation had died down: 'I have never taken for a movement of the whole people what was really nothing more than a premeditated conspiracy by a few individuals'.[52] This self-delusion remained with him until the end: in a long review of the events in Belgium, written in late November 1789, he was still telling himself that it had not been his fault – the mass of the people would not have reacted against his reforms if their evil leaders had not sought to defend their own selfish vested interests by pretending that everyone's property and religion were at risk.[53]

In that same document he pointed his finger at those he believed to be the real culprits – the so-called agents of his will, who had let him down so badly by their feeble irresolution. There was something in this. The governors-general do seem to have panicked at a crucial moment in May 1787; the civilian and military authorities did argue among themselves; and Joseph was indeed right to suspect that his sister maintained a secret correspondence highly critical of his policies with his brother and heir, Leopold of Tuscany.[54] On the other hand, Joseph had no understanding of, or sympathy for, the difficulties they all faced in trying to impose policies which contravened custom and constitution and which were rejected vehemently by the great majority of local people. The most distressing aspect of his policy towards Belgium was his constant call for severity. Again and again he called for tougher action: 'there's no need to be afraid of setting an example of terror', he told d'Alton, 'and you should never threaten without acting, and still less should you shoot over their heads or fire blanks'.[55]

Whatever the morality of such advice, it was correct from a prudential point of view only if there were enough soldiers to make it work. There never were. When Joseph eventually decided – at one minute *past* midnight – to substitute pacification for coercion, he did so on the grounds that no troops could be spared from the other fronts of the beleaguered Habsburg Monarchy.[56] The armed forces of all branches in Belgium never amounted to more than 18,000 during the crisis, a pitifully inadequate number to deal with more than two-and-a-quarter million disaffected subjects. Moreover, many of these troops were native-born Belgians, understandably reluctant to exert themselves against their fellow-countrymen and correspondingly prone to resignation and desertion. Despite Joseph's pre-emptive strike in late July 1789, when he raised the pay of NCOs and privates by one kreuzer a day, this demoralised force proved easy meat for the insurgents when the fighting began in earnest.[57]

The loss of the Belgian provinces was seen as an unmitigated disaster by Joseph – and rightly so. It provided the most crushing illustration imaginable of his personal and political limitations. Contrary to what Joseph liked to believe, Belgium was no stagnant backwater but one of the most prosperous, dynamic and advanced parts of Europe. It was just because its people had an accurate assessment of their achievements and prospects that they resented Joseph's reforming intrusion – in just the same way that they then rejected their own radicals and, even more emphatically, the French revolutionaries in the 1790s.[58] In view of most historians' predilection for linking conservatism to social, economic and cultural backwardness, Joseph might reasonably be forgiven for that failure of understanding, but there was no excuse for his wilful rejection of the much sound advice on offer. When Kaunitz counselled caution, at the very start of the crisis, Joseph called it 'cowardice'. In a letter bordering on the hysterical, written from the Crimea in June 1787, he told his chancellor that not even the angel of death could make him sign a document granting concessions to the Belgian rebels: 'You will send this humiliating document back to the governors torn-up, as it deserves to be, just to show what I think about this business. And anyone who dares to speak to me in this tone of voice is the friend of neither Joseph nor the Emperor'. His familiar hyper-sensitive response to anything which seemed to impugn either his dignity or that of the state was also given an airing: 'There are occasions when one must listen only to what one's courage tells one to do, and this is one of them; if I soften, then I shall lose for the rest of my life the respect due to my person and to my state'.[59]

What Joseph certainly should have foreseen was the sharp deterioration in the international situation. With the three great continental powers either preoccupied with war (the Habsburg Monarchy and Russia) or immobilised by bankruptcy and incipent revolution (France), the way was clear for the Prussians to start fishing in troubled waters, especially as they now enjoyed the support of the only great maritime power remaining: Great Britain. The brilliantly successful invasion of the Dutch Republic in the autumn of 1787 gave the new king, Frederick William II, the opportunity to give the law to Europe and the confidence to seize it.[60] By provoking the Belgian revolt, Joseph played straight into Prussian hands. His only hope of escape was to bring the Turkish war to a quick and victorious conclusion.

. . .

THE WAR AGAINST THE TURKS

Joseph knew that only too well. As he told the Prince de Ligne, whom he sent to Russia to serve as liaison officer in the autumn of 1787, the objectives of the allies had to be secured by two campaigns at the most.[61] On the face of it, this should not have been too challenging an assignment. The reforms of the previous two decades put at Joseph's disposal the largest, best-trained and best-equipped army the Monarchy had ever boasted. For their part, the Russians had defeated the Turks so often and so easily in the war of 1768–74 that it was reasonable to assume that they could do it again.

By the time the Turkish declaration of war of 17 August 1787 reached Vienna, the season was so advanced that there was no question of beginning a campaign that year. So although he recognised the *casus fœderis* at once, Joseph decided not to declare war formally until the following spring. In the meantime, however, he planned a bold pre-emptive strike – a surprise night-attack on the great Turkish fortress of Belgrade, in both symbolic and military terms the key to the Balkans. If this enterprising venture had succeeded, the course of the war – and much else besides – would have been very different, but it was frustrated by the untimely descent of a thick fog which prevented the commandos arriving at their rendezvous on time (or so Joseph claimed).[62]

When the war proper opened in the spring of 1788 the strategic position of the Austrian army had deteriorated, thanks to events on the Russian front. The mobilisation of the Russian army, always a lengthy and haphazard business, was going badly, seriously impeded by the poor harvest of 1787 and the unusually severe winter which followed. The immobilisation of the Black Sea fleet by a terrible storm in October put the Russian commander-in-chief, Prince Potemkin (who lacked self-confidence anywhere outside the bedroom), firmly on the defensive. Defeatist enough to consider evacuating the Crimea, he had no intention of sending an army to the Danube to help his Austrian allies. Any chance that the Baltic fleet might be sent round via the Mediterranean, as in 1769, was scuttled by a British refusal to cooperate and intelligence reports that the mercurial Gustavus III of Sweden was planning an invasion of Russia through Finland.[63]

In other words, for the foreseeable future Joseph was on his own. No sooner had he arrived at the front, in March 1788, to take over personal command of the operations, than he began what became a tediously repetitive threnody about inadequate support from his ally, for example: 'it is simply intolerable that the Russians should remain inactive for so long, and thus bring down on my head the entire Turkish army'.[64] He therefore felt obliged to devise a defensive strategy, holding the line against the Turks until his ally was ready for a joint offensive. He placed his main army, commanded by himself with the assistance of Field Marshal Lacy, on the Danube between Peterwardein (now called Petrovaradin, opposite Novi Sad) and Semlin (Zemun, opposite Belgrade). This was flanked by two army corps to the west, one in Croatia in the region of Dubica and the other in Slavonia along the river Sava, and by three army corps to the east, one in the Banat of Temesvár (Timişoara), another in Transylvania and another in south-eastern Galicia. Together they comprised ninety-four battalions of infantry and sixty-three divisions of cavalry – approximately 245,000 men, 37,000 horses and 800 pieces of artillery.[65] Joseph also hoped to create a diversion behind the Turkish lines by inciting the Christians of Montenegro and bribing the Pasha of Scutari (now Shkodër in northern Albania) with the promise of large grants of land if Bosnia were conquered.[66]

What then followed was a classic illustration of Clausewitz's concept of 'friction' (known in the Anglo-Saxon world more colloquially as 'Murphy's law'), as almost everything that could go wrong did go wrong. Supplies of food and forage were inadequate from the very start, due to poor roads made worse by bad weather, the after-effects of the harvest-failure of 1787 and the ill-will of the Magyar gentry who controlled the army's hinterland.[67] As the latters' disaffection grew with the approach of the tax reform,[68] so did their enthusiasm for sabotaging the war-effort. By the autumn of 1789 Joseph was having to consider detaching units from the field army to extract supplies from the reluctant Hungarians by force.[69]

Another familiar creeping problem was illness, in every premodern war a more formidable foe than the human enemy and nowhere more so than in the malaria-ridden Balkans. In July 1788 Joseph reported that the number of sick was rather high but not yet dangerous, and that no one had actually died yet, but by the following month an epidemic afflicting the army corps in Slavonia required the construction of a new field-hospital.[70] From then the toll mounted relentlessly. Although casualties inflicted by the Turks were always light, it has been estimated by the official historian of the war that between June 1788 and May 1789 172,000 soldiers fell ill, of whom some 33,000 died.[71]

Filling the gaps in the ranks proved difficult, especially as the rate of desertion was 'very annoying', as Joseph put it in August 1788.[72] Several thousand Serbs fleeing from Turkish atrocities were incorporated in 'free corps' of irregulars and sent back to exact revenge, but the usual obstruction by the Hungarian local authorities prevented the conscription of regulars.[73] As early as June 1788 Joseph was writing home calling for major reinforcements: twenty-seven battalions of infantry and three regiments of cavalry, together with the appropriate number of artillery, draught animals and equipment. All this was clearly going to be very expensive, he pointed out, especially as he had incurred already a great deal of extraordinary expenditure due to the raising of free corps, the care of 50,000 refugees, the construction of dams, bridges and fortifications and the purchase of ships for coastal operations. He instructed his ministers to put their heads together and devise a scheme for raising the money – and they were not to adopt the soft option of relying solely on more loans, because 'every patriot who wishes to enjoy protection, honour and advantage in the state must in these circumstances reach into his pocket for an extraordinary contribution'.[74] It was now that the folly of his alienation of the Belgians became apparent, for their money-market was the traditional and most productive source of war finance. At the end of the year he lamented that attempts to borrow money in Belgium (and the Dutch Republic) at 4 per cent had failed.[75]

Despite all the effort and expense, the campaign of 1788 never really got started. On 18 July Joseph wrote to General d'Alton: 'I have nothing to report from here, my dear general, except that we are waging a guerrilla war every day against the mosquitoes and that we all defend ourselves as best as we can against fever and diarrhoea, because as for the Turks – well, they seem to have forgotten us, and we shall do the same to them'.[76] This facetious complacency betrayed a dangerous ignorance of what was going on around him. He had already complained to Kaunitz about the impossibility of securing reliable intelligence, asking him rather pathetically to pass on any information which might come his way about Turkish troop movements.[77] With the plan to raise Montenegro proving an expensive failure – the Pasha of Scutari promptly executed the Austrian agents and sent their heads to the Turkish Grand Vizier at Sofia[78] – Joseph settled down to await events. He did not have to wait long. Allowed the opportunity to pick their spot in the Austrian defensive cordon, the Turks suddenly attacked, on 7 August, near Old Orsova on the Danube. They then put a bridge across the river at Kladovo and poured into the Banat of Temesvár, devastating it as only they knew how. Caught flat-footed, Joseph moved east from Semlin with a detachment of about 30,000 men to eject them. However, his tentative advance soon ground to a halt, quickly turning into a retreat, punctuated by a humiliating collapse of discipline during the night of 20-21 September when a brawl between hussars and infantry over the sale of brandy was mistaken for a Turkish attack and caused a panic.[79] Joseph was beside himself with anger, disappointment and grief, lamenting to Kaunitz that it was heart-breaking to see how fifty years of toil to make the Banat flourish had been destroyed in a few days. He estimated that at least half of the region had been ruined by Turkish looting and burning. What he felt, he added, when he considered the likely consequences and the contempt which would be heaped on him and his army, could be experienced but not described.[80]

As so often, his despair was overdone. The Turks soon withdrew from the Banat and hostilities virtually ceased for the year at the end of November, 1788, with both armies retiring into winter quarters. On balance, the campaign had not gone so badly. If the crucial prize of Belgrade remained in Turkish hands, Austrian armies had operated successfully in Croatia and Slavonia, where the important fortresses of Dubica and Novi had been captured. On the eastern front, both the Transylvanian and Galician corps had made forays deep into Moldavia and Wallachia, capturing Khotin on the upper Dniestr and Jassy (Iasi).[81] Moreover, although Joseph continued to rail against his Russian allies, there were signs that they would be able to play a more active part in the next campaign. The Swedish invasion in July 1788 had soon come to a halt, when the Finnish officers mutinied and the Danes opened up a second front. Indeed, only the diplomatic intervention of Prussia and Great Britain saved Gustavus III from total disaster. The armistice they mediated in September relieved, if it did not end, pressure on Catherine the Great in the north. Better news still came at the end of the year when at long last the Russians captured the great Turkish fortress of Ochakov, which controlled the estuary of the Dniepr and was the key to the Black Sea coast between the Bug and the Dniestr.[82]

If Joseph had had to worry only about the Turks, he might have viewed the next campaign with confidence. Alas, by this time the baleful effects of the Habsburg Monarchy's geopolitical situation were beginning to make themselves felt once again. Not surprisingly, it was from Prussia that the new threat came. A protracted struggle for influence at the anarchic court of Frederick William II had ended with the victory of Ewald Count von Hertzberg, who believed that the time was ripe for rounding off the first partition of Poland. He believed that Prussia could intervene diplomatically in the war in the east to secure peace by means of an interlocking series of exchanges. In return for an international guarantee of their remaining European possessions, the Turks would cede the principalities of Moldavia and Wallachia to the Habsburg Monarchy, which would return Galicia to Poland, which would cede their cities of Danzig and Thorn, plus surrounding territory, to Prussia.

Joseph had known all about the Hertzberg plan for some time and was determined never to accept it in any shape or form. Forgetting his brief flirtation with the idea of a *rapprochement* after the death of Frederick the Great in 1786,[83] he was now prepared to wage war '*à toute outrance*' rather than allow Prussia 'one single village'.[84] Joseph need not have worried; as neither the Turks nor the Poles were inclined to play the roles allocated to them in Hertzberg's complex scenario, there was no prospect of his scheme being put into practice. As that became clear, Frederick William II became more receptive to the forward policy being urged by the hawks at his court: with the war going badly for the Austrians and with discontent at home reaching crisis proportions, was this not the time to invade from the north and settle acounts with the old enemy once and for all? Prussian agents were already hard at work fomenting unrest in Belgium, Galicia and Hungary and sending back reports that the Habsburg Monarchy was on its last legs. From July 1788

Joseph knew that the Prussian envoy to Vienna, Baron Jacobi, was in contact with dissident nobles in Hungary.[85] The final collapse of France and the impending revolt in Belgium (about which the Prussians received advance warning) gave the green light: in August 1789 Frederick William II took the decision to invade the Habsburg Monarchy in the following spring.[86] He also authorised negotiations for offensive alliances with Turkey and Poland and the payment of a large subsidy to Gustavus III, put pressure on the British to send a fleet to the Baltic and ordered an intensification of the campaign of subversion inside the Habsburg Monarchy.[87]

In short, Joseph faced the prospect of a war on several different fronts – in the Balkans against the Turks, in the north-east against the Poles, in the north-west against the Prussians, in Italy against the Spanish and the Piedmontese, and in Belgium, Galicia and Hungary against his own subjects. No wonder that many contemporaries believed that the Habsburg Monarchy would share the fate of France. But rescue was at hand. The campaign of 1789 turned out to be one of the most glorious in the annals of Habsburg military history. Joseph's intention to return to the front in the spring was frustrated by what proved to be his terminal illness, so Field Marshal Hadick was placed in charge of the main army. Old and ill, he soon proved inadequate and was replaced on 28 July 1789 by Field Marshal Gideon von Laudon, a veteran of the Seven Years War with a reputation for being both aggressive and lucky – two qualities notoriously in short supply among the Austrian high command.[88]

The plan of campaign called for only the flanking armies to take the initiative, in Croatia and Wallachia respectively. The main army was to sit tight, lulling the Turks into a sense of false security. Only a Russian victory or the onset of autumn, when the Turks would begin to drift home, would be the signal for it to begin its main objective – the siege and capture of Belgrade.[89] The first success came on 8 July when Laudon's Croatian army captured the important fortress of Berbir (Bosanka Gradisca) on the Sava and advanced into Bosnia. Meanwhile the Russians were beginning to stir in the east and on 31 July a joint Austro-Russian force commanded by Prince Coburg and General Suvorov defeated a large Turkish army at Fokshani (Focşani) in Moldavia. At about the same time, the army corps under Prince Hohenlohe in Transylvania and the detachment of the main army under Clerfayt in the Banat began to advance. Victories now came thick and fast. On 16 September the bombardment of Belgrade began; on 21 September Coburg and Suvorov won another crushing victory in Moldavia at Martinesci on the river Rymnik, inflicting heavy casualties; on 30 September the assault on Belgrade began, leading to the capitulation of the Turkish garrison on 8 October; on the same day Hohenlohe defeated at Porceni what proved to be the last Turkish offensive on the Transylvanian front; on 11 October Semendria (Smederevo) surrendered to Laudon and the Turks also evacuated Passarowitz; and on 10 November Coburg captured Bucharest.[90]

Credit for this brilliant campaign belongs in part to Joseph. The fact that the military situation improved only after he had returned to Vienna tempts one to conclude that he alone had been responsible for the failures of the previous year. It is certainly the case that his strategy of forming a thin defensive cordon along his southern frontier invited the Turks to punch through it when and where they chose. It was only when commanders such as Coburg and Hohenlohe concentrated their forces and went on the offensive that the tide turned.[91] This was the gist of Kaunitz's criticisms, to which Joseph replied reasonably and cogently that it was easy to devise strategy sitting in an armchair in Vienna, that the Russian war-effort had been far weaker than anyone had anticipated, while that of the Turks had been far stronger.[92] He might also have added that the cordon strategy derived from his senior military adviser, Field Marshal Lacy. Joseph could certainly have claimed the credit for the siege of Belgrade, for Laudon had been reluctant to undertake such a risky operation until he received a direct order from Vienna to get started.[93] More generally, the training, discipline and infrastructure of the Austrian army eventually proved decisively superior to those of their enemy – and for that achievement Joseph's reforms of the past two decades were largely responsible. As death approached in the autumn of 1789 he was still very much in command of his armies and still showing his usual remarkable command of detail and dedication to duty.[94]

. . .

BACK FROM THE BRINK

The end of the 1780s was a difficult period for all European governments. A run of poor harvests and the disruption of relief supplies by the war in the Baltic created hardship and social unrest everywhere. In the Habsburg Monarchy, the additional abrasion caused by the unsuccessful campaign of 1788, the supplementary war taxes, increased conscription and the cumulative effect of Joseph's reforms gave cause for anxiety. Part of the crisis atmosphere which settled on the closing years of the reign was generated by the development of the police force. This dated back to 1782 when a reorganisation of the government of Lower Austria brought Johann Anton von Pergen to the fore as president of the province. Thanks to his ambition and enthusiasm for police matters, the scope of his powers increased both geographically and substantively. The climax came in March 1789 when Joseph's characteristic love of 'complete uniformity' prompted him to give Pergen responsibility for police matters in the entire Monarchy. Provincial governors were told to implement his instructions to the best of their ability.[95]

A more sinister development was Joseph's growing penchant for using his police in what can only be called a despotic manner to counter what he believed to be subversion. Indeed, one historian has alleged that 'Joseph allowed Pergen to introduce all the worst features of a police state into the Habsburg Monarchy'.[96] This is a patent exaggeration. Although the interception of mail, encouragement of informers and use of *agents provocateurs* were certainly as offensive to contemporaries as to posterity, the police were as much, if not more, concerned with social welfare as they were with law enforcement, while the 'political criminals' (*Staatsverbrecher*) taken into custody were few in number (seven) and by no means the innocent victims portrayed in some accounts.[97] It may be readily agreed that Joseph was capable of disturbing acts of cruelty, perhaps pathologically so, as when he personally condemned the mentally deranged Piarist priest Remigius Fravo to sixty years imprisonment for his plan to convert Frederick William II of Prussia to Catholicism and to place him on the Hungarian throne, or when he ordered his governor of Galicia to set 'a terrible example' to stifle a conspiracy there.[98] However, to speak of Joseph in the same terms applied to twentieth-century monsters, or even the French revolutionaries in their worst moments, is to debase the coinage of horror.

Joseph too overshot the target. In Belgium there was open revolt, in Hungary and Galicia there were preparations to follow suit, elsewhere in the Monarchy the nobility became increasingly restive as the date for the implementation of the dreaded tax decree drew near. But Vienna was relatively calm. In the late summer of 1788 there was an eruption of violence on the streets of Vienna, when bakers refused to sell bread at the prices dictated by the government.[99] Much has been made of this incident by historians seeking to show that the old regime was confronted by a progressive and popular movement, but this was no confrontation between people and authorities, but rather between the bakers and an *alliance* of people and authorities. It was Joseph who intervened to order that eleven bakers deemed guilty of profiteering be displayed in the stocks.[100] This may well have been a despotic use of executive privilege, but it did consolidate the government's reputation for prompt intervention in times of scarcity to maintain bread prices at affordable levels. In June of the following year, Joseph ordered immediate action to temper the worst effects of the harvest failure which threatened: all export of grain was prohibited and import dues were lifted; relief supplies were to be brought from Swabia via the Danube and from Poland via Galicia.[101] For this reason, that terrible paranoid belief in a *pacte de famine* which inflicted so much violence on revolutionary France was mercifully absent from the Habsburg Monarchy.

The major reason for the contrasting experiences of the two countries during this period, however, lay in the very different structures of their two capitals. Vienna was first and foremost a 'residential city' (*Residenzstadt*), a city whose *raison d'être* was the residence within its walls of the Habsburg Monarchy's court and government, the great ecclesiastical institutions and the town-houses of the nobility (or 'palaces', as they preferred to call them). Once the defeat of the last Turkish siege in 1683 had brought security, a great building boom transformed the city's appearance permanently, as any stroll through the old city inside the 'Ring' will confirm. By 1720 no fewer than 200 palaces of various kinds had been built in and around the city, doubling by 1740.[102] The conspicuous consumption of the

Habsburg court, the prelates, the magnates and the lesser nobility created an economy in their own image, a web of luxury trades and luxury-services which drew to Vienna the labour to serve them. As the most authoritative contemporary survey recorded: 'The great majority of the nobility in the city are courtiers or civil servants. Taken as a whole, the nobility owns great wealth and spends freely, which is a blessing for the working population, especially in a place like Vienna where there is a large number of manufacturers, artisans and other labourers'.[103]

Although the development of manufacturing industries in the suburbs pointed the way to the future, in the reign of Joseph II the capital was still very much wedded to the old order. The relationship between privileged orders and the working population was intimate, amicable and mutually beneficial – for once, that over-worked scientific metaphor 'symbiosis' really does apply. The resources drawn by the consumers from all over the Habsburg Monarchy brought a prosperity which impressed all foreign travellers. 'The number of poor is much smaller than at Paris, and, probably, than at London', wrote J.C. Riesbeck, 'Everything, even the clothing of the lowest servant-maid, bespeaks a great degree of affluence. The prodigality of the higher nobility, the many, and great appointments paid by the court, and the extensive commerce of the middling classes, greatly assists the circulation of money'.[104] Vienna was also lucky in being blessed with a fertile hinterland and the opportunity to draw supplies easily and quickly via the Danube from both Germany and Hungary. Even after six years of revolutionary warfare, Ernst Moritz Arndt could write in 1798: 'All the basic necessities of life are excellent here, available in superfluity, and cheap in the same degree. Rich Hungary sends oxen, pigs, grain, wine and flour in great quantities, while the surrounding regions are among the most naturally fertile in the German Empire'.[105] Together with the fierce attachment to traditional forms of religion which also attracted the notice of visitors, this socio-economic nexus created a culture as resistant to revolution as it is possible to imagine.[106] It must be remembered that the French equivalent of Vienna was not Paris, but Versailles – which was a *counter*-revolutionary city.

. . .

CELEBRATION AND DEATH

It was to this restive, disaffected but basically loyal residential city that good news at last began to arrive during the late summer of 1789. The news of Coburg's victory at Fokshani was the occasion for a public celebration, as was the news of the more spectacular triumph at Martinesci. Joseph took good care that no one in Vienna was ignorant of these very welcome tidings by broadcasting them throughout the city by a courier accompanied by two dozen postillions with horns and by ordering Te Deums to be sung in the military church, complete with a battalion of grenadiers to fire salvos and two dozen pieces of artillery to fire salutes at appropriate moments during the service.[107]

So it was to a city 'already drunk with joy from previous victories' achieved in a campaign which was 'unequalled in history', as Lorenz Hübner put it, that the news of the fall of Belgrade came on 12 October.[108] As this crucial episode has been wilfully ignored by many who write about the period, it is desirable to devote a little space to putting the record straight.[109] As Johann Pezzl recorded, General Kleebeck rode into Vienna with the first news at seven in the morning: 'and now began a victory celebration which lasted for three days and which I now describe to show foreigners how such things ought to be done, for three days like these we had never witnessed before'. By the time the travel-weary general made a second ceremonial entry at twelve noon, the whole city knew about it, so the streets and squares were lined by the sort of cheering crowds last seen when Pius VI visited the city. All work stopped, houses were illuminated and the dancing and singing went on through the night. The normally torpid Viennese were still celebrating two days later, when a great Te Deum was held in St Stephen's cathedral: 'The Emperor was accompanied by full court ceremonial, by the gentlemen-of-the-bedchamber, by the great court dignitaries and by the noble life-guard. Every window and every street was filled to bursting-point with spectators. When the Sovereign reached the Kohlmarkt, a hundred thousand hands applauded him, and when he reached the Graben, the joyful applause rang out towards him with redoubled force'. At midnight, as the celebrations reached their climax, a procession of 900 students marched from the university to the imperial palace to honour Joseph with 'a majestic serenade'.[110] To put these events in perspective, it should be recalled that just one week earlier a crowd of Parisians had marched on Versailles, had captured Louis XVI and his family and had taken them back to captivity and eventual execution in Paris.

The war was unpopular only when it was unsuccessful. It had begun in a blaze of popularity and bellicosity.[111] This can be well illustrated by the example of Mozart, who composed no fewer than five pieces specifically to celebrate the success of Austrian arms, using texts which were patriotic to the point of jingoism:

I would dearly love to be the emperor,

I would shake the East,

The muslims would tremble,

Constantinople would be mine.

His collaborator Emanuel Schikaneder, the librettist of *The Magic Flute*, was even more violent:

Now then, German brothers, gird up your courage!

Pursue the Turks, squirt out their blood![112]

In other words, the war itself had never been unpopular. It had been the failures of 1788 which had turned public opinion against it – and the victories of 1789 made it popular once more. Moreover, it was popular not only with the Viennese. As Field Marshal Laudon made his way back from the front, in December 1789, he was lionised by the Hungarians, especially by the inhabitants of Pest, who turned out in their thousands to give him a hero's welcome. On their behalf the chief magistrate recited a panegyric: 'May God bless, may God reward Your Excellency – That is our prayer and that shall be the daily prayer of our children and our children's children. And above all may God bless and preserve our Most Gracious Monarch and always grant him for his army commanders like Your Excellency!'[113]

If the victories of the autumn brought the Habsburg Monarchy back from the brink, the situation was still perilous. Joseph knew only too well that the Prussians were preparing to enter the war in the spring of 1790, together with the Poles, who were busy reforming their institutions. He also knew that this resurgence of Poland would divert the attention of his Russian allies. He also knew of course that his French ally had collapsed and that the central axiom of revolutionary foreign policy was Austrophobia.[114] The situation inside the Monarchy was still critical – Belgium was lost and it remained likely that the Polish nobility in Galicia and the Magyar gentry in Hungary would rise in revolt if a Prussian army hove into view.

It was in this last crisis of his life that Joseph showed himself at his best – sensible, flexible, resolute and decisive. His strategy had three parts. Firstly, he drew up a plan for meeting the challenge of a war on two fronts, sending 88 infantry battalions and 52 cavalry regiments to face the Prussians and Poles in the north, keeping 124 and 68 respectively to hold the Turks in the south, and leaving 24 and 4 to deal with the interior. The detailed gloss which accompanied these dispositions showed his usual remarkable grasp of the geography of his dominions and is surprisingly upbeat in tone. He reasoned that the Prussians would have to divide their forces too, to keep an eye on the Russians, while it was certain that their allies in the League of Princes would remain neutral. He concluded that the situation was difficult but by no means hopelesss. At all events, he was determined not to give up a square inch of territory to Prussia without a fight.[115]

The second initiative was diplomatic. It was well known in Vienna that the British were less than enthusiastic about the expansionist plans of their Prussian ally and also wanted to see Belgium eventually restored to Austrian rule, out of fear that an independent state would quickly fall under the control of France. On 6 December 1789, therefore, Kaunitz began a campaign to separate the British from the Prussians by offering to restore the old Belgian constitution, to make peace with the Turks on 'moderate terms' and even to conclude a defensive alliance with Great Britain.[116] For the time being, there was only a chilly response from London, but a development had been set in train which would lead to the British turning from ally of Prussia to neutral mediator. Unlike Kaunitz, who believed that just one more campaign might inflict total defeat on the Turks, Joseph was prepared to cut his losses by using the autumn victories to secure peace.[117]

The third leg of his strategy for survival was political. He was under no illusions about the scope and intensity of the discontent caused by his reforms, especially among the privileged classes. On 13 January 1790 his minister of police, Count Pergen, had delivered a devastating report on the state of public opinion.[118] According to the Bavarian ambassador, 'The unanimous opinion here is that only his [Joseph's] death can save the Monarchy'.[119] So Joseph bit the bullet and began to dismantle the most unpopular of his innovations, suspending the tax decree and restoring the old order in Hungary (only religious toleration, the new parochial organisation and the abolition of serfdom remained).[120]

This vigorous combination of resistance and concession began the process which restored stability to the Habsburg Monarchy. It was an impressive display of political skill and determination, all the more so because it was the work of a dying man. The years of over-exertion, especially the toll taken by those countless exhausting journeys, had finally laid Joseph low. What eventually killed him was the tuberculosis contracted at the front in 1788. He returned to Vienna at the end of the year suffering from a nagging cough and shortness of breath.[121] In March the following year, just as he was getting ready to return to the front, a high temperature and violent fits of coughing blood nearly carried him off. Believing that his last hour had come, he made careful arrangements for an orderly transfer of power to his sucessor. Then he rallied, and even began to put on a little weight, until an extremely painful operation to deal with an anal abcess put him back in bed again. His own recognition that he would never recover seems to have come on 9 October 1789, when he gave the order for the return of his personal belongings from the front. By December he was suffering again from a high temperature, terrible fits of coughing and was having to struggle constantly to breathe. Characteristically, he worked on until the end, which came at 5.30 on the morning of 20 February 1790.

·   ·   ·

NOTES

1. The full text of the censorship law, together with Joseph's 'Grund-Regeln zur Bestimmung einer ordentlichen künftigen

189

Bücherzensur', on which it was based, are reprinted by Hermann Gnau, *Die Zensur unter Joseph II.*, (Strasbourg and Leipzig, 1911), pp. 254–68. This paragraph – number three – is on page 257.

2. Oskar Sashegyi, *Zensur und Geistesfreiheit unter Joseph II.* (Budapest, 1958), p.29.

3. Leslie Bodi, *Tauwetter in Wien. Zur Prosa der österreichischen Aufklärung 1781–1795* (Frankfurt am Main, 1977), p.53.

4. Fred Hennings, *Das josephinische Wien* (Vienna and Munich, 1966), p. 66.

5. Bodi, *Tauwetter in Wien*, p. 159. See also the examples in Paul P. Bernard, *The limits of enlightenment. Joseph II and the law* (Urbana, 1979), ch. 3.

6. Handbillets, vol. 13 (51), no. 760, to Councillor von Beer, 19 July 1789, fo. 438; no. 1101, to Count Kollowrat, 17 October 1789, fo. 653; Marianne Lunzer, 'Josephinisches und antijosephinisches Schrifttum', in Erich Zöllner (ed.), *Öffentliche Meinung in der Geschichte Österreichs* (Vienna, 1979), p. 58.

7. Handbillets, vol. 8 (31), no. 1075, to Count Cobenzl, 28 December 1784, fo. 1010; vol. 9 (36), no. 26, to Count Pergen, 10 January 1785, fo. 15.

8. Rudolf Payer von Thurn (ed.), *Joseph II. als Theaterdirektor* (Vienna and Leipzig, 1920), p. 60.

9. Bodi, *Tauwetter in Wien*, p. 121.

10. Jürgen Habermas, *The structural transformation of the public sphere. An inquiry into a category of bourgeois society* (Cambridge, 1989), ch.1

11. Denis Silagi, *Jakobiner in der Habsburger Monarchie* (Vienna and Munich, 1962), pp. 31–2.

12. Eva Huber, 'Zur Sozialstruktur der Wiener Freimaurerlogen im Josephinischen Jahrzehnt', in *Aufklärung und Geheimgesellschaften*, ed. Helmut Reinalter (Munich, 1989), p. 173.

13. *Meine Gedanken über die Broschüre: Warum wird Kaiser Joseph von seinem Volk nicht geliebt?* (Vienna, 1787), p.3.

14. Handbillets vol. 3 (41), no. 60, to Count Cavriani, Brünn, 9 September 1786, fos 82–3.

15. See above, pp. 93–4.

16. Gottlieb Mohnike, 'Briefwechsel zwischen Kaiser Joseph dem Zweiten und Clemens Wenzeslaus, Churfürsten von Trier', *Zeitschrift für die historische Theologie*, 4, 1 (1834), 285.

17. Handbillets vol. 9 (36), no. 1043, to Count Kollowrat and *in simili* to Count Palffy, Field Marshal Hadick, Kaunitz, 11 December 1785, fos 916–19.

18. Ibid. This episode provides a good illustration of the central argument of Reinhart Koselleck, *Critique and crisis. Enlightenment*

and the pathogenesis of modern society (Oxford, New York and Hamburg, 1987).

19. Otto Erich Deutsch, 'Kaiser Josef II. und die Freimaurer. Nach Akten des Haus-, Hof- und Staatsarchivs', *Wiener Geschichtsblätter*, 20 (1965), 491.

20. Lorenz Hübner, *Lebensgeschichte Josephs des Zweyten, Kaiser der Deutschen, oder Rosen auf dessen Grab* (Salzburg, n.d. [1790]), pp. 206–7, 223–4.

21. See above, pp. 101–3.

22. Huber, 'Zur Sozialstruktur der Wiener Logen', p. 183.

23. Ignaz de Luca, *Beschreibung der kaiserlichen königlichen Residenzstadt Wien, Ein Versuch*, 2 vols (Vienna, 1785–7), II, 295–323.

24. Ernst Wangermann, *The Austrian achievement 1700–1800* (London, 1973), p. 119.

25. Ibid., p. 119.

26. Bodi, *Tauwetter in Wien*, pp. 268, 277, 312, 320, 328. It is a measure of the integrity of this fascinating if flawed book that it supplies the evidence to disprove its central thesis itself.

27. *Kaiser Joseph wird doch geliebt. Eine kleine Antwort auf die kürzlich erschienene Schrift: Warum wird Kaiser Joseph von seinem Volke nicht geliebt?* (Vienna, 1787), p. 5.

28. Ibid., p. 11; *Meine Gedanken über die Broschüre*, p. 12.

29. The most outspoken representative was the anonymous author of *Warum bekömmt Wucherer nicht fünfzig Prügel??? Ein Pendant zu der Frage: warum wird Kaiser Joseph von seinem Volke nicht geliebt?* (Vienna, 1787).

30. Kálmán Benda, 'Probleme des Josephinismus und des Jakobintertums in der Habsburgischen Monarchie', *Südostforschungen*, 25 (1966), 45; Kálmán Benda, 'Die ungarischen Jakobiner', in Walter Markov (ed.), *Maximilien Robespierre 1758–1794* (Berlin, 1958), p. 442; Laszlo Sziklay, 'Lesegesellschaften und Akademien im Rahmen des nationalen Erwachens der Völker Ostmittel- und Südosteuropas', in Otto Dann (ed.), *Lesegesellschaften und bürgerliche Emanzipation* (Munich, 1981), p. 217.

31. Peter F. Sugar, 'The influence of the Enlightenment and French Revolution in eighteenth-century Hungary', *Journal of Central European Affairs*, 17, 4 (1968) 337, 344.

32. *Betrachtungen über das jetzige Toleranzwesen in denen Kayserl. oesterreichischen Ländern* (Vienna, 1783).

33. Hübner, *Lebensgeschichte Josephs des Zweyten*, p. 70; Joseph von Sonnenfels, *Gesammelte Schriften*, vol. 6 (Vienna, 1784), unpaginated preface.

34. Bodi, *Tauwetter in Wien*, p. 245.

35. Karl Grünberg, *Die Bauernbefreiung und die Auflösung des guts-herrlich-bäuerlichen Verhältnisses in Böhmen, Mähren und Schlesien*, 2 vols (Leipzig, 1894, 1893[*sic*]), II, 337.

36. Volkmar Braunbehrens, *Mozart in Vienna* (Oxford, 1991), p. 228.

37. Derek Beales, 'Court, government and society in Mozart's Vienna', p.2.

38. Christopher McIntosh, *The Rose Cross and the age of reason. Eighteenth-century Rosicrucianism in central Europe and its relationship to the Enlightenment* (Leiden, 1992), ch. 4.

39. Handbillets, vol. 11 (45), no. 2, to Count Mercy, 2 January 1787, fo. 1.

40. McIntosh, *The Rose Cross*, p. 136.

41. See above, pp. 143–6.

42. Walter W. Davis, *Joseph II: an imperial reformer for the Austrian Netherlands* (The Hague, 1974), pp. 236–40.

43. See above, pp. 153–4.

44. See especially his letters to Belgioioso of 3 June, 6 June and 16 June, and to Kaunitz of 6 June, 16 June and 23 June – Handbillets, vol. 11 (45), nos 443, 447–50, 458. The letters to Kaunitz are reprinted in Beer, pp. 264–72.

45. Handbillets vol. 11 (45), no. 953: 'Points d'instruction pour le Général Commandant aux Païs-Bas Feldzeugmeister Comte d'Alton', November 1787, fos 840–3.

46. The fullest account in English is to be found in Davis, *Joseph II*, chs 8–10, but still invaluable is Henri Pirenne, *Histoire de Belgique*, vol. 5 (Brussels 1920).

47. Handbillets vol. 10 (40), no. 757, to Count Belgioioso, 15 October 1786, fo. 579.

48. Ibid., vol. 13 (51) no. 810, 4 August 1789, fos 468–9.

49. Ibid., no. 854, to General d'Alton, 15 August 1789, fo. 494; no. 1051, to Count Trauttmansdorff, 8 October 1789, fo. 624. The latter letter is reprinted in Schlitter, p. 418.

50. Handbillets, vol. 13 (51) no. 1118, to General d'Alton, 23 October 1789, fo. 667. See also his further letter, no. 1143, fo. 684, which is undated but located between two documents dated 31 October 1789, in which he 'flatters himself' that apart from a bit of looting from dissidents coming over the Dutch frontier, they would get through without a major incident.

51. Ibid., vol. 11 (45), no. 437, to Count Belgioioso, Kherson, 28 May 1787, fos 344–5.

52. Ibid., no. 1030, 24 November 1787, fo. 890 and reprinted in Schlitter, pp. 16–18.

53. Handbillets, vol. 13 (51) no. 1216, 'Réflexions sur les arrangemens à prendre aux Païs Bas pour parvenir à une Constitution stable', undated but located between two documents dated 22 November 1789, fo. 769.

54. For Joseph's suspicions, see ibid., no. 496, to Count Trautt-mansdorff, 25 April 1789, fo. 279, reprinted in Schlitter, pp. 238–9, and for details of the highly critical, not to say abusive, remarks on Joseph's policies in the correspondence between the archduchess and Leopold, see Adam Wandruszka, *Leopold II*, 2 vols (Vienna and Munich, 1964–5), II, 202–19.

55. Handbillets, vol. 11 (45), no. 953: 'Points d'instruction pour le Général Commandant aux Païs-Bas Feldzeugmeister Comte d'Alton', November 1787, fos 840–3.

56. Ibid., vol. 13(51), no. 1236, to Kaunitz, 26 November 1789, fos 799–800.

57. Ibid., no. 710, to General d'Alton, 27 June 1789, fo. 401; no. 796, to General d'Alton, 29 July 1789, fo. 462; no. 1236, to Kaunitz, 26 November 1789, fo. 799; no. 1333, 'Schilderung von der gegenwärtigen Lage der Monarchie', 22 December 1789 fos. 856–8; no. 1338, to Count Philipp von Cobenzl, 24 December 1789, fo. 865. Acccording to Oskar Criste, *Kriege unter Kaiser Joseph II.*, (Vienna, 1904), p. 237, at the end of November 1789 there were 13,100 infantry and 1,049 cavalry in the Austrian Netherlands.

58. J. Craeybeckx, 'The Brabant revolution: a conservative revolt in a backward country?', *Acta Historiae Neerlandica*, 4 (1970), *passim*.

59. Handbillets, vol. 11 (45), no. 458, to Kaunitz, Leopol, 23 June 1787, fos 397–8.

60. On the Prussian invasion of the Dutch Republic, see above, p. 154.

61. Handbillets, vol. 11 (45), no. 840, to the Prince de Ligne, 13 October 1787, fo. 765.

62. Ibid., no. 1075, to Count Ludwig Cobenzl, 11 December 1787, fo. 928; Criste, *Kriege unter Kaiser Joseph II.*, p. 153.

63. Isabel de Madariaga, *Russia in the age of Catherine the Great* (London, 1981), pp. 393–7.

64. Handbillets, vol. 12 (47), no. 467, to Count Philipp Cobenzl, Semlin, 27 April 1788, fo. 296.

65. J. Nosinich and L. Wiener, *Kaiser Joseph II. als Staatsmann und Feldherr* (Vienna, 1885), p. 326; Wilhelm Edler von Janko, *Das Leben des kaiserlich königlichen Feldmarschalls Gideon Ernst Freiherrn von Laudon* (Vienna, 1869), p. 400.

66. Handbillets, vol. 12 (47), nos 440 and 468, to Kaunitz, Semlin, 20 and 27 April 1788, fos 282, 297–9. There is a good deal of correspondence in this fascicle relating to the undercover mission to Montenegro of Captains Vukassovich and Pernet.

67. Ibid., no. 111, to Count Zichy, 25 January 1788, fo. 79; vol. 13 (51), no. 2, to Field Marshal Hadick, 2 January 1789, fo. 1; no. 249, to Field Marshal Hadick, 26 February 1789, fo. 157; no.

524, to Count Zichy, 1 May 1789, fo. 292; no. 567, to Feldzeug-meister Wallis, 13 May 1789, fo. 314; no. 568, to Count Zichy, 13 May 1789, fos 314–16; no. 907, to Count Palffy, 31 August 1789, fo. 525.

68. See above, pp. 106–12.

69. Handbillets, vol. 13 (51), no. 1125, to Field Marshal Hadick, 24 October 1789, fo. 670.

70. Ibid., vol. 12 (47), no. 837, to Prince Dietrichstein, Semlin, 5 July 1788, fo. 512; no. 1044, to Field Marshal Hadick, Semlin, 12 August 1788, fo. 621.

71. These barely credible figures are supplied by Criste, *Kriege unter Kaiser Josef II.*, p. 222 n. 3, and repeated by Lorenz Mikoletzky, '"Der Bauern Gott, der Bürger Not, des Adels Spott, liegt auf den Tod". Kaiser Josephs II. langes Sterben aus eigener und fremder Sicht', *Mitteilungen des österreichischen Staatsarchivs*, 39 (1986), 18.

72. Handbillets, vol. 12 (47), no. 1152, to Field Marshal Count von Wartensleben, Caransebes, 31 August 1788, fo. 671.

73. Paul P. Bernard, 'Austria's last Turkish war: some further thoughts', *Austrian History Yearbook*, 19–20, pt. 1 (1983–84), 21–2; Handbillets, vol. 12 (47), no. 1185, to Count Palffy, Hova, 10 September 1788, fo. 689; vol. 13 (51), no. 819, to Count Palffy, 6 August 1789, fo. 475.

74. Ibid., vol. 12 (47), no. 766, to Count Chotek, Semlin, 25 June 1788, fos 476–8.

75. Ibid., no. 1548, to Count Kollowrat, 15 December 1788, fo. 870.

76. Ibid., no. 905, to General d'Alton, Semlin, 18 July 1788, fo. 547.

77. Ibid., no. 516, to Kaunitz, Semlin, 7 May 1788, fo. 330.

78. Ibid., no. 874, to Count Szapary, Semlin, 12 July 1788, fo. 529. A year later Vukassovich's Montenegrin free corps, which had proved more trouble than it was worth, was disbanded – ibid., vol. 13 (51), no. 809, to Field Marshal Laudon, 4 August 1789, fo. 468.

79. Criste, *Kriege unter Kaiser Josef II.*, pp. 162–5.

80. Handbillets, vol. 12 (47), no. 1203, to Kaunitz, Ilova, 20 September 1788, fos 697–8; no. 1220, to Mercy, Lugos, 29 September 1788, fo. 709.

81. Criste, *Kriege unter Kaiser Josef II.* pp. 166–75.

82. Madariaga, *Russia in the age of Catherine the Great*, pp. 396, 405.

83. See above, p. 151.

84. Joseph to Count Mercy, 7 January and 4 August 1788, Arneth and Flammermont, II, 151–2, 186.

85. Robert Gragger, *Preußen, Weimar und die ungarische Königskrone* (Berlin and Leipzig, 1923), p. 16.

86. Friedrich Carl Wittichen, *Preußen und die Revolutionen in Belgien und Lüttich* (Göttingen, 1905), pp. 25–30.
87. Robert Howard Lord, *The second partition of Poland. A study in diplomatic history*, (Cambridge, Mass., 1915), pp. 119–20.
88. Laudon had not distinguished himself, however, in the War of the Bavarian Succession – Beales, p. 415.
89. Handbillets, vol. 13(51), no. 215, 'Hauptentwurf zu dem bevorstehenden Feldzuge mit eintretendem Frühjahr: nähmlich am 15ten April', fos 136–9; no. 494, 'Kurze Betrachtungen über die anfangende Campagne 1789' [23 April], fos 272–6.
90. Criste, *Kriege unter Kaiser Josef II.*, pp. 195–220.
91. Ibid., p. 223.
92. Joseph to Kaunitz, Ilova, 15 September 1788, Beer pp. 315–19. For Kaunitz's trenchant criticisms of Joseph's conduct of the war, see his letters of 10 August 1788, 10 June, 29 July, 31 July 1789, ibid., pp. 299, 332, 336, 338.
93. Criste, *Kriege unter Kaiser Josef II.*, pp. 199, 224.
94. See, for example, his long letter to Field Marshal Hadick on recruiting arrangements of 19 November 1789, which shows that he knew his army inside out – Handbillets, vol. 13 (51), no. 1200, fos 752–60.
95. Ibid., vol. 13(51), no. 300, 9 March 1789, fo. 182.
96. Wangermann, *The Austrian achievement*, p. 166.
97. See the two works by Paul P. Bernard – *The limits of enlightenment. Joseph II and the law* (Urbana, 1979) and *From the Enlightenment to the police state. The public life of Johann Anton Pergen* (Urbana and Chicago, 1991) for an important revision of the 'black legend' perpetrated by Ernst Wangermann, especially in his *From Joseph II to the Jacobin trials*, 2nd edn. (Oxford, 1969).
98. Bernard, *From the Enlightenment to the police state*, p. 153; Handbillets, vol. 12 (47), no. 983, to Count Brigido in Galicia, Semlin, 1 August 1788, fos 589–90.
99. Bernard, *The limits of enlightenment*, p. 52.
100. Ibid.
101. Handbillets, vol. 13 (51), no. 670, to Count Kolowrat and Count Palffy, Laxenburg, 17 June 1789, fo. 374.
102. Felix Czeike, *Geschichte der Stadt Wien* (Vienna, 1981), p. 124.
103. Ignaz de Luca, *Beschreibung der kaiserlichen königlichen Residenzstadt Wien. Ein Versuch*, 2 vols (Vienna, 1785–7), I, 52.
104. J.C. Riesbeck [*sic*], *Travels through Germany in a series of letters*, 3 vols (London, 1787), II, 8. For other examples, see T.C.W. Blanning, *Joseph II and enlightened despotism* (London, 1970), pp. 88–9, 148–50, and de Luca, *Beschreibung der kaiserlichen königlichen Residenzstadt Wien*, II, unpaginated preface. For modern confirmation that the presence of free-spending consumers

allowed the working class to live well, see Roman Sandgruber, 'Einkommensentwicklung und Einkommensverteilung in der zweiten Hälfte des 18. Jahrhunderts – Einige Quellen und Anhaltspunkte', *Österreich im Europa der Aufklärung*, I, 252.

105. Ernst Moritz Arndt, *Reisen durch einen Theil Teutschlands, Italiens und Frankreichs in den Jahren 1798 und 1799*, vol. 6 (Leipzig, 1803), p. 288.

106. For comments on the religiosity of the Viennese, see – for example – John Moore, *A View of Society and Manners in France, Switzerland and Germany*, 4th edn, 2 vols (Dublin, 1789), II, 279, and Wilhelm Ludwig Wekhrlin, *Denkwürdigkeiten von Wien (1777)* in *Schriften 1772–1789*, ed. Alfred Estermann, vol. 1 (Nendeln, 1978), p. 70.

107. Handbillets, vol. 13 (51), no. 840, to Feldzeugmeister von Colloredo, 12 August 1789, fo. 489; no. 1019, to Feldzeugmeister von Wallis, 30 September 1789, fos 596–7.

108. Hübner, *Lebensgeschichte Josephs des Zweyten*, pp. 490, 492.

109. The chief offenders are Ernst Wangermann (*From Joseph II to the Jacobin trials*) and Helmut Reinalter (*Aufgeklärter Absolutismus und Revolution* (Vienna, Cologne and Graz, 1980)), who although claiming to write about the political situation in the late 1780s simply do not mention the successes of the 1789 campaign or the celebrations in Vienna, although presumably they must be aware of them. See also Hans Wagner's strictures on this mortal sin of omission in his review of the German translation of Wangermann's book, published in *Mitteilungen des Instituts für österreichische Geschichtsforschung*, 76 (1968), 245–6.

110. Johann Pezzl, *Skizze von Wien*, vol. 6 (Vienna and Leipzig, 1790), pp. 313–19. There are several other contemporary accounts in the same vein. One of the best was that given by the Archduchess Elizabeth in letters to her husband, extracts from which are reprinted in Criste, *Kriege unter Kaiser Joseph II.*, p. 218 n. 2. These events also unleashed a torrent of pamphlets in celebration of the capture of Belgrade; see, for example, Lorenz Leopold Haschka, *Ode nach der Eroberung Belgrads* (Vienna, 1789) or J.M. Armbruster, *Joseph der Zweyte, Keyser der Deutschen. Ein Denkmal* (Vienna, 1790) or Berthold Eichele, *Siegerpredigt nach der Einnahme Belgrads* (Linz, 1789).

111. Richard Kralik, *Geschichte der Stadt Wien und ihrer Kultur*, 3rd edn (Vienna, 1993), p. 349.

112. Derek Beales, *Mozart and the Habsburgs*, Stenton lecture, University of Reading, 1993. This very important revisionist lecture corrects all manner of myths concerning Mozart.

113. Willhelm Edler von Junker, *Das Leben des kaiserlich königlichen Feldmarschalls Gideon Ernst Freiherrn von Laudon* (Vienna, 1869), p. 471.

114. On the international situation in the autumn of 1789, see T.C.W. Blanning, *The origins of the French revolutionary wars* (London, 1986), pp. 51–60.

115. Handbillets vol. 13 (51), no. 1173, 'Betrachtungen wie bei einem doppelten Krieg mit den Türken, den Preußen und Pohlen, die Truppen eingetheilt und die Länder defendirt werden können' [12 November 1789], fos 721–33.

116. A.F. Pribram (ed.), *Österreichische Staatsverträge: England*, vol. 2: *1749–1813*, (Vienna, 1913), pp. 154–6.

117. See the exchange of letters reprinted in Beer, especially Kaunitz's bellicose letter of 13 November 1789, p. 351.

118. The memorandum is reprinted in full in August Fournier, 'Joseph der Zweite', in August Fournier, *Historische Studien und Skizzen* (Prague and Leipzig, 1885), pp. 167–78.

119. Viktor Bibl, *Kaiser Joseph II. Ein Vorkämpfer der großdeutschen Idee* (Vienna and Leipzig, 1943), pp. 283, 293.

120. Elisabeth Bradler-Rottmann, *Die Reformen Kaiser Josephs II.* (Göppingen, 1973), pp. 50–1.

121. Handbillets, vol. 12 (47), no. 1342, to Count Trauttmansdorff, Semlin, 28 October 1788, fo. 760. Reprinted in Schlitter, pp. 144–5. The harrowing course of Joesph's illness can be followed best through his letters in Schlitter. See also Mikoletzky, 'Kaiser Josephs II. langes Sterben', *passim*.

CONCLUSION

'That was very good of him' was the reported reaction of Kaunitz to the news that Joseph had died.[1] His bitterness is at least understandable in view of the diplomatic disasters of the 1780s. Although the two men had agreed on the central axioms of the Monarchy's foreign policy – the alliances with Russia and France – Kaunitz had been alienated increasingly by the baleful effects of Joseph's state-building. In a memorandum prepared for the Council of State as long ago as 1761, Kaunitz had argued that it would be both dangerous and difficult to attempt to turn the Habsburg Monarchy into a unitary state.[2] Events after 1780 confirmed his prediction all too clearly. His attempt to rebuild and expand Habsburg influence in the Holy Roman Empire was hampered and then destroyed by Joseph's repeated violation of the imperial constitution.[3] The international ramifications of other domestic initiatives, notably the Belgian fiasco, together with what Kaunitz believed to be the inept conduct of the war, reduced him to utter despair. He wrote to Count Mercy on 6 January 1790: 'Everything is as bad as it possibly can be and there is little hope for the future, despite all my best efforts. It is frightful that despotic obstinacy has reduced this great monarchy to its present state'.[4] Yet only six weeks later, he ascribed *'très grandes qualités'* to Joseph, and although he told Count Trauttmansdorff on returning from the funeral that it was the first time for years that he had approached the Emperor with a feeling of relief, he also felt obliged to add that he had been 'a great man'.[5]

This ambivalence was widely shared. As the flood of pamphlets unleashed by his death demonstrated, it was only among the most reactionary defenders of the old order that unqualified

198

condemnation was to be found. Even when criticising his haste or his radicalism, the great majority of pamphleteers and preachers found many aspects of his policy to praise. They singled out his concern for social outcasts: 'You, the poor, the afflicted, the disabled, the helpless, the crippled, the sick, was he not your father, your support, your Samaritan, who poured balm on your wounds?'.[6] They singled out his liberation of the human spirit:

> If your grandchildren should ask you: why was it that just before the end of the eighteenth century men began to write and talk what they believed to be true? Oh! Then answer them from a full heart and with sparkling eyes: 'Because it was at this time that God put an Emperor on the throne who regarded all men as his brothers and sought to make them happy' – and then allow warm tears of deeply-felt gratitude to flow from your eyes in the presence of your grandchildren, so that such a fire may be lit in their souls that a grateful memory of Emperor Joseph II may never be extinguished in the hearts of our German posterity.[7]

They praised his promotion of agriculture and protection of peasants; his admission of the public to the imperial parks and art collections; his improvement of street-lighting and theatres; his immediate personal appearance at the scene of any disaster; his construction of new hospitals and institutions for the handicapped.[8] They praised him for being a devout Catholic, even advancing his introduction of toleration and the general seminaries as evidence of his deep piety.[9] Above all, they praised his military reforms which had driven terror of Austrian arms 'deep into the bowels of the Ottoman Porte' and had won the most glorious campaign of the century.[10]

It would be tedious to enumerate all the eulogies of Joseph II, but in view of the current historiographical emphasis on his unpopularity, there is a need to set the record straight. The following extract from a sermon preached by the pastor of the Protestant community in Vienna must suffice as an example:

> Through Joseph, God raised the glory and prestige of the house of Austria, together with the fortunes and prosperity of its extensive provinces; through Joseph He gave an improved organisation to the internal structure of the state and the administration of justice and a greater strength to

the military; through Joseph He attended to the promotion of trade and industry, of arts and sciences; through Joseph He turned barren wastes into happy homes and fertile fields; through Joseph he restored to a large number of the inhabitants of his territories their natural human and civil rights; through Joseph He purged from religion the many abuses and accretions which prevented its beneficent power from reaching the hearts of men; through Joseph He disseminated the spirit of toleration and forbearance among the various denominations in these territories and also inspired emulation in other countries and states. And God also broadcast many a seed through this prince which will germinate in the future and bear many wonderful fruits for us and our successors.[11]

One man who did not share this enthusiasm for Joseph's achievement was his brother Leopold, hitherto Grand Duke of Tuscany and now the new ruler of the Habsburg Monarchy. Leopold had detested Joseph personally with an intensity that was unusual even among royal brothers and had opposed his policies with equal vehemence. Although an enlightened reformer himself, he was fiercely critical of many of Joseph's most cherished projects, especially the attempt to modernise Belgium and the Russian alliance.[12] Yet when he arrived in Vienna in March 1790, he found himself obliged to continue the strategy adopted by Joseph during the last months of his life and described at the end of the last chapter.

Even before he left Florence, Leopold had adopted that strategy's first instalment – the attempt to separate Great Britain from Prussia. In an audience with the British envoy hastily arranged on the very day that news of the death of Joseph arrived, Leopold could not have been more forthcoming, saying that his esteem for George III was boundless; that the 'unfortunate' alliance with France was dead; that the old alliance between Great Britain and the Habsburg Monarchy should be restored forthwith; that Joseph's death had changed totally 'the Way of Thinking and the Mode of Acting of the Court of Vienna'; that he himself was 'wholly inclined for Peace' and would make any honourable sacrifice to obtain it; that he disapproved of the Russian alliance and Russian plans for expansion; that he would restore the pre-Josephist *status quo* in Belgium and Hungary; and that he would observe all treaties.[13] Although the British did not fall into his arms, they did set about restraining their Prussian ally, by making it clear that they would not recognise the independence of the 'United States of Belgium' and that they preferred a settlement of the war in the east on the basis of the *status quo ante bellum* – in other words, without any territorial gains for Prussia. On 8 March 1790 the Austrian envoy to London, Count Rewiczky, was able to report the good news that the British foreign secretary, the duke of Leeds, had hinted that Great Britain would overrule Prussia if Frederick William II remained adamant.[14]

As soon as he reached Vienna, Leopold also launched a peace initiative in the direction of Prussia. In a personal letter to Frederick William II, he asked for better relations and offered to end the war with the Turks on moderate terms. The next four months saw intense diplomatic activity, during the course of which the British moved from being an ally of Prussia to being a neutral mediator between Prussia and Austria. The result was the Convention of Reichenbach of 27 July 1790, by which Frederick William II agreed to demobilise his army of invasion and Leopold agreed to make peace with the Turks on the basis of the *status quo ante bellum*.[15] The crisis which had begun three years earlier with the Turkish declaration of war on Russia was over.

In the words of the most authoritative Prussian historian of the episode, if Reichenbach was 'one of the most dazzling triumphs of English diplomacy', for Prussia it was a humiliation.[16] But what did it mean for the Habsburg Monarchy? On the one hand, Leopold had been obliged to give up all those territorial gains which the Austrian armies had made in the great autumn offensive of 1789, including Belgrade. On the other hand, he had won peace abroad and with it peace at home. The death of Joseph had done nothing to calm the Magyar gentry of Hungary. On the contrary, they thought they now saw the opportunity to win total independence from the Habsburg yoke. So long as it seemed certain that a Prussian army would be coming south to aid their struggle for independence, so long did they maintain their martial posture. But when Reichenbach both ruled out the possibility of external assistance and paved the way for an end to the Turkish war, they were faced by quite a different situation. Now the tables were turned, and aspiring insurgents had to consider the prospect of certain retribution from an army of battle-hardened Austrian veterans, fired by their victories against the Turks.

To aid their sensible decision not to start a rebellion, Leopold continued Joseph's policy of dismantling the more unpopular reforms. In a grand symbolic gesture, he went to Budapest to be crowned King of Hungary, accompanied by several senior members of the Habsburg family, all wearing the Hungarian national costume which had recently become popular as a visual protest against Joseph's centralising and Germanising policies.[17] The same policy of demonstrative reconciliation was also pursued in Bohemia, where Leopold also had himself crowned king, and in the other restive German-speaking provinces, especially Styria and the Tyrol. This should not be regarded as capitulation. What lent added conviction to the concessions Leopold made was the simple fact that he actually believed in them for their own sake, as well as for prudential reasons. On the other hand, he always made it clear that inside his urbane Florentine rhetoric there lurked the iron fist of coercion. In Hungary he showed special imagination and skill in playing off Slavs against Magyars, and peasants and town-dwellers against the nobility.[18] The fate of the privileged orders in France – dramatised by the abolition of noble titles on 19 June 1790 – was an awful warning to their colleagues in the Habsburg Monarchy not to push their sovereign too far.

Belgium remained to be subdued. Its fate demonstrates more eloquently than any other episode the true nature of the crisis in the Habsburg Monarchy at the end of the 1780s. So long as the Turkish war preoccupied the Austrian military, so long could the citizens of the United States of Belgium live on in their fool's paradise (although its calm was soon shattered by the violent ejection of the radical wing by the conservative majority). As soon as the Convention of Reichenbach brought the Balkan war to an end, the appearance of Nemesis could not be long delayed. She came in the shape of General Bender's modest force of 30,000 men, sent in the autumn of 1790 to re-establish Habsburg control. After the insurgent leaders had gallantly but unwisely rejected Leopold's generous offer of the old constitution and an amnesty, the Austrian soldiers experienced no difficulty in occupying the entire country in a matter of days.[19] In other words, the crisis of the Habsburg Monarchy was both caused and cured by international relations.[20] It provides a classic example of the primacy of foreign policy.

What had allowed Leopold to negotiate the Convention of Reichenbach, and thus to maintain the integrity of his inheritance, had been first and foremost the military victories of the previous autumn. For them Joseph deserves the lion's share of credit, for it was he who had done most to create the army which won them. For the same reason, he also should be placed at the head of any roll of honour of victors over revolutionary-Napoleonic France. So often were the Austrians defeated by the latter – at Jemappes, Fleurus, Lodi, Arcola, Marengo, Hohenlinden, Ulm, Austerlitz and Wagram (to list only the more celebrated French victories) – that it is easy to forget that it was they who won in the end. It was the Habsburg Empire (as the Habsburg Monarchy became in 1804, following Francis II's assumption of the title 'Emperor of Austria') which took control of central and southern Europe in 1815. Napoleon observed contemptuously that the Habsburgs were always one idea and one army behind the rest of Europe, but in the end it was he who ran out of ideas and armies.[21]

Joseph's radical reform programme of the 1780s also ensured that the confrontation between his state and the French Revolution would not become a Manichaean ideological struggle between black reaction and red revolution. He himself adopted an objective attitude towards events in France, pouring his habitual scorn with equal relish on both parties. As he told Count Trauttmansdorff in August 1789: 'It is in my interest to be perfectly neutral in this business, no matter what may happen to the King and Queen, and I shall certainly not intervene'.[22] An approach from the younger of Louis XVI's two brothers, the comte d'Artois, was rebuffed with the firm statement 'I am certainly neither a democrat nor an aristocrat'.[23] The marked similarities between his own programme and that of the French Revolution made his sobriquet 'the revolutionary emperor' a contemporary cliché. It was an image he propagated himself, encouraging, for example, the distribution of a pamphlet which argued that the French were only demanding from below what Joseph had sought to introduce from above for many years.[24] As a result, all those in the Monarchy who believed in progressive change also believed that the best way forward was through reform from above, a conviction which became a central axiom of the political culture of central Europe. In his play *The Hotheads* (*Die Aufgeregten*), Goethe made his supporter of the French Revolution say:

BREME	All I can tell you – and these people know it – is that the prince himself wants a revolution.
MAGISTER	The prince?
BREME	He has the same way of thinking as Frederick and Joseph, the two monarchs all true democrats should worship as their saints.[25]

In recent years there has been an intense hunt for supporters of the French Revolution who did not accept even the most enlightened of rulers but sought a democratic republic. The effort has been prodigious, but the results have been meagre – rarely in the field of historical scholarship has so much attention been lavished by so many on so few. In the Habsburg Monarchy attention has centred on the 'Jacobin conspiracy' unearthed in 1794. If Macartney's verdict – 'an almost ludicrously childish affair of a few men who had done nothing more than plant a "tree of liberty" in a sequestered valley outside Vienna and dance around it, singing tipsy catches in praise of liberty'[26] – is unduly dismissive, the attention paid to the episode certainly owes more to late twentieth-century politics than to late eighteenth-century reality. Never more than a handful, the 'Jacobins' were for the most part Josephists disillusioned by the more conservative path taken by Francis II after his accession in 1792. Not even the most visionary of wishful thinkers can turn them into a threat to the state.[27]

Political dissidents did eventually increase to become a movement to be reckoned with – but not until the years before 1848, by which time a great deal of reactionary water had flowed under the bridge, washing intelligentsia away from state. Significantly, they took Joseph with them. A good example was Grillparzer's poem 'The Emperor's statue', in which Joseph II addresses his faithless successors, threatening to descend from his pedestal to pass judgment on them for having wrecked his achievements.[28] Eventually, even the Habsburg dynasty listened: perhaps the most eloquent tribute from posterity was the addition of 'Joseph' to the official name of the eighteen-year-old Archduke Francis when he became emperor on 2 December 1848 in an attempt to borrow his great-great-uncle's posthumous prestige.

By that time it was much too late. With the advantage of hindsight we can see that Joseph II was the last person the Habsburgs should have been looking to for credibility. The history of the Monarchy in the fifty-eight years since Joseph's death had shown all too clearly how mistaken his programme had been. Not all the revisionist historiography can disguise the fact that by the middle of the nineteenth century the Habsburg Empire had fallen a long way behind the rest of German-speaking Europe, especially Prussia. In large measure this was due to intractable geopolitics, which no man could alter, but Joseph had certainly made an unpromising situation worse. His obsessive concern with demographic increase, aided and abetted by his egalitarianism, had led him to continue and to intensify his mother's policy of protecting the peasantry. The result was an economy based on small holdings aimed at self-sufficiency rather than the market, a recipe for social and economic conservatism. As the Prussians were to show after 1806, a modern, productive economy demanded not the emancipation of the peasants but the emancipation of the *landowners*. In the 1860s Prussia achieved European hegemony at the expense of two powers – the Habsburg Empire and France. It was no accident that both were retarded by social and economic structures still anchored in small-scale subsistence peasant agriculture. Both had finally chosen to take this route at about the same time – the Habsburg Monarchy under Joseph II and France during the Revolution.[29]

If Joseph became the 'peasant's God' at the expense of putting his country in lead boots, in other sectors his enthusiastic programme of modernisation pulled out its roots. By seeking to impose standardisation, centralisation, secularisation, Germanisation – and all the other '-isations' associated with modernisation – Joseph was certainly attempting the impossible, given the wonderful diversity of the Monarchy. That can be readily grasped. What is less apparent, perhaps, is that the attempt was fundamentally misconceived. The Habsburg Monarchy was not a state, it never became a state and it never could have become a state. The only way forward to political stability, social harmony, economic prosperity and cultural vitality was to recognise that fundamental fact and make a virtue out of necessity. Writing from the vantage point of the closing years of the twentieth century, it is certainly easier to see that a multi-national empire held together by a single dynasty whose justification was the guarantee of mutual recognition of diversity is a more attractive option than the other solutions which have been tried – and are being tried. With chilling foresight, Prince Charles Schwarzenberg in 1891 asked a radical Czech nationalist the following question: 'If you and yours hate this state...what will you do with your country, which is too small to stand alone? Will you give it to Germany or to Russia, for you have no other choice if you abandon the Austrian union'.[30] One wonders what he would have said to those Slovaks who have successfully destroyed Czechoslovakia or to those national groups which have destroyed Yugoslavia.

· · ·

NOTES

1. Viktor Bibl, *Kaiser Joseph II. Ein Vorkämpfer der großdeutschen Idee* (Vienna and Leipzig, 1943), p. 292.
2. Dickson, I, 240.
3. Karl Otmar Freiherr von Aretin, *Heiliges römisches Reich. Reichsverfassung und Staatssouveränität*, 2 vols (Wiesbaden, 1967), I, 161, See above, pp. 147–50.
4. Arneth and Flammermont, II, 291–2.
5. Ibid., p. 294; Lorenz Mikoletzky, *Joseph II. Herrscher zwischen den Zeiten* (Göttingen, 1979), p. 98.
6. J.J. von Knauer, *Trauerrede auf Josephs den II.* (Laibach, 1790), p. 12; [Ignaz Aurel Fessler], *Empfindungen der Dankbarkeit des edler denkenden Wieners, in Bezug auf die Gute und Gerechtigkeit Josephs des Zweyten. Bei Gelegenheit des Eintrittes deren Kranken in das Hauptspital den 16. August 1784* (Vienna and Berlin, 1784), pp. 6–7, 24–32.
7. Johann Gottfried Heinrich Müller, *Versuch, das Landvolk über herrschend-tägliche Vorurtheil und Aberglauben natürlich denken lernen*, 2 vols (Vienna, 1791), II, 6.
8. F.[ranz]F.[riedrich]E.[ntner] von E.[ntnersfeld], *Trauerrede über das allerbetrübteste Hinscheiden Josephs des Zweyten* (Vienna, 1790), pp. 22–7.
9. Joseph Lauber, *Lob- und Trauerrede auf den betrübten Todesfall Josephs des Zweiten, römischen Kaisers, gehalten da die Olmützer hohe Schule den 13. April 1790; die feyerliche Exequien für den hohen Verblichenen hielt* (Brünn, n.d.).
10. Joseph Scheller, *Trauerrede auf Joseph den Zweyten* (Vienna, 1790), pp. 5–6. On the same militarist theme, see also Knauer, *Trauerrede auf Joseph den II.*, Joseph Oehler, *Kurze Lebensbeschreibung Josephs des Zweyten* (Vienna, 1790) and *Zuruf eines patriotischen Oesterreichers an seinen neuen Monarchen Leopold II.* (Reichenbach, 1790).
11. Johann Georg Fock, *Predigt bei Veranlassung des Todes unsers geliebten Kaisers Josephs des Zweiten über Psalm 116. v. 15. am Sonntage*

Reminiscere in dem Bethause der hiesigen Augsburgischen Confessions-verwandten gehalten (Vienna, 1790), pp. 23–4.

12. Adam Wandruszka, *Leopold II.*, 2 vols (Vienna and Munich, 1964–5), II, 82–100, 202–231.

13. BL Add. MSS 35,542, Lord Hervey to the duke of Leeds, Florence, 28 February 1790, fos 78–83.

14. Staatskanzlei, England, Berichte, 1790, no. 304.

15. The best detailed account of this episode in English is to be found in Robert Howard Lord, *The second partition of Poland, A study in diplomatic history*, (Cambridge, Mass., 1915). For a shorter account, see T.C.W. Blanning, *The origins of the French revolutionary wars* (London, 1986), pp. 54–5, 82–4.

16. F.K. Wittichen, 'Die Politik des Grafen Hertzberg 1785–1790', *Historische Vierteljahrschrift, 9* (1906), 192.

17. Wandruszka, *Leopold II.*, II, 312–13.

18. Ibid., pp. 277–89. See also Denis Silagi, *Jakobiner in der Habsburger Monarchie* (Vienna and Munich , 1962), pp. 88–96.

19. Wandruszka, *Leopold II.*, II, 317–20.

20. Among contemporary German historians, this has been grasped most clearly – as one might expect – by Volker Press, 'Österreich, das Reich und die Eindämmung der Revolution in Deutschland', in Helmut Berding (ed.), *Soziale Unruhen in Deutschland während der Französischen Revolution* (Göttingen, 1988), p. 243.

21. Kurt Peball, 'Zum Kriegsbild der österreichischen Armee und seiner geschichtlichen Bedeutung in den Kriegen gegen die Französische revolution und Napoleon I. in den Jahren von 1792 bis 1815', in Wolfgang von Groote and Klaus-Jürgen Müller (eds), *Napoleon und das Militärwesen seiner Zeit* (Freiburg in Breisgau, 1968), p. 139.

22. Handbillets, vol. 13 (51), no. 830, 10 August 1789, fo. 482; reprinted in Schlitter, p. 344.

23. Joseph to the comte d'Artois, 30 October 1789, Arneth and Flammermont, II, 278.

24. Ernst Walder, 'Zwei Studien über den aufgeklärten Absolutismus', *Schweizer Beiträge zur allgemeinen Geschichte*, 15 (1957), 134.

25. *Goethes Werke*, hrsg. im Auftrage der Großherzogin Sophie von Sachsen, 133 vols (Weimar, 1887–1912), XVIII (1895), 57.

26. C. A. Macartney, *The Habsburg Empire 1790–1918* (London, 1969), p. 157.

27. This has not prevented wildly inflated claims being made about them by some historians, notably Ernst Wangermann and Helmut Reinalter, who make up in repetition and assertion what they lack in evidence. Anyone contemplating reading Wangermann's *From Joseph II to the Jacobin trials*, (2nd edn, Oxford, 1969)

should first read Hans Wagner's review of the German translation, published in *Mitteilungen des Instituts für österreichische Geschichtsforschung*, 76 (1968), 245–6. Anyone contemplating reading Helmut Reinalter's *Aufgeklärter Absolutismus und Revolution* (Vienna, Cologne and Graz, 1980) should first read Grete Klingenstein's review in *Historische Zeitschrift*, 235 (1982), 434–5. Much shorter, judicious and authoritative assessments of the true scope and significance of radicals in the Habsburg Monarchy can be found in Walter Markov, 'I giacobini dei paesi absburgici', *Studi storici*, III, 3 (1962), Kveta Mejdricka, 'Die Jakobiner in der tschechischen öffentlichen Meinung', in *Maximilien Robespierre 1758–1794* (Berlin, 1958) and Kálmán Benda, 'Probleme des Josephinismus und des Jakobinertums in der Habsburgischen Monarchie', *Südostforschungen*, 25 (1966). The best overall account is Denis Silagi's, *Jakobiner in der Habsburger Monarchie* (Vienna and Munich, 1962), which shows that the 'Jacobin conspiracy' actually began as a *government* operation.

28. Ilsa Barea, *Vienna* (London, 1966), p. 123.
29. A. J. P. Taylor, *The Habsburg Monarchy 1809–1918* (London, 1948), p. 20; Hans-Ulrich Wehler, *Deutsche Gesellschaftsgeschichte*, vol. I: *Vom Feudalismus des Alten Reiches bis zur defensiven Modernisierung der Reformära 1700–1815* (Munich, 1987), pp. 404–27.
30. Quoted in Arthur J. May, *The Habsburg Monarchy 1867–1914* (Cambridge, Mass., 1965), p. 199.

FURTHER READING

Three books which have been referred to often in the course of this present work dominate the field: R.J.W. Evans, *The making of the Habsburg Monarchy 1550–1700. An interpretation* (Oxford, 1970), which is essential to any understanding of the Habsburg Monarchy in the eighteenth century; P.G.M. Dickson, *Finance and government under Maria Theresa 1740–1780*, 2 vols (Oxford, 1987), which is an extraordinary achievement of meticulous scholarship and a mine of insight and information; and Derek Beales, *Joseph II*, vol. I: *In the shadow of Maria Theresa 1741–1780* (Cambridge, 1987), by far the best biography of Joseph II in any language, both in terms of scholarship and readability. Also crucial is Beales' article 'The False Joseph II', *The Historical Journal*, 18, 3 (1975). The best general survey available in any language is Charles Ingrao's *The Habsburg Monarchy 1618–1815* (Cambridge, 1994).

There are now several good histories of Germany in the period, all of which have something useful to say about the Habsburg Monarchy. The best are Mary Fulbrook, *A concise history of Germany* (Cambridge, 1990); John Gagliardo, *Germany under the old regime 1600–1790* (London, 1991); James J. Sheehan, *German history 1770–1866* (Oxford, 1990) and Michael Hughes, *Early modern Germany 1477–1806* (London, 1992). Two older works with plenty about Joseph, despite the chronology suggested by their titles, are A.J.P. Taylor, *The Habsburg Monarchy 1809–1918. A history of the Austrian Empire and Austria-Hungary* (London, 1948) and C.A. Macartney, *The Habsburg Empire 1790–1918* (London, 1968). An abbreviated but revised version of the latter was published in 1978 with the title *The house of Austria: the later phase 1790–1918*. His collection of documents –

The Habsburg and Hohenzollern dynasties in the seventeenth and eighteenth centuries (London, 1970) – is better on Maria Theresa than on Joseph. Ernst Wangermann, *The Austrian achievement 1700–1800* (London, 1973) contains many attractive illustrations.

The best general history of international relations in the period is Derek McKay and H.M. Scott, *The rise of the great powers 1648–1815* (London, 1983). An alternative view can be found in Jeremy Black, *The rise of the European powers 1679–1793* (London, 1990). More specifically on the international relations of the Habsburg Monarchy are important monographs by Karl A. Roider, *Austria's eastern question 1700–1790* (Princeton, 1982), Paul P. Bernard, *Joseph II and Bavaria: Two eighteenth century attempts at German unification* (The Hague, 1965), H.W.V. Temperley, *Frederic the Great and Kaiser Joseph* (reprinted, 1968), Karl A. Roider, *Baron Thugut and Austria's response to the French Revolution* (Princeton, 1987) and M.S. Anderson, *The Eastern Question 1774–1923* (London, 1966). There is a good deal on Joseph's foreign policy in T.C.W. Blanning, *The origins of the French revolutionary wars* (London, 1986). The fateful Russian alliance is dealt with most authoritatively in Isabel de Madariaga, *Russia in the age of Catherine the Great* (London, 1981). Articles with a bearing on Joseph's foreign policy are Isabel de Madariaga, 'The secret Austro-Russian treaty of 1781', *Slavonic and East European Review*, 38 (1959), M.S. Anderson, 'The great powers and the annexation of the Crimea, 1783–1784', *Slavonic and East European Review*, 37 (1958), T.C.W. Blanning, 'George III, Hanover and the Fürstenbund of 1785', *The Historical Journal*, 20, 2 (1977), Jeremy Black, 'British policy towards Austria, 1780–93', *Mitteilungen des österreichischen Staatsarchivs*, 42 (1992) and Jerzy Łojek, 'The international crisis of 1791: Poland between the Triple Alliance and Russia', *East Central Europe*, 2 , 1 (1975).

On the vexed question of the relationship between Joseph's reform programme and the Enlightenment, see T.C.W. Blanning, *Joseph II and enlightened despotism* (London, 1970), H.M. Scott, 'Reform in the Habsburg Monarchy', in H.M. Scott (ed.), *Enlightened absolutism. Reform and reformers in later eighteenth-century Europe* (London, 1989) and Derek Beales, 'Was Joseph II an enlightened despot?', in *The Austrian Enlightenment and its aftermath*, Austrian Studies 2, ed. Ritchie Robertson and Edward Timms (Edinburgh, 1991). There is also much of value in three short works by Paul Bernard: *Joseph II* (New York, 1968), *Jesuits and Jacobins: Enlightenment and enlightened despotism in Austria* (Illinois UP, 1971) and *The Limits of enlightenment. Joseph II and the law* (Urbana, 1979) and in his more substantial *From the Enlightenment to the police state. The public life of Johann Anton Pergen* (Urbana and Chicago, 1991).

On Hungary there are two cooperative enterprises: Ervin Pamlenyi (ed.), *A history of Hungary* (London, 1975), which is particularly useful on economic matters, and Peter F. Sugar (ed.), *A history of Hungary* (London, 1990). C.A. Macartney, *Hungary. A short history* (Edinburgh, 1962) is short but to the point. Something can still be garnered from the old book by H. Marczali, *Hungary in the 18th century* (Cambridge, 1910), but the single most illuminating work is undoubtedly B.K. Király, *Hungary in the late 18th century* (New York, 1969). Poorly translated but informative is Domokos Kosary, *Culture and society in eighteenth-century Hungary* (Budapest, 1987). A rare article on the Hungarian enlightenment is George Barany, 'Hoping against hope: the enlightened age in Hungary', *American Historical Review*, 76, 2 (1971). Two good studies on the periphery of the Kingdom of Hungary are Gunther Rothenberg, *The military border in Croatia 1740–1881* (Chicago, 1966) and Karl A. Roider, 'Nationalism and colonisation in the Banat of Temesvar, 1718–1778', in *Nation and ideology. Essays in honour of Wayne S. Vucinich* ed. Ivo Banac, John G. Ackerman and Roman Szporluk (New York, 1981).

On Bohemia there is a brief but penetrating overview by R.J.W. Evans, 'The Habsburg Monarchy and Bohemia', in Mark Greengrass (ed.), *Conquest and coalescence: The shaping of the state in early modern Europe* (London, 1991). His general article 'Joseph II and nationality in the Habsburg Lands', in *Enlightened absolutism. Reform and reformers in later eighteenth-century Europe*, ed. H.M. Scott (London, 1990) should also be consulted. Other brief accounts can be found in A.H. Herrmann, *A history of the Czechs* (London, 1975) and H.F. Schwarz, 'Bohemia under the Habsburgs', *A handbook of Slavic studies*, ed. L.I. Strakhovsky (Cambridge, Mass., 1949) and J.F. Zack, 'The Czech enlightenment and the Czech national revival', *Canadian Review of Studies in Nationalism*, 10 (1983). More substantial but difficult to read is Robert J. Kerner, *Bohemia in the 18th century. A study in political, economic and social history with special reference to the reign of Leopold II 1790–1792* (New York, 1932). A special issue of

Austrian History Yearbook – 3, 1 (1967) – was devoted to various ethnic groups in the Habsburg Monarchy as 'integrating and disintegrating forces'. On Galicia, there is something to be found in Norman Davies' excellent general history of Poland: *God's playground. A history of Poland*, vol. 1: The origins to 1795 (Oxford, 1981) and R.H. Lord, *The second partition of Poland. A study in diplomatic history* (Cambridge Mass., 1915), although the latter is essentially a diplomatic history (and a very good one). On the Belgian provinces, the best short account is in E.H. Kossmann, *The Low Countries 1780–1940* (Oxford, 1978). Much more detailed are W.W. Davis, *Joseph II: An imperial reformer for the Austrian Netherlands* (The Hague, 1974) and Janet L. Polasky, *Revolution in Brussels 1787–1793* (London, 1987), although the most valuable single piece available in English on the Belgian troubles is an article by J. Craeybeckx, 'The Brabant revolution: a conservative revolt in a backward country?', *Acta Historiae Neerdlandica*, 4 (1970). There is a good chapter in R.R. Palmer, *The age of the democratic revolution*, vol. II (Princeton, 1964).

Little is available in English on the Italian possessions but something can be gleaned from Stuart Woolf, *A history of Italy 1700–1860. The social constraints of political change* (London, 1979); Dino Carpanetto and Giuseppe Ricuperati, *Italy in the age of reason* (London, 1987); Derek Beales, *The Risorgimento and the unification of Italy* (London, 1970); J.M. Roberts, 'Enlightened despotism in Italy', in *Art and ideas in eighteenth-century Italy. Lectures given at the Italian Institute 1957–58, Pubblicazioni dell' Istituto Italiano di Cultura di Londra*, vol. 4 (Rome, 1960) and M.S. Anderson, 'The Italian reformers', in *Enlightened absolutism. Reform and reformers in later eighteenth-century Europe*, ed. H.M. Scott (London, 1990). There is also a good deal on Italy in Franco Venturi, *The end of the old regime in Europe 1768–1776: The first crisis* (Princeton, 1989) and *The end of the old regime in Europe 1776–1789* (Princeton, 1991). On more specific topics: D.M. Klang, *Tax reform in eighteenth-century Lombardy* (New York, 1977); D.A. Limoli, 'Pietro Verri, a Lombard reformer under enlightened absolutism and the French Revolution', *Journal of Central European Affairs*, 18 (1958); Franco Venturi, 'Church and reform in Enlightenment Italy: the sixties of the 18th century', *Journal of Modern History*, 48, 2 (1976); Alexander Grab, 'Enlightened despotism and state building: the case of Austrian Lombardy', *Austrian History Yearbook*, 20 (1984) and

Miriam J. Levy, *Governance and grievance: Habsburg policy and the Italian Tyrol in the eighteenth century* (West Lafayette, 1988).

Long neglected by historians writing in English, there are now some good studies of the economy of the Monarchy available. Although perhaps unduly revisionist, David F. Good's, *The economic rise of the Habsburg Empire 1750–1914* (Berkeley, 1984) is strongly recommended. There is much useful information to be found in John Komlos, *Nutrition and economic development in the eighteenth-century Habsburg Monarchy* (Princeton, 1989). Books dealing mainly with the nineteenth century but which also look backwards are John Komlos (ed.), *Economic development in the Habsburg Monarchy in the 19th century* (New York, 1983); Ivan T. Behrend and György Ranki, *Economic development in East-Central Europe in the 19th and 20th centuries* (New York, 1974); Ivan T. Behrend and György Ranki, *The European Periphery and industrialisation 1780–1914* (Cambridge, 1982). There are several detailed articles by Arnost Klima available in translation, notably 'Mercantilism in the Habsburg Monarchy, with special reference to the Bohemian lands', *Historica*, 11 (1965); 'Industrial growth and entrepreneurship in the early stages of industrialisation of the Czech lands', in *Economic development in the Habsburg Monarchy in the 19th century*, ed. John Komlos (New York, 1983), 'Industrial development in Bohemia 1648–1781', *Past and Present*, 11 (1957), and 'Agrarian class structure and economic development in pre-industrial Bohemia', *Past and Present*, 85 (1979). Two important articles by Hermann Freudenberger are 'Industrialisation in Bohemia and Moravia in the 18th century', *Journal of Central European Affairs*, 19 (1960) and 'The woollen-goods industry of the Habsburg Monarchy in the 18th century', *Journal of Economic History*, 20, 3 (1960), to be read together with his monograph *The industrialisation of a Central European city – Brno and the fine woollen industry in the 18th century* (Edington, 1977). Other articles on the economic history of the Monarchy are Richard L. Rudolph, 'The pattern of Austrian industrial growth from the 18th to the early 20th century', *Austrian History Yearbook*, 11 (1975); I. Kallay, 'Management of big estates in Hungary between 1711 and 1848', *Studia Historica*, 148 (1980); and Nachum Gross, 'The industrial revolution in the Habsburg Monarchy, 1750-1914', *The Fontana economic history of Europe*, ed. Carlo M. Cipolla, vol. 4: *The emergence of industrial societies*, part 1 (London, 1973).

On the nobilities of the Monarchy there are two articles in the collection edited by Albert Goodwin: *The European nobility in the 18th century*, 2nd ed (London, 1967), namely H.G. Schenk on 'Austria' and C.A. Macartney, on 'Hungary' and Robert A. Kann, 'Aristocracy in the 18th century Habsburg Empire', *East European Quarterly*, 7 (1973-4). On the peasantry there is precious little, William E. Wright, *Agrarian reform in eighteenth-century Bohemia* (Minnesota, 1966) being more satisfactory than Edith Murr Link, *The emancipation of the Austrian peasant 1740-1798* (New York, 1949). Bela Király, 'The emancipation of the serfs of East Central Europe', *Antemurale*, 15 (1971) is difficult to find. On social reform, strongly recommended is James van Horn Melton, *Absolutism and the eighteenth-century origins of compulsory schooling in Prussia and Austria* (Cambridge, 1988). An important aspect of Joseph's social policy is dealt with in Paul P. Bernard, 'The limits of absolutism: Joseph II and the *Allgemeines Krankenhaus* (General Hospital)', *Eighteenth-century Studies*, 9 (1975-6).

On Joseph's relations with the Church, the starting-point is Owen Chadwick, *The popes and European revolution* (Oxford, 1981). It may be supplemented by the specialised work of W.W. Davis, 'The origins of religious Josephism', *East Central Europe*, 1 (1974); Charles H. O'Brien, 'Ideas of religious toleration at the time of Joseph II. A study of the Enlightenment among Catholics in Austria', *Transactions of the American Philosophical Society*, new series, 59, 7 (1969); Paul P. Bernard, 'Joseph II and the Jews: the origins of the toleration patent of 1782', *Austrian History Yearbook*, 4–5 (1968–9) and Grete Klingenstein, 'Modes of religious tolerance and intolerance in eighteenth-century Habsburg politics', *Austrian History Yearbook*, 24 (1993). Concise overviews are Jean Berenger, 'The Austrian Church' and Bela K. Király, 'The Hungarian Church', both in *Church and society in Catholic Europe of the 18th century*, ed. William J. Callahan and David Higgs (Cambridge, 1979). Especially valuable is Peter Dickson, 'Joseph II's reshaping of the Austrian Church', *The Historical Journal*, 36, 1 (1993). The article by Ernst Wangermann, 'Reform Catholicism and political radicalism in the Austrian Enlightenment', in *The enlightenment in national context*, ed. Roy Porter and Mikulas Teich (Cambridge, 1981) is marred by a reductionist emphasis on the growth of scepticism.

There is no volume in English devoted to the military history of the Monarchy under Joseph. The subject is best approached through Christopher Duffy, *The army of Maria Theresa. The armed forces of imperial Austria, 1740–1780* (London, 1977). General histories of relevance are Michael Howard, *War in European history* (Oxford, 1976), Geoffrey Best, *War and society in revolutionary Europe 1770–1870* (London, 1982), Hew Strachan, *European armies and the conduct of war* (London, 1983) and André Corvisier, *Armies and societies in Europe 1494–1789* (Bloomington and London, 1979). Three important articles are Robert A. Kann, 'The social prestige of the officer corps in the Habsburg Empire from the 18th century to 1918' and Zoltan Kramar, 'The military ethos of the Hungarian nobility 1700–1848', both in *War and society in East Central Europe*, ed. Bela K. Király and Gunther E. Rothenberg, vol. 1 (New York, 1979), and Gunther E. Rothenberg, 'The Habsburg army and the nationality problem in the 19th century, 1815–1914', *Austrian History Yearbook*, 3, 1 (1967).

Alas there is no general cultural history. Part of the gap can be filled by William M. Johnston, *The Austrian mind: An intellectual and social history* (London, 1972); Ilsa Barea, *Vienna* (London, 1966); Peter Horwath, 'Literature in the service of enlightened absolutism: the age of Joseph II (1780–1790)', *Studies on Voltaire and the eighteenth century*, 56 (1967) and Klaus Epstein, *The genesis of German conservatism* (Princeton, 1966). An original and important article is James van Horn Melton's, 'From image to word: cultural reforms and the rise of literate culture in eighteenth-century Austria', *Journal of Modern History*, 58, 1 (1986). There are, however, many distinguished works on music. Especially valuable for repairing the damage done by the film *Amadeus* are Volkmar Braunbehrens, *Mozart in Vienna* (Oxford, 1991) and Derek Beales, *Mozart and the Habsburgs* (Stenton lecture, University of Reading, 1993). Good general accounts are to be found in John A. Rice, 'Vienna under Joseph II and Leopold II', in Neal Zaslaw (ed.), *The classical era. From the 1740s to the end of the eighteenth century* (London, 1989) and Giorgio Pestelli, *The age of Mozart and Beethoven* (Cambridge, 1984). On Mozart the best introduction is Stanley Sadie, *The New Grove Mozart* (London, 1982).

CHRONOLOGY

1740 Death of Charles VI, accession of Maria Theresa 20 October
Invasion of Silesia by Frederick II of Prussia, 16 December

1741 Birth of Joseph, 13 March; Prussian victory at Mollwitz, 10 April; Spain, France and Bavaria declare war on Maria Theresa

1742 Charles Albert of Bavaria elected Holy Roman Emperor as Charles VII
Peace with Prussia, end of first Silesian war

1744 Prussia re-enters war

1745 Peace of Dresden with Prussia, end of second Silesian war

1748 Peace of Aachen with France brings the war of the Austrian Succession to an end

1749 Domestic reforms directed by Count Haugwitz begin

1756 First treaty of Versailles between France and the Habsburg Monarchy
Frederick the Great's pre-emptive strike against the Habsburg Monarchy through Saxony begins the Seven Years War

1760	Creation of the Council of State (*Staatsrat*); new wave of reforms begins; Joseph marries Isabella of Parma
1762	Death of the Tsarina Elizabeth (January); Russia withdraws from war
1763	Treaty of Hubertusburg ends the Seven Years War on the continent Death of Joseph's wife Isabella
1764	Alliance between Russia and Prussia Joseph elected King of the Romans
1765	Joseph marries Josepha Maria of Bavaria Death of Francis I; Joseph becomes Holy Roman Emperor and co-regent of the Habsburg Monarchy
1767	Death of Joseph's second wife Josepha Maria
1768	War between Russia and the Ottoman Empire
1769	Joseph's meeting with Frederick the Great
1770	Joseph's second meeting with Frederick the Great
1772	Partition of Poland by Russia, the Habsburg Monarchy and Prussia
1773	Dissolution of the Jesuits
1775	Peasant revolt in Bohemia Bukovina annexed
1777	Joseph's visit to France Death of Elector Max Joseph of Bavaria, 30 December
1778	Frederick the Great invades Bohemia, 5 July
1779	Peace of Teschen ends the war of the Bavarian Succession, 13 May
1780	Joseph visits Catherine the Great
1781	Alliance between Russia and the Habsburg Monarchy

Joseph visits the Austrian Netherlands
Relaxation of censorship
Religious toleration for Protestants and Greek Orthodox is introduced
Emancipation and assimilation of Jews begins
Dissolution of 'useless' religious orders begins
Abolition of personal serfdom
Judicial reform begins

1782   Pius VI travels to Vienna
Police reorganised under Count Pergen
Creation of new parishes begins

1783   General Seminaries established
Reform of poor laws
Commutation of labour dues (*robot*) introduced
First plans for a comprehensive fiscal and urbarial reform
Reorganisation of the diocesan structure of the Habsburg Monarchy begins; Russia annexes the Crimea
Joseph begins his attempt to open the river Scheldt to international shipping

1784   Germanisation edict
Reform of secondary and higher education
New burial regulations
Peasant revolt in Transylvania
General Hospital opened in Vienna
Joseph begins his attempt to exchange his possessions in the Netherlands for Bavaria
Attempt by an Austrian ship to force the passage of the Scheldt fails after the Dutch fire on it, 6 October

1785   Joseph abandons the Bavarian exchange on learning of French opposition; Land survey begins
Administrative reorganisation of Hungary
League of German Princes formed by Frederick the Great

Dispute with the Dutch Republic over the Scheldt is settled

Freemasonry placed under government supervision

1786   Death of Frederick the Great, 17 August

1787   Comprehensive reform of administrative and judicial institutions in the Austrian Netherlands

New penal code

Joseph meets Catherine the Great

Disturbances in the Austrian Netherlands

Ottoman Empire declares war on Russia, 17 August; Joseph recognises the *casus fœderis*

Prussia invades and occupies the Dutch Republic, 13 September

1788   Joseph takes command of the army against the Turks, March

Triple alliance between Great Britain, Prussia and the Dutch Republic

War against the Turks goes badly

Sweden invades Russia, July

Prussia begins conspiracy with Hungarian dissidents

Joseph returns to Vienna from the front, November

1789   Tax reform

Revolution in the Austrian Netherlands

Prussia decides to invade Habsburg Monarchy in spring of 1790

Prussia negotiates alliances with Poland and the Ottoman Empire

Successes in the war against the Turks

Capture of Belgrade, 8 October

Capture of Bucharest, 10 November

1790   Joseph revokes reforms in Hungary, 28 January

Death of Joseph, 20 February

Convention of Reichenbach removes threat of Prussian invasion, 27 July

The Habsburg Monarchy at the time of Joseph II.
After: D. Beales, *Joseph II*, vol 1, (Cambridge University Press).

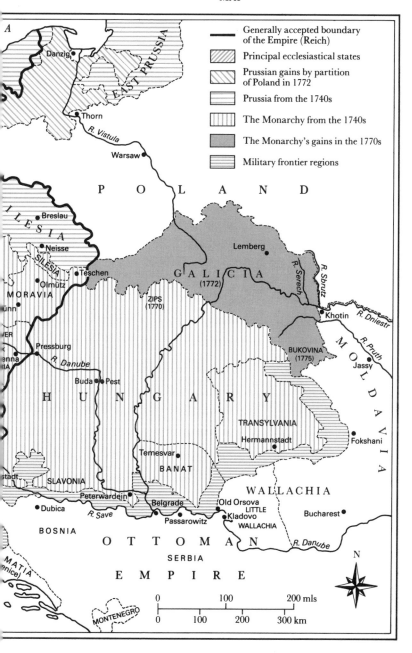

Generally accepted boundary of the Empire (Reich)

Principal ecclesiastical states

Prussian gains by partition of Poland in 1772

Prussia from the 1740s

The Monarchy from the 1740s

The Monarchy's gains in the 1770s

Military frontier regions

INDEX